Achiev

Primary English

Teaching Theory and Practice

7th edition

LIVERPOOL JMU LIBRARY

3 1111 01468 6503

Achieving QTS

Primary English

Teaching Theory and Practice

7th edition

Jane Medwell • David Wray • Hilary Minns •
Elizabeth Coates • Vivienne Griffiths

Los Angeles | London | New Delhi
Singapore | Washington DC

Learning Matters
An imprint of SAGE Publications Ltd
1 Oliver's Yard
55 City Road
London EC1Y 1SP

SAGE Publications Inc.
2455 Teller Road
Thousand Oaks, California 91320

SAGE Publications India Pvt Ltd
B 1/I 1 Mohan Cooperative Industrial Area
Mathura Road
New Delhi 110 044

SAGE Publications Asia-Pacific Pte Ltd
3 Church Street
#10–04 Samsung Hub
Singapore 049483

Editor: Amy Thornton
Development editor: Jennifer Clark
Production controller: Chris Marke
Project management: Deer Park Productions,
   Tavistock, Devon, England
Marketing manager: Catherine Slinn
Cover design: Wendy Scott
Typeset by: C&M Digitals (P) Ltd, Chennai, India
Printed by: Henry Ling Limited at The Dorset
   Press, Dorchester, DT1 1HD

MIX
Paper from
responsible sources
FSC
www.fsc.org   FSC™ C013985

© Jane Medwell, David Wray, Hilary Minns, Elizabeth
Coates and Vivienne Griffiths 2014

First published in 2001 by Learning Matters Ltd.

Second edition published in 2002.
Reprinted in 2002, 2003, 2004 (twice) 2005
and 2006. Third edition published in 2007.
Reprinted in 2007 and 2008. Fourth edition
published in 2009. Reprinted in 2009
(twice). Fifth edition published in 2011.
Reprinted in 2011 (twice). Sixth edition
published in 2012. Seventh edition published 2014.

Apart from any fair dealing for the purposes
of research or private study, or criticism or review,
as permitted under the Copyright, Designs
and Patents Act 1988, this publication may be
reproduced, stored or transmitted in any form,
or by any means, only with the prior permission
in writing of the publishers, or in the case of
reprographic reproduction, in accordance with
the terms of licences issued by the Copyright
Licensing Agency. Enquiries concerning
reproduction outside those terms should be sent to
the publishers.

Library of Congress Control Number: 2014937401

British Library Cataloguing in Publication Data

A catalogue record for this book is available from
the British Library.

ISBN: 978-1-4462-9521-2
ISBN: 978-1-4462-9522-9 (pbk)

At SAGE we take sustainability seriously. Most of our products are printed in the UK using FSC papers and boards. When
we print overseas we ensure sustainable papers are used as measured by the Egmont grading system.
We undertake an annual audit to monitor our sustainability.

Contents

1
Introduction

About this book

This book has been written to address the needs of trainees on all courses of primary initial teacher training in England and other parts of the UK. By the end of their course of initial training, trainees are required to have developed a defined set of professional attributes, professional knowledge and understanding and professional skills. Such teaching skills are required to meet the Teachers' Standards (2013) and seek the award of Qualified Teacher Status (QTS) or its equivalent. The book will also be useful to Newly Qualified Teachers (NQTs) and other professionals working in education who have identified aspects of their English teaching that require attention.

This book has been written with the requirements of the Teachers' Standards firmly at its core. This book aims to address the essential skills of English teaching which relate specifically to Teachers' Standard 3: Demonstrate good subject and curriculum knowledge, specifically for primary teachers:

- have a secure knowledge of the relevant subject(s) and curriculum areas, foster and maintain pupils' interest in the subject, and address misunderstandings
- demonstrate a critical understanding of developments in the subject and curriculum areas, and promote the value of scholarship
- demonstrate an understanding of and take responsibility for promoting high standards of literacy, articulacy and the correct use of standard English
- demonstrate a clear understanding of systematic synthetic phonics.

Features of the main chapters of this book include:

- clear links with the Teachers' Standards;
- references to required English knowledge and understanding;
- research summaries that give insights into how the theory of English teaching has developed, including seminal studies on oracy and literacy;
- examples of practice in the classroom to illustrate important points;
- suggestions for embedding ICT in your practice;
- reminders of how planning for teaching English fits in with the bigger picture, across the curriculum and with other aspects of school life;
- reflective tasks and practical activities for you to undertake;
- a summary of key learning points;
- suggestions for further reading.

For those undertaking credits for a Master's Degree, we have included suggestions for further work and extended study at the end of each chapter in a section called 'M-Level Extension'. The book also contains a glossary of terms.

Each chapter addresses the teaching of particular areas of English, such as reading and writing. The subject knowledge that primary teachers need in order to become effective teachers of English and literacy is addressed in the companion volume, *Primary English:*

Knowledge and Understanding (Learning Matters SAGE, 2014). However, the authors of this book have also attempted to make clear the knowledge you will need in order to carry out successful English teaching.

What is primary English and why is it taught?

There is a good deal of consensus about what we want children to achieve in primary English, but it can still be difficult to define primary English as a subject. For the purposes of this book, we feel that primary English is about children acquiring the skills, knowledge and attitudes to become empowered readers, writers, speakers and listeners.

Teaching primary English involves ensuring children learn the skills and processes of **literacy** and **using spoken language**, but these are not always defined simply. Literacy can be construed as having the skills necessary for effective reading and writing, but this raises many questions. What degree of expertise must one achieve to be 'literate'? Are some people more literate than others, and what do we mean by this? Does literacy involve reading certain texts and not others? What about media literacy – the ability to 'read' and be critical about media such as TV, social networking and other internet sources?

The National Curriculum looks very broadly at literacy, aiming for all children to be able to read and write a full range of texts. They should learn not only to decode and encode written English, but also to be critical about what they read so that they can identify the stance of the author and the intended effects on the reader. The National Curriculum aims for children to read a wide range of texts, including electronic texts. In writing, too, the aims of the National Curriculum are not only for children to be able to write in a technical sense, but also for them to be able to write to express themselves and achieve their purposes for writing.

In spoken language, it is also important to recognise that children need to be able to listen not only to the literal sense of what is said, but also to listen critically and evaluate the veracity, relevance and intent of what they hear – to become critical listeners. The National Curriculum aims to empower children to become critical speakers, too, so that they are able to speak appropriately and effectively in a whole range of situations, whatever the purpose of their speech.

To use reading, writing, speaking and listening skills, children need a great deal of knowledge. They need to know about the technical aspects of speaking, listening, reading and writing if they are to be able to use them effectively. These 'technical aspects' include a vast range of specialised knowledge, for instance knowing the sounds of English, knowing about word order in sentences and knowing how to listen for the key points from a text. The most important and complex knowledge children must gain is knowledge about how to orchestrate their skills and understanding about reading, writing, speaking and listening effectively. To do this, children need to know about successful texts – these can be written examples of literature or non-fiction, spoken discussions or reports. If children have clear, effective models they can analyse why these are effective and begin to make their own texts effective. All this knowledge is part of primary English.

In addition to skills and knowledge, primary English also involves attitudes. We aim for children to find reading fiction an enjoyable experience, so that they will be motivated to do more. We aim for children to find non-fiction persuasive, interesting or useful. We aim for children to learn from listening and to speak powerfully. These are only a few of the attitudes towards the use of literacy and spoken language that we aim for children to develop. The texts by themselves will not develop useful attitudes in children. It is the way the texts are treated by teachers and children that develops attitudes.

Primary English is about empowering children with a range of skills, knowledge and attitudes for schooling and life. Primary English involves studying and creating spoken and written texts. English texts and language are worth studying for themselves and also as a gateway to every other subject in the curriculum.

The Teachers' Standards

In this book we are focusing mainly on the skills needed to plan, manage, monitor and assess learning in English, including literacy.

Curriculum context

The primary curriculum is changing in 2014 and this sort of change may very well happen several times in your career as a teacher. You need to know about the new curriculum and a good deal about what your children have already learnt and how they have been taught. Here we have included a brief summary of information about the primary National Curriculum programmes of study, and the Early Learning Goals for children in the Early Years Foundation Stage.

English in the National Curriculum

English in the National Curriculum is organised on the basis of five key stages: Foundation Key Stage (part of the Early Years Foundation Stage) for 3–5-year-olds; Key Stage 1 for 5–7-year-olds (Years 1 and 2); and Key Stage 2 for 7–11-year-olds (Years 3 to 6) refer to primary and Early Years teaching. The components of the Foundation Key Stage are set out as Early Learning Goals (ELGs), which set targets for the end of the Foundation Stage and stepping stones, which set out how children can achieve ELGs. Key Stages 1 and 2 include Programmes of Study, which set out the English that children should be taught. These Programmes are organised over four age phases:

- Key Stage 1 – Year 1;
- Key Stage 1 – Year 2;
- Lower Key Stage 2 – Years 3 and 4;
- Upper Key Stage 2 – Years 5 and 6.

Within each age phase the material to be taught is split into 5 strands:

- Reading – word reading;
- Reading – comprehension;
- Writing – transcription;
- Writing – composition;
- Writing – vocabulary, grammar and punctuation.

There are also requirements for the teaching of spoken language which span Years 1 to 6, and two statutory appendices – one about spelling and one about vocabulary, grammar and punctuation – which give an overview of the specific features that should be included in teaching the programmes of study.

The National Curriculum is intended to be a minimum statutory entitlement for children and schools have the flexibility and freedom to design a wider school curriculum to meet the needs of their pupils and to decide how to teach it most effectively. As *The National Curriculum in England* (DfE, 2013a) itself puts it:

> The national curriculum is just one element in the education of every child. There is time and space in the school day and in each week, term and year to range beyond the national curriculum specifications. The national curriculum provides an outline of core knowledge around which teachers can develop exciting and stimulating lessons to promote the development of pupils' knowledge, understanding and skills as part of the wider school curriculum.

All schools are required to set out their school curriculum for English on a year-by-year basis and make this information available online. You need to know about the English curriculum of your training settings and how this relates to the National Curriculum. This will be the basis of your planning and assessment.

Statutory assessment of English attainment after the introduction of the 2014 National Curriculum is undergoing some phased changes. In 2015 onwards the statutory assessment of primary pupils, in English, will involve reporting of assessment at the end of Key Stage 1 and Key Stage 2. This assessment will include teacher assessment and some tests.

At the end of Key Stage 1 in 2015, schools may order and use the Key Stage 1 tests and tasks for English in 2014 and 2015, but they do not have to and many schools will make their own arrangements to assess reading, writing, speaking and listening. Schools are required to report the results in the summer. In addition, Year 1 pupils must do the nationally set, but teacher-administered, phonics screening check.

At the end of Key Stage 2 in 2015, Year 6 pupils will do Key Stage 2 tests in English, including nationally developed tests of English reading and English spelling, punctuation and grammar (SPaG), and teacher-administered assessments of writing.

In 2016 a new national assessment regime will be introduced which will dispense with the National Curriculum levels and sub-levels. The new approach to assessment will aim to assess annual progress and will be related to the content of the 2014 National Curriculum. In the light of these changes, we have focused in this book on giving you insights into the development of the theory behind the core areas of English teaching that you will need to inform your practice as you plan to promote the literacy of the children you work with and to ensure that they develop effective speaking and listening skills, and become successful readers and writers.

The Early Years Foundation Stage

The Early Learning Goals (DfE, 2012) describe what most children should achieve by the end of their Reception year. This document identifies features of good practice during the Early Years Foundation Stage and sets out the early learning goals in three prime areas and six specific areas of learning. One of the prime areas is that of Communication and

Language (including Listening and Attention, Understanding and Speaking) and one of the specific areas is Literacy (including Reading and Writing).

There are thus five areas within the Early Learning Goals which specifically concern us in the present book. These are:

- listening and attention;
- understanding;
- speaking;
- reading;
- writing.

English also includes exploring and using media and being imaginative. Specific reference will be made to these Early Learning Goals where relevant in the book.

At the end of the EYFS (the end of Reception), all providers of Early Years care and education complete the Early Years Foundation Stage profile, which summarises and describes children's attainment at the end of the EYFS. It is based on ongoing observation and assessment in the three prime and four specific areas of learning, and the three learning characteristics. This book discusses how you can include this as a part of your practice and offers an underpinning rationale for your assessment.

Outcomes

By using this book to support your developing teaching skills you will be able to teach primary English and Communication Language and Literacy successfully. We hope that your own reading and writing of English will fuel your enthusiasm for teaching English and, especially, that you will develop a lifelong love of the excellent children's literature available to children today. This is part of your stock in trade. Your enthusiasm is an invaluable asset to a teacher and can bring English alive for children. We hope you will design challenging, stimulating and engaging activities for children which will teach them the richness and power of English.

FURTHER READING   FURTHER READING   **FURTHER READING**   FURTHER READING

To support you in understanding the curriculum context, you may find it helpful to refer to some of the following documentation:

DfE (2012) *Statutory Framework for the Early Years Foundation Stage*. Runcorn: DfE. (https://www.education.gov.uk/publications/standard/AllPublications/Page1/DFE-00023-2012)

DfE (2013) *2014 Key Stage 2 Tests*. (http://education.gov.uk/schools/teachingandlearning/assessment/keystage2/b00208296/ks2-2013/ks2-2014)

DfE (2013) *The National Curriculum in England*. London: DfE. (https://www.gov.uk/dfe/nationalcurriculum)

DfE (2013) *The 2014 National Curriculum*. London: DfE. (https://www.gov.uk/government/collections/national-curriculum)

DfE (2013) *Teachers' Standards*. London: DfE. (https://www.gov.uk/government/uploads/system/uploads/attachment_data/file/208682/Teachers__Standards_2013.pdf)

2
Learning English

TEACHERS' STANDARDS

A teacher must:

2. **Promote good progress and outcomes by pupils**

   - demonstrate knowledge and understanding of how pupils learn and how this impacts on teaching

3. **Demonstrate good subject and curriculum knowledge**

   - have a secure knowledge of the relevant subject(s) and curriculum areas, foster and maintain pupils' interest in the subject, and address misunderstandings
   - demonstrate an understanding of and take responsibility for promoting high standards of literacy, articulacy and the correct use of standard English, whatever the teacher's specialist subject

This chapter will consider general trends in the way children learn language and draw parallels between literacy and oracy learning. It looks at how you as a teacher can best support children's development as language learners and teach children the range of skills, knowledge and attitudes they need to become effective readers, writers, speakers and listeners. Later chapters focus on how these general strategies are used for different aspects of literacy and oracy teaching at the different primary age phases.

Most of us learned our first language so early in our lives that we do not remember doing so and therefore we are able to take this immense learning achievement for granted. When we look at teaching language to others, however, we need to review and establish what it is important to know and be able to do in language. It is important that children use language effectively, automatically and without having to give undue attention to it, but it is also important that they, and you as their teacher, are able to take a close look at language and examine ways of using it more effectively.

REFLECTIVE TASK

1. List six things you have read and four conversations you have taken part in during the past 24 hours.

   Are you surprised by the range of topics covered?

2. You are in an airport in Greece but you do not speak, read or write Greek. You need to find your way to the car hire area.

Why are you 'lost'?

What is language?

What can you do?

What do you know about Greek?

3. Read this passage:

Impairments in _____ are overtly manifested in children who exhibit errors in their speech production that are _____ for their age. Phonology is an aspect of linguistic _____ concerned with both the rules governing the ordering of _____ into meaningful units and the _____ phonetic qualities in which meanings are transmitted (Grunwell, 1990). Language _____ include phonological impairments that occur either in isolation or with other _____ problems (Bishop and Edmundson, 1987; Leonard, 1982).

The relationship between _____ skills and reading has received a great deal of attention in light of the body of research that has indicated that deficits in phonology can be directly linked to _____ disabilities (see Catts, 1989). During the _____ phase, the first stage of formal reading instruction, there is a heavy _____ on a phonological processing method to access _____. Words are broken into graphemes, graphemes are converted into phonemes, and phonemes are blended into _____ to form words. To perform this process successfully, adequate _____ awareness (phonics) skills are required (Blachman, 1989; Catts, 1989; Snyder and Downey, 1991). Children with reading _____ have been found to be poor in tasks that tap _____ awareness: these include sound counting, sound deletion (say 'dog' without the 'd'), sound _____ (reversal of phonemes), and sound _____ (e.g. categorising words by their beginning sounds) (Blachman, 1989).

Can you get the full meaning from this passage? If not, why is this?

What strategies do you use to work out the meaning?

Language is functional and meaning orientated

If you look at your list of readings, you will find that all the reading you did was meaningful and had some purpose – to provide enjoyment or amusement, to inform you or to persuade you. When you try to read a sign, you have an expectation of the meaning and function (or purpose) of the sign. In the third task above, you may have been able to supply missing words on the basis of the meaning – your existing knowledge of the subject or ability to work out a plausible meaning. This is called using **semantic cues** or information. By recognising the purpose of a text, we can make appropriate language choices.

REFLECTIVE TASK

REFLECTIVE TASK

The work of Halliday (1978, 1985) and his theory of 'Functional Systemic Linguistics' has been very important in recent years in informing practice in literacy teaching. Halliday's emphasis has been on looking at what language lets us do in the world – its function. Halliday's work has introduced a range of important insights, many of which have been a strong influence on the teaching of literacy and oracy.

- It has emphasised that language is not just a means of communicating. It is also a way of making meanings and understanding the world. Language is a way of achieving what we want in our culture.
- Halliday looked at the ways language is related to problem solving, thinking and understanding. He emphasises that ways of using language are at the heart of understanding the ideas and concepts of any knowledge area – this has real implications for how we use language in teaching. For instance, if we want children to think and learn problem solving like mathematicians, they need to learn and use the language and ideas internalised by mathematicians. You, in learning to become a teacher, will learn the language of teaching. This is not just jargon, it is a crucial tool in enabling you to think and problem solve as a teacher and learn the concepts and ideas shared by other teachers.
- Halliday has given the world the concept of 'texts' – meaningful chunks of written **or spoken** language. He argues strongly that the level at which we operate in the real world is not the word or the sentence but the level of the whole text. We, as teachers, need to respond to texts in terms of their success or failure at achieving their purpose for a given audience.
- Halliday has emphasised 'genres' – forms of language – which are valued in different contexts. This has led to the study of appropriate genres for children to be taught.
- Halliday has developed awareness of the relationship between author, purpose and linguistic choice. By making the linguistic choices involved in constructing a written text, or by uttering a spoken text, we are using our knowledge of the purpose of the text and the range of language elements available to us. As teachers, we want to teach children to be aware of how language choices change as the audience and purpose of a text change. So, children writing a newspaper report for other children will make different language choices from those writing a letter to the local council. Halliday's work has given many authors a framework for considering how texts work and how children might best learn to create and respond to texts.

Language is a code

Language might be described as the set of symbols we use to represent our immediate lives as well as experiences and ideas far away from us. Language even lets us represent abstract concepts (such as language or thought). It is certainly a very flexible and creative code. The basic units that carry meaning in English are phonemes and graphemes. At the **word** and **sub-word level**, around 45 basic sound units (phonemes) and the 26 letters of the English language, along with spaces, pauses, punctuation marks and intonation, can be combined in a multitude of ways. You cannot read Greek signs if you do not know the basic units of Greek code. In reading, we call using the links between known symbols and sounds using **graphic and phonic cues**. In the second task above, you did not know these basic facts about the Greek language and so you could not extract the full meaning from the Greek signs, but there are probably many things you could understand about a Greek sign. As an English user you knew the function of signs and expected them to contain useful information. You had a concept of word and letter, and even though you could not read the words, you knew in which direction the text proceeded. In a more sophisticated way you knew that there were likely to be sentences and that the word order would be significant. These insights were not enough to allow you to understand the Greek text fully, but they do remind you that all these ideas are important for young children who will understand some, but not all, aspects of the sophisticated code of language. (For more on phonemes and graphemes, see Chapter 3 of our companion volume *Primary English: Knowledge and Understanding* (Learning Matters SAGE, 2014.)

There are also **sentence level** codes that help us to understand language. In the third task above, you probably guessed some of the missing words because you knew so much about the sentence structure around those words that you could predict from the syntax. The code of language at sentence level is called grammar and it is a very powerful way of making meaning. Although spoken language is actually clause driven, rather than reliant on the full sentences of writing, this also has a clear grammar and syntax. We call using known syntactic structures in reading using **syntactic cues**.

At a whole **text level** the codes of language include the ways in which written or spoken text types are structured for their purposes. As an experienced language user, you would know the purpose of a sign or of the texts you have written.

Children learning language

Interesting insights into how children acquire their early knowledge about the workings of literacy can be gained from considering some of the processes through which they learn their first spoken language. While learning to talk is not the same as learning to be literate, both processes clearly have much in common, because spoken language has much in common with written language. Written language also differs in important ways from spoken language, and awareness of these differences is in itself an important feature of becoming literate.

The table below, adapted from that given in David Crystal's *Encyclopaedia of the English Language* (1995: p. 291) summarises some of the differences between spoken and written language.

Differences between speech and writing	
Speech is time-bound, transient and part of an interaction in which both speaker and listener are usually present.	Writing is space-bound, permanent and the result of a situation in which the writer is usually distant from the reader.
The spontaneity of most speech makes it difficult to plan in advance. The pressure to think while talking produces looser construction, repetition and rephrasing. Long utterances are divided into manageable chunks, but sentence boundaries are often unclear.	Writing allows repeated reading and analysis, and promotes the use of careful organisation. Units of discourse (sentences, paragraphs) are usually easy to identify through punctuation and layout.

Differences between speech and writing	
Because participants are typically in face-to-face interaction, they can rely on such cues as facial expression and gesture to aid meaning. Speech tends to rely on words that refer directly to the situation, such as 'that one', 'in here', 'right now'.	Lack of visual contact means that participants cannot rely on context to make their meanings clear. Most writing therefore avoids the use of expressions that pin it to the here and now.
Many words and constructions are characteristic of speech, such as long, conjoined sentences, vocabulary which may have no standard spelling (whatchamacallit), slang and grammatical informality (isn't, they've).	Some words and constructions are characteristic of writing, such as multiple use of subordination in the same sentence, and the use of precise vocabulary.
Speech is very suited to social functions, such as passing the time of day, or any situation where casual and unplanned discourse is desirable.	Writing is very suited to the recording of facts and the communication of ideas, and to tasks of memory and learning.
There is an opportunity to rethink an utterance while it is in progress. However, errors, once spoken, cannot be withdrawn.	Errors and other perceived inadequacies in writing can be eliminated in later drafts without the reader ever knowing they were there.
Unique features of speech include intonation, contrasts of loudness, tempo, rhythm and other tones of voice.	Unique features of writing include pages, lines, capitalisation, spatial organisation and several aspects of punctuation.

How does having learnt spoken English help the literacy learner?

How is learning written English different from spoken English?

Some of the processes by which children learn spoken language apply to the acquisition of literacy. Children, from the moment they are born, are surrounded by spoken language. One of the most noticeable facts about babies is that people talk to them long before anyone could expect these babies to understand what is being said, and the remarkable thing about the way people talk to babies is that they generally do it meaningfully. Of course, there is a certain amount of 'goo-gooing', but, more often, the talk will be similar to, 'Who's going to see his Grandad? Yes, he is. Oh, there's a clever boy.' Many babies spend almost the whole of their waking lives being played with; play which almost inevitably is accompanied by talk. This talk may not be in totally adult forms but is invariably meaningful. In addition to this, young children are also surrounded by talk that is not directly addressed to them. Again, such talk is invariably meaningful and much of its sense is obvious from its context. Children, then, begin life bathed in meaningful talk.

Because the talk that surrounds them is meaningful, young children are receiving continual demonstrations of the purposes of spoken language. If an adult says to a child, 'Who's dropped his ball then? There we are. Back again', and returns the ball, the adult is demonstrating the connection between talk and the action it refers to. When the child says, 'Daddy blow', and the adult responds with, 'Yes, Daddy will blow the whistle now', the demonstration is not only of the connection between language and action, but also of an appropriate form of speech. Children receive millions of demonstrations of meaningful talk, not only directed at them, but also taking place around them. From these demonstrations, they have to work out how the system of language works so that they can begin to take part in it.

Of course, the simple fact of witnessing demonstrations of language would not be sufficient to turn children into language users unless some other factors were also present. First among these is engagement, that is the desire on the part of children to take part in the language behaviour they see around them. This desire arises because children witness the power of language in the world and want to share in it. They see, for example, that if you can ask for a biscuit rather than just scream loudly, you are more likely to get what you want. They also see that using language in ways that achieve the effects they want is not something so difficult that they are unlikely to master it. On the contrary, language is presented to them from the very first as something they **can** do. This produces a crucial expectation of success, which we know to be vitally important in actual achievement. There is plenty of evidence that children, both in and out of school, achieve very much what they are expected to achieve by other people. It is likely that this works because children internalise others' expectations about them and come to hold these expectations of themselves. The most familiar example of this concerns children whom adults label as 'not very clever' and who come to believe this of themselves. Because they do not believe they can 'be clever', they stop trying to be.

In the case of spoken language, however, every child is expected to be able to master it (unless some medical condition makes this impossible). Asking any parent the question 'Do you expect your child to learn to talk?' is likely to produce only a very puzzled response. The question seems ludicrous because the answer is so obvious. Because the adults around them believe so firmly that they will become talkers, the children themselves come to believe they will do it, and they do, generally effortlessly.

When children are learning to talk, it is highly unlikely that the adult expert talkers that surround them will decide to administer a structured programme of speech training. Adults who have tried to be even a little systematic in helping children to develop language have found that it simply does not work. The following much quoted exchange between child and caregiver is an example of what can happen.

Child: Nobody don't like me.
Mother: No, say 'Nobody likes me'.
Child: Nobody don't like me. [Eight repetitions of this dialogue]
Mother: No, now listen carefully: say 'Nobody likes me'.
Child: Oh! Nobody don't likes me.
(This exchange comes from the work of David McNeill. It is quoted in Crystal, 1987: p. 234.)

Instead of this situation, in which the adult has tried to take responsibility for what the child should learn, it is much more usual for the child to take the responsibility. Learning to talk is the child's task, which can be supported by adults but is not sequenced, structured or taught by them. The majority of adults implicitly accept this and rarely try to force the pace when children are learning to talk, but instead take their lead from the child's performance.

During this learning, nobody expects children to perform perfectly from the very beginning. If children had to wait until they had perfect control of all facets of spoken language before speaking, they would not produce any speech until at least nine or ten years of age. What in fact happens is that children produce spoken language forms that are approximations to adult forms, and these approximations gradually become closer and closer to the desired end product. 'Baby talk' is not only accepted by caregivers but is actually encouraged by being received with amusement and pride. It is also usually responded to as a meaningful utterance, and elaborated by the adult into a more fully developed form. When a child says, for example, 'Daddy, you naughty', the adult is much more likely to respond with something like, 'Oh, fancy saying Daddy is naughty. He's a good Daddy', rather than, 'No. Say "Daddy, you are naughty"'. The adult responds to the child's attempts at fully-fledged speech forms by interpreting and adding meaning rather than by correcting them. Approximations are accepted and responded to by adults, and gradually children realise for themselves that they are approximate and how to make them more 'adult'.

Any learning, to be effective, requires a great deal of practice on the part of the learner, and learning to talk is no exception. For the vast majority of children this is no problem at all. They are constantly surrounded by talk and are expected and given chances to join in with it. Even when by themselves they carry on practising, from early babbling in which language sounds are practised to later oral accompaniments to actions such as play. Significantly, this practice occurs for completely different purposes than to help children learn to talk. Adults rarely hold conversations with babies and young children because they know this is good for their language development. Nor do children talk to themselves when playing because they think this will make them better talkers. Both activities occur for more fundamental, human reasons. Conversations take place because there is something to converse about and children are included in the conversation that accompanies everyday action from very early in their lives. Children talk to themselves because this is how they represent their actions to themselves and how they reflect on these actions. This kind of talk becomes more and more elliptical and eventually fades altogether, occurring inside the head as 'inner speech'. It is the beginning of thought.

For all the importance of the above processes in children's growing capacity to produce meaningful speech, none of them would work were it not for the fact they all operate in a two-sided situation. Children are immersed in language, receive a myriad of demonstrations of it, are expected to try to emulate these and are given freedom and opportunities to do it at their own pace and level of approximation, but the crucial factor is that all this happens in the context of real dialogue with other people. Adults talk, not just across children, but also to them; they expect children to talk back to them, and when they do, adults respond. This constant interaction is at the heart of growing language use, and it is the need for interaction that comes first. Relationships need to be developed and things need to be achieved together. Language comes into being as a means of helping these things happen. It is therefore learned as a means of coping with the demands of being human.

Because of the interactive nature of language learning, the process inevitably involves response. Children respond to adult language, and adults respond to children's attempts at language. Such response not only reaffirms the relationship that forms the context of the talk, but also gives children feedback about their language and, perhaps, a more elaborated model on which to base future language.

The development of insights into literacy

The same processes that underpin the development of spoken language can also be seen to underpin the development of children's early insights into and use of literacy.

The vast majority of children are surrounded by literacy from their earliest years. Here are just a few of the manifestations of this:

- they consume things from packaging covered in print, from soft drink cans to chocolate bar wrappers;
- they wear print, from clothes labels to T-shirt slogans;
- they accompany their parents shopping in printed surroundings and come into contact with signs, from 'Car Park' to 'Play Centre', and printed packages, from cereal boxes to juice cartons;
- they watch print on screen: on television and as part of computer packages;
- they see print used in their homes, from shopping lists to telephone directories, and recipes to newspapers.

This environmental print is not there simply by accident, but because it communicates messages. Children are thus surrounded by meaningful print. They are also continually being given demonstrations of people using this print. They see adults:

- following instructions on packages and making their food;
- reading newspapers, magazines or books, and reacting with laughter, anger, sadness, etc.;
- consulting telephone directories, and dialling numbers guided by print;
- reading computer screens and bank machines;
- finding their way around supermarkets by following the signs;
- and so on, ad infinitum.

These are illustrations that print can affect the way you feel, can act as a guide to action, or can be used for the sheer pleasure of using it. As a result of these constant demonstrations of literacy, most children come to value engagement in literacy. This shows itself in all kinds of ways. Some children learn that there is little point in saying 'I want a burger' unless you are near a place that sells them, which you know because of the signs outside. (American researchers have suggested that virtually every American two- to three-year-old can 'read' well-known burger bar signs!) Others will proudly produce a page covered in scribble and say 'I've written a story'. The three-year-old girl who sat for three-quarters of an hour absorbed in the pages of a book that was on her knee, upside down, had learnt to value the literacy behaviour she had witnessed in adults, even if she had not quite yet worked out how to do it. Any Reception teacher will testify to the fact that most of their new charges come to school wanting to learn to read above all things. Their engagement with literacy is usually high.

EMBEDDING ICT EMBEDDING ICT **EMBEDDING ICT** EMBEDDING ICT **EMBEDDING ICT**

When teaching children in the Early Years, remember to build on their high levels of engagement by giving them opportunities to interact with a wide range of media and technologies. Include an electronic till, a basic calculator and an up-to-date looking telephone or mobile in the role-play area. When planning guided play activities, include the choice of listening to a pre-recorded story independently and ensure that all children have a turn at completing programs on the computer, for example to practise their shape or letter recognition. The digital camera or camera-phone is not only one of the very best recording tools for the Early Years teacher, but also for the pupil who wants to make meaning. Photocopy or scan and print out the children's work to include in a class book or to be sent home to share with parents.

You might also visit the Lend Me Your Literacy website (http://lendmeyourliteracy.com/) where children's written work can be posted for the whole world to see. The benefits of this for children's feelings about writing need hardly be described!

Before they reach school, most children have few grounds not to believe that they will be successful in their encounters with literacy. The majority of three-year-olds will cheerfully 'read' a book, even if what they say does not match to the actual printed words. They will also 'write', using scribble or the letters of their name to signify meaning. Because they have received so many demonstrations of literacy in so many contexts, they come to believe that there is nothing to it. Everyone else can do it, so they can too, or even if they are aware they have not quite got the hang of it yet, it is only a matter of time until they do. It is a sad fact that the first time many children begin to doubt that they will master the activities of reading and writing is when their school experience shows them that these things are difficult and failure is possible.

In the early lessons that children learn about literacy, it is unlikely that adults will make too many demands on them to perform in particular ways. The choice of whether to attend to the literacy demonstrations around them and whether to try to copy them or not is left to the children. They therefore, as with spoken language, have responsibility for their own learning. Of course, parents often do attempt more direct teaching of reading and writing with young children than they do of speaking. This is only natural, given the high status of literacy and parents' perceptions that the ability to read and write is linked with success in later life. Most parents will, however, take the lead from their children in terms of how long their teaching will last, when they have done enough and, indeed, what this teaching will consist of. Again, the child has a large amount of responsibility for the process.

Adults also rarely expect the 'reading' and 'writing' of their young children to be perfect. A two-year-old who makes up a spoken story in response to looking at a captioned picture book is more likely to receive praise for this effort than an exhortation to be more careful and get the words right. Similarly, children who present their parents with scribbled 'letters' are likely to have their attempts taken seriously, with the parents pretending to 'read' the message, and not to be admonished for their poor handwriting or spelling. In the same way that children are allowed 'baby-talk' that approximates to adult speech, they are allowed 'baby-reading' and 'baby-writing'.

In addition to being surrounded by demonstrations of literacy, many children get a great many opportunities to take part in it, at however rudimentary a level. Almost all children 'write', whether it be with pencil, felt tip, crayon, paint brush or chalk. Most of them also 'read', whether from books, comics, TV screens or advertisements. The three-year-old who proudly displays a new T-shirt with a cartoon character on the front is using the ability to derive meaning from printed symbols. The two-year-old who picks up the tube of sweets rather than the indigestion tablets is making discriminations on the basis of print.

Reading and writing, in rudimentary forms, are part of most young children's play activities simply because they are such a significant part of their worlds.

Finally, many of children's early interactions with print take place in collaboration with an experienced adult. This is done so naturally that many adults are almost unaware of it. Some examples will show it in action.

- A mother is shopping with her two-year-old boy who sits in a seat in the shopping trolley. He reaches out and picks up a packet of cornflakes. He says, 'Bix, Mummy.' The mother replies, 'No. We don't want cornflakes. We want wheat biscuits. See. Here we are.' She has given feedback on his interpretation of print, and helped him learn more about this process.
- A father is standing at a bus stop with his three-year-old son. A bus draws up and the little boy moves forward. The father says, 'No. We want the bus for Warwick Street. This goes to Haslam Road, look.' He points to the indicator on the bus. He is demonstrating which items of print it is important to attend to.
- A mother is playing 'Shops' with her three-year-old daughter. She asks to 'buy' several things, and helps her daughter find each item in the shop. Each time the child finds the right item, the mother praises her with, 'Yes. That's the toothpaste.' Again, the child is being helped to make links between objects and their print representations.

Of course, children vary in the quantity of interactions of this kind they experience with their parents. Where they receive a great many, the children are in fact being treated as apprentice print users, an experience which almost certainly helps them develop into independent print users later. The concept of apprenticeship is an important one in trying to understand the growth of early literacy, and essentially involves the actions of an expert being copied and experimented with by a less expert apprentice. Learning takes place naturally and almost undetectably, yet it clearly does take place.

The experience of literacy that children get at home is probably not sufficient to ensure they develop into fully competent experts in all the ways literacy is used in the modern world. While it is true that most children make a start on the process of becoming literate before they arrive at school, there is a great deal that they still have to learn. However, they have made an important start before they ever enter school. Although school has a vital role to play in the development of literacy, it can still learn a great deal from an examination of the learning processes at work in the home that we have just discussed. The attractiveness of these processes is in their naturalness. The fact that nobody, parents or children, consciously plans these processes suggests that there is something in them that is fundamental to effective human learning. If this is so, these processes represent a very good place to start in planning the teaching that happens in school. As children learn in school, they do become more independent and more able to deal with abstracts, so they can extend their range of learning strategies, but it makes sense to build on the insights they bring with them from pre-school experience.

Halliday (1978, 1985) emphasised three aspects of language learning: learning language, learning through language and learning about language. Very young children are engaged in doing all these right from the beginning. As their vocabularies expand (learning language) they learn about using language for the social purposes in their environment (learning about language) and in doing so they learn about the world and their place in it (learning through language). We build on this learning when they come to nursery and school. To do this, we need to teach all three of Halliday's aspects of language.

- Teachers need to offer children more language to learn – more, varied text types (spoken and written), a wider range of words, new ways of organising language, and the conventions of standard written English at text, sentence and word levels.
- Teachers need to help children to learn about language – to reflect on and analyse how texts work and to speak and write new texts. By learning about language, children will become more flexible users of language.
- Teachers need to help children learn through language. Children need to learn the language of the subjects they study so that they can learn the concepts of those subjects. Children also need effective oracy and literacy skills so that they can have access to other subjects.

THE BIGGER PICTURE THE BIGGER PICTURE **THE BIGGER PICTURE** THE BIGGER PICTURE

When you are planning spoken language and literacy work for your class, remember to include activities to promote all three of Halliday's three aspects of language, but not just in your plans for communication and language. Children can be offered more language to learn as they undertake activities in mathematics and personal, social and emotional development. They can be helped to learn about language through widening their vocabulary and accessing information texts as they gain knowledge through understanding the world. They can learn through language as they take part in sessions to support their creative and their physical development.

RESEARCH SUMMARY RESEARCH SUMMARY **RESEARCH SUMMARY** RESEARCH SUMMARY

Cambourne (1988) systematically observed toddlers in experimenter-free settings and recorded their talk with caregivers, friends, neighbours and in a range of different settings. He identified certain conditions in the language-learning environment which he considered 'necessary' conditions for language learning to occur. Cambourne suggests that these conditions are essential for early literacy learning in classrooms. These eight conditions are summarised as follows.

- **Immersion**: Language learning involves being immersed in language. Babies are immersed in language (and involved in it) from birth. In classrooms, children can be immersed in literacy and oracy.
- **Demonstration**: To learn language, children need demonstrations of why they use language, how they use language and what language to use. Demonstrations of talking, listening, reading and writing are essential in literacy teaching to show children at all levels what they can do, why they should do it and how to go about it.
- **Engagement**: Immersion and demonstration are not sufficient conditions for language learning. The child must be engaged and take part or else learning will not occur.
- **Expectations**: Parents give very clear signs that they expect their babies to learn to talk. Teachers need to have clear, high expectations in literacy and oracy learning.
- **Responsibility**: Babies learning to talk initiate much of the talk and take responsibility; similarly, children need to participate in decision-making in school language learning.
- **Employment**: Young children use language long before they have a perfect mastery of it and 'practise' in situations like babbling and pre-sleep monologues; similarly, young literacy learners need plenty of chances to use language for a purpose and to practise.
- **Approximations**: Parents accept approximations from young children and see in them signs of development. Teachers, too, must accept approximations as part of learning literacy.
- **Response**: Parents respond positively and give meaning-based, but usually correct, responses to children's approximations. Feedback is very important in early literacy and oracy work.

Language learning for children with EAL

The conditions of language and literacy learning discussed above are just as powerful for children whose first language is not English but, clearly, they have language-learning experience in one language at home and in another at school. Moreover, much of the literacy-focused activity they may have done in home settings will not have been in English or about literacy in English. These children may have a huge range of positive experiences of literacy in another language and will have a foundation in language about literacy, key stories or rhymes. However, these may not be in English.

Children become bilingual very effectively if they are offered plenty of opportunities to develop their English language skills in ways which are age appropriate for them. Ideally, children will start to become bilingual from very early in their lives and in Early Years settings, through play and interaction with adults and other children. The big challenge for teachers is that children with EAL do not fit one pattern. They may start to learn English at different ages and with different language and personal experiences and this means it is very important to differentiate to meet their needs. In an Early Years setting, this may still mean teaching language through the conditions discussed above and making additional efforts to use gestures, role plays and play activities to share language. The research evidence suggests that it is spoken language proficiency which is the most important aspect of language learning for young EAL pupils.

RESEARCH SUMMARY RESEARCH SUMMARY **RESEARCH SUMMARY** RESEARCH SUMMARY

The National Literacy Panel on Language-Minority Children and Youth in the USA examined peer-reviewed studies dating from 1980 to investigate the development of literacy in language-minority children and youth, and cross-linguistic relationships. The report (August and Shanahan, 2006) points to very different developmental trends in word-level aspects of literacy (e.g., decoding, spelling) as compared with text-level skills such as reading comprehension.

Language-minority students frequently develop word-level skills to the same degree as their monolingual peers, but significant differences tend to remain in text-level skills. The panel also concluded that what they term 'oral language proficiency' explained minimal amounts of variance in word-level skills but played a much greater role in reading comprehension in English for second-language students. The panel points out that oral vocabulary knowledge plays a 'crucial role' (2006: p. 46) in reading comprehension.

This finding, which has also been reported in the UK, emphasises that early language development is the key to later comprehension success. Children with EAL may learn word level aspects of literacy like phonics particularly well, because they have metalinguistic capabilities monolinguals lack, but the development of comprehension is a longer-term prospect which is founded on oral language use.

A SUMMARY OF **KEY POINTS**

➢ **Language is functional and orientated towards meaning.**
➢ **Language is encoded meaning and successful use of it demands the ability to decode.**

> ➤ The codes of language occur at three levels: word, sentence and text.

> ➤ There are a number of processes that characterise children's learning of spoken language, such as immersion in meaningful talk and the use of approximations.

> ➤ Early, pre-school learning of literacy and language relies on similar processes.

> ➤ Oral language proficiency is particularly important for learners with EAL and is a key objective of their Early Years education.

M-LEVEL EXTENSION > > M-LEVEL EXTENSION > > M-LEVEL EXTENSION

Use the eight conditions for language learning as developed by Cambourne (see above) as a checklist against which to evaluate the literacy-learning environment in a classroom with which you are familiar. Try to make judgements about the extent to which the children in this classroom:

- are immersed in literacy;
- receive demonstrations of expert literate behaviour;
- are engaged with literacy;
- are expected to succeed in literacy;
- are given responsibility for their own literacy learning;
- gain practice in using literacy;
- are allowed to approximate to the forms of adult use of literacy;
- receive regular responses from adults to their use of literacy.

Having made your judgements consider whether any of the eight aspects could be improved and how you would approach this with a class of your own. You may wish to read the next chapter as you do this.

FURTHER READING FURTHER READING FURTHER READING FURTHER READING

August, D. and Shanahan, T. (eds) (2006) *Developing literacy in second-language learners: Report of the National Literacy Panel on Language-Minority Children and Youth*. Mahwah, NJ: Lawrence Erlbaum.

Crystal, D. (2010) *The Cambridge Encyclopaedia of Language* (3rd edn). Cambridge: Cambridge University Press.

DfE (2013) *The National Curriculum in England*. London: DfE. (https://www.gov.uk/dfe/nationalcurriculum)

DfE (2013) *Teachers' Standards*. London: DfE. (https://www.gov.uk/government/uploads/system/uploads/attachment_data/file/208682/Teachers__Standards_2013.pdf)

Geekie, P., Cambourne, B. and Fitzsimmons, P. (1999) *Understanding Literacy Development*. Stoke-on-Trent: Trentham.

Halliday, M.A.K. (2004) *An Introduction to Functional Grammar* (3rd edn). London: Edward Arnold.

3
Effective English teaching

TEACHERS' STANDARDS

A teacher must:

3. **Demonstrate good subject and curriculum knowledge**

   - have a secure knowledge of the relevant subject(s) and curriculum areas, foster and maintain pupils' interest in the subject, and address misunderstandings
   - demonstrate a critical understanding of developments in the subject and curriculum areas, and promote the value of scholarship
   - demonstrate an understanding of and take responsibility for promoting high standards of literacy, articulacy and the correct use of standard English, whatever the teacher's specialist subject
   - if teaching early reading, demonstrate a clear understanding of systematic synthetic phonics

4. **Plan and teach well structured lessons**

   - impart knowledge and develop understanding through effective use of lesson time
   - promote a love of learning and children's intellectual curiosity
   - contribute to the design and provision of an engaging curriculum within the relevant subject area(s).

5. **Adapt teaching to respond to the strengths and needs of all pupils**

   - have a secure understanding of how a range of factors can inhibit pupils' ability to learn, and how best to overcome these
   - have a clear understanding of the needs of all pupils, including those with special educational needs; those of high ability; those with English as an additional language; those with disabilities; and be able to use and evaluate distinctive teaching approaches to engage and support them.

8. **Fulfil wider professional responsibilities**

   - take responsibility for improving teaching through appropriate professional development

Introduction

In the previous chapter, we considered the key features of language and some of the conditions that support language learning. From these, it is possible to draw out some important strategies for teaching English in the primary school. We suggest that the following teaching strategies are features of successful literacy and spoken language teaching at all key stages, but these teaching strategies will, of course, operate rather differently in the Early Years, and each of the first two key stages. We will provide some examples of how this works.

Offer frequent demonstrations

In teaching literacy and spoken language, the teacher has to offer **demonstrations**, or models, of all aspects of what is being taught, because the processes are largely invisible and it would be hard for children to infer them without a model. In reading, it is important to demonstrate what reading involves. This means reading enlarged texts so that the children can see the text and read it with the teacher. Big books are popular in the Early Years and at Key Stage 1 for this reason. At Key Stage 2, posters and overhead projectors allow teachers and children to share texts. The use of interactive whiteboards increasingly facilitates the sharing of texts for all ages.

In demonstrations of reading children need to see all aspects of reading, for example:

- **the content** – the meaning of the passage and how it is encoded, including the direction of text, the concept of a word, and the structures of particular text types;
- **the skills of reading** – how the experienced reader works out words or meanings and the strategies used;
- **the reader's response to reading** – teachers need to demonstrate how the purpose of the text affects the reader. If it is a story, what is enjoyable, and why? If it is a persuasive text, what persuades, and how?

The same is true of demonstrations of writing. Teachers can model writing right from the beginning of Nursery provision. This involves demonstrating:

- **appropriate content** – what goes into each type of writing and how to generate and order ideas;
- **the skills of writing** – in the early stages this will involve demonstrating handwriting and spacing, spelling and layout. Later, children need to see idea generation, revision and reordering of ideas, and editing and changing of texts;
- **knowledge of the features of the text type** – knowing what the text aims to achieve and how to choose structures, words and ideas to suit the reader.

In speaking and listening teachers also have an important role to play in demonstrating the use of Standard English, especially as many children may not actually speak Standard English but will have a home dialect or language of their own. Teachers initially model Standard English through their speech with children, but later in school will also model its use by discussing when Standard English is, and is not, a good language choice. Role play and hot seating are strategies that involve modelling the use of English. As well as modelling a particular variant of English, the teacher will also model how to achieve particular speech purposes – a report, a discussion or a storytelling. Speech, especially intonation, is a very important aid to making sense and using grammar for reading for early readers.

Demonstrations, or models, are very important in literacy and spoken language in showing children what to do and how to do it, but they are only useful if children are able to make the links between demonstrations and their own work. Talk is one way to help them do this.

Talk about language

It is important to be able to talk about language choices with children in group, whole-class and individual situations. Talking about language choices and their effects helps children to become better at using language for a purpose. It is important to have a shared vocabulary about language (a **meta-language**) so that issues can be dealt with clearly. Naturally, talk about language becomes more abstract the more experienced the children are, but it would be a mistake to think that only older children can discuss language. The youngest children use terms such as 'story', 'dictionary', 'word', 'letter', 'sound' or 'phoneme' (depending on your preference) and older children can use a very wide range of terms clearly. It is also apparent that many teachers of literacy, at all levels, use a great many technical terms with their pupils.

RESEARCH SUMMARY   RESEARCH SUMMARY   **RESEARCH SUMMARY**   RESEARCH SUMMARY

Wray and Medwell (2002), in their Effective Teachers of Literacy study, found evidence of the following terms being used by literacy teachers.

- **Word level**: alphabet, alphabetical order, rhyme, definition, beginning sound, middle sound, end sound, vowel, word, letter, sound, blend, magic e, homophone, synonym, digraph, prefix, spelling string.
- **Sentence level**: capital letter, full stop, sentence, speech mark, inverted comma, noun (thing word), adjective (describing word), contraction, apostrophe, word order, dialogue, conversation, apostrophe, question mark.
- **Text level**: predict, picture, caption, label, paragraph, planning, drafting, revising (plan, draft, revision), story, instructions, report, headings, ending, opening, character, setting, alliteration, ingredients, list, fiction, non-fiction, layout, address, salutation, skimming, scanning, highlight, key word, meaning, expression, image, simile.
- **Range of text types**: poem, author, illustrator, paperback and hardback, nursery rhyme, cover, ISBN, picture, script, play, recipe, dictionary, appreciation, comparison.

It is important, when discussing language, to make sure you are actually discussing how a language element works in the context of a passage: often a shared or guided reading or writing passage or a piece of the child's own work. Simply offering children definitions of language units does little to further their understanding.

Make learning goals clear

It is important to be quite clear about what you want children to learn and why. For you, as a teacher, this is vital to planning effective lessons. For the children as learners, it helps them to understand what they learn and to make links between their understandings. For very young children, objectives will be simpler than for older children but it is still essential to make them clear.

In English lessons for children at Key Stages 1 and 2, many teachers write the objectives of a lesson in a way that is clearly visible for the children. This is useful, as long as you check that children have read and understood these objectives, that they are checking their learning against them and that they are considering when they might use this piece of learning again. Successful English teachers often check these things in whole-class introductions and plenaries.

Have high expectations and targets

Literacy learning is less instinctive than learning to speak and listen: literacy, for example, is not a 'natural' human activity in the same way that learning spoken language is. There are no human societies in which using spoken language is not almost universally learnt, but there are some societies in which not everyone becomes literate. However, literacy is a very normal activity in our society and so it is quite appropriate to signal to children that you expect them to learn the processes involved. Indicating to children that they are likely to find an activity or skill impossible or very difficult can inhibit their progress. As children progress through schooling, it is important to set targets for groups and individuals so that they can focus on improving particular aspects of the very complex processes of literacy and spoken language use. The key to doing this is to assess children's progress diagnostically.

Use language purposefully

Whenever possible, children should understand the purpose of the text they are reading or creating. This gives them a clear view of the reader or author and enables them to make appropriate language choices and responses. It is also good practice for children to see examples of the text type they are working on, examine how that text works and then create that type of text. This is a useful cycle because it gives children a clear context for language study. When you are studying a word or sentence level element of language, it is important for children to understand how they will use this element and what its contribution is to the whole text.

Play with language

Play is a vital learning process for young children and it is, in itself, a purposeful activity for them. When young children play with language, they are able to explore its purposes, forms and the reactions of others to their use of language. Language play is an important part of the Early Years and Key Stage 1 classrooms.

IN THE CLASSROOM

Mrs S has set up a dramatic play area in her Reception/Y1 class. She changes the theme regularly so that children have three different play settings each term. In the final part of the winter term, just before Christmas, the class have been studying 'people who help us' and have had visits from people in the community, including a postman. Mrs S has made the dramatic play area into a post office for the children to use. To do this, she has introduced a suitable table to be a counter and placed on it a till and play money, a post-person's hat, some scales, envelopes and paper and 'pretend' stamps. She has collected a variety of forms for purposes such as TV licences and passport applications from the real post office and made them available in the class post office. The teaching assistant in the school has made a set of parcels of various shapes and sizes, containing a range of items, which each bear the name and address of a child in the class. The children are encouraged to write letters, take them to the post office, 'buy' stamps and post letters to friends in the class post-box. A designated post-person distributes class letters when the class gathers on the mat. Groups of children are given a designated time in the dramatic play area. In this area, they can adopt the roles of customer, recipient of a letter or parcel, post office cashier or post-person. In one hour of observing the children, they use language in a variety of ways.

- Children fill out forms and practise 'writing' official documents. They are not all able to use correct letter formation but it is noticeable that one child points out to another that you only write in the spaces on forms.
- Children take forms and letters to the cashier and 'buy' stamps, engaging in the ritualised conversation used in such transactions. They are remarkably aware of the sort of language used, such as 'Can I help you?' and 'I would like two first-class stamps, please.'
- Two children use the scales and balance to work out whose parcel is heavier. Then they experiment with rolling, rattling and shaking to work out what could be in the parcels. They use a wide range of mathematical and descriptive language and show quite clearly that they are thinking through their talk.
- Several children use the paper and envelopes to make and send Christmas cards. It is clear that they know how such cards look and that they only have to write a short message in them. The children 'address' the envelopes and post them.
- Mrs S comes over to the post office and asks if she is in time to come and collect her monthly pension money. The 'cashier' says she has just a few minutes but must hurry. She stamps Mrs S's 'book' and gives her some money, saying 'closing time now, please go out quickly' as she does it. Mrs S thanks her politely and leaves.
- The 'cashier' closes and tidies the post office, grumbling to himself as he does so about the untidiness of customers. He is looking at the post office from someone else's point of view. He then counts the money and writes down how many forms he has got left.

This is a fairly typical dramatic play area. Other settings you may encounter include a home area, a garden centre, a space ship, a boarding kennel, a hairdresser's, a toy or grocery shop, a café or restaurant, a newsagent's and a supermarket. All these settings offer huge potential for literacy and language play. They all demand certain types of conversation and provide literacy artefacts that let children experiment with a variety of literacy acts, such as reading newspapers and catalogues and writing letters, menus, shopping lists and so on. It is important to note that Mrs S participates in the play, signalling her expectations and offering children models of language and ideas for new roles and actions.

EMBEDDING ICT EMBEDDING ICT **EMBEDDING ICT** EMBEDDING ICT **EMBEDDING ICT**

When you are developing a dramatic play area such as the ones described above, remember to make these as realistic and up to date as possible by including a range of information and communication technologies. If you are planning a shop, include an electronic till and a modern telephone handset. In the hairdressing salon or boarding kennel, include a laptop so that the children can take bookings and make appointments. In a coffee shop or restaurant, include a calculator to add up the bills. In a hotel reception area, include the computer so that the children can print out customers' accounts.

It is not only the younger children who play with language. Word play is important for older primary children, and nonsense poetry, rhymes, riddles and puns are all text types included for study, experience and enjoyment in literacy sessions for older primary children.

Practise language use

Literacy and spoken language include a variety of skills that become better with practice. However, the term practice does not mean that children have to do endless, repetitive, decontextualised exercises. The use of language exercises to learn little bits of language has presented problems in the past. The chief problem is that a skill or knowledge item practised in an exercise may not transfer into the child's everyday repertoire and may not be used in other work – in which case, it is not useful to the child. Perhaps the best example of this is the child who spells a word correctly in a spelling test, then immediately gets it wrong in a piece of **extended writing**. To avoid this, it is best to focus on the study of language in the context of whole texts. If a child has looked at a language element in a text and will go on to use that language element in creating a similar text, then working with it using an exercise can be useful. It is important to remember that play tasks and writing and discussion tasks in other subject areas are also good practice of literacy and spoken language skills.

THE BIGGER PICTURE THE BIGGER PICTURE THE BIGGER PICTURE THE BIGGER PICTURE

When you are planning opportunities for children to practise language use, think about the text types that you will need to choose for them to read and write. Think more widely than just your sessions in English. Don't forget about primary and secondary source materials in history, geography and RE, information texts of different kinds in science and art, persuasive materials in personal, social and health education and citizenship, and opportunities to use instructional writing in design technology and PE. Cross-curricular planning such as this can help to consolidate new literacy and spoken language skills meaningfully and reinforce the need for children to use them in all contexts as they talk, read and write for a purpose.

Develop independence

As children develop as both literacy and spoken language learners, they move from dependence on more experienced language learners to independence. There are various levels of independence that will probably be used each time a new text type is encountered, so that children read it first with a great deal of support, explore the language of the text, write texts of that type with support and then write independently.

In planning your classroom, you can also give children the opportunity to be independent learners. This means involving children in taking responsibility for organising resources, selecting activities and using the literacy resources around them, such as spelling prompts, reminder sheets and dictionaries.

Offer feedback

Having offered children clear messages about what you want them to learn, you must then offer clear feedback about their progress, both in writing and verbally. The quality of your feedback is important. If you simply praise indiscriminately, children will soon learn that your feedback does not mean much. When offering feedback about work or to questions, it is important:

- not to praise wrong answers – thank the child for offering the answer but say they are not right and offer more support to get the answer or task right;
- to offer specific praise, which makes it clear what has been learned or achieved, rather than general comments such as 'good' or 'well done' – ticks tell children almost nothing;
- to praise improvements in performance for individuals, which will not be the same as for the class as whole;
- to take positive feedback opportunities to look forward to the next target.

When marking written work, feedback should relate to the criteria you set for the task – either specific criteria for that task, class targets or individual targets.

Celebrate success

Finally, celebrate the literacy and spoken language success of your class. One way of celebrating work is to get children to perform or read out work to the class or a group. This is also a chance to teach your children to comment positively on other children's work. Simply pointing out improvements in performance or using reward or house point charts also celebrates children's success. In literacy, high quality displays of work celebrate children's success, but remember to display the work so that others can read it. Think about the children's eye levels. Try to choose a range of achievements to display, including handwriting, composition and planning tasks, as this will allow you to display the successes of a wider range of children.

RESEARCH SUMMARY RESEARCH SUMMARY **RESEARCH SUMMARY** RESEARCH SUMMARY

The *Effective Teaching* report (Ko and Sammons, 2013) presents a thorough review of the research literature on effective teaching and suggests that effective teachers:

- are clear about teaching goals;
- are knowledgeable about curriculum content and the strategies for teaching it;
- communicate to their learners what is expected of them, and why;
- make expert use of existing teaching materials in order to devote more time to practices that enrich and clarify the content;
- are knowledgeable about their learners, adapting teaching to their needs and anticipating misconceptions in their existing knowledge;
- teach meta-cognitive strategies and give learners opportunities to master them;
- address higher- as well as lower-level cognitive objectives;
- monitor learners' understanding by offering regular appropriate feedback;
- integrate their teaching with that in other subject areas;
- accept responsibility for learner outcomes.

RESEARCH SUMMARY RESEARCH SUMMARY **RESEARCH SUMMARY** RESEARCH SUMMARY

One of the most significant research-based books about teaching was published in 2012. John Hattie's *Visible Learning for Teachers* is a thorough account of his meta-analysis of the effects on student achievement of a host of teaching interventions. Hattie distils the results of evaluations of these interventions into what he refers to as 'effect sizes', that is, the size of the effect that the intervention has had on learner achievement. An effect size bigger than zero meant that achievement was raised by the intervention. However, in many cases, achievement would have gone up anyway, just through things such as learners growing older and more mature, so Hattie sets the bar for an effect size to be significant rather higher than zero. He uses the figure of 0.4 as an effect size to take notice of. If an intervention has an effect of 0.4 or higher, then it might be worth other teachers adopting it.

In the appendix to his book, Hattie lists, in order of effect size, those interventions whose effects on achievement have been researched. The highest effect size (and thus, according to Hattie's argument, the most effective teaching intervention) is 'Self-reported grades/Student expectations', with an effect size of 1.44, which we might take to mean getting learners to grade their own achievements in particular tasks and set themselves high targets for future tasks.

Interventions which are particularly relevant to the material presented in this book were found to have the following effect sizes.

Intervention	Effect size
Classroom discussion	0.82
Reciprocal teaching	0.74
Meta-cognitive strategies	0.69
Prior achievement and knowledge	0.65
Self-verbalisation and self-questioning	0.64
Comprehension programs	0.60
Phonics instruction	0.60
Peer tutoring	0.55
Cooperative vs competitive learning	0.54

A SUMMARY OF **KEY POINTS**

Successful literacy and spoken language teaching includes a range of key strategies.

➢ **The teacher has to offer frequent demonstrations or models of all aspects of what is being taught, including speaking, listening, reading and writing.**

➢ **It is important for children to be able to talk about language choices in whole-class, group and individual situations and they need a shared vocabulary or meta-language to do so.**

➢ **It is important to make learning goals clear – to share with children what you want them to learn and why.**

➢ **You need to have high expectations of all children and to set targets for groups and individuals to achieve.**

> ➢ Children need to use language purposefully and to see how different text types are used before attempting to write in that genre themselves.

> ➢ Young children need opportunities to play with language in order to explore its purposes, forms and the reactions of others to their use of it.

> ➢ You should provide a range of meaningful contexts for children to practise language use, including outside of English sessions.

> ➢ You can help children to learn to develop independence by helping them to read a new text type together with a great deal of support, explore the language of the text and write texts of that type with support before they go on to write one independently.

> ➢ Children need high quality feedback about their progress, both verbal and written.

> ➢ You should celebrate children's success in spoken language and literacy in a range of ways.

M-LEVEL EXTENSION > > M-LEVEL EXTENSION > > M-LEVEL EXTENSION

Compare the approach to, and organisation of, literacy teaching in schools in which you have worked so far.

- Do schools teach literacy through a discrete literacy lesson?
- What variations have you seen in how their literacy teaching is organised?
- How did the schools rationalise their particular approaches?

FURTHER READING FURTHER READING FURTHER READING FURTHER READING

DfE (2013) *Teachers' Standards*. London: DfE. (https://www.gov.uk/government/uploads/system/uploads/attachment_data/file/208682/Teachers__Standards_2013.pdf)

Hattie, J. (2012) *Visible Learning for Teachers*. London: Routledge

Ko, J. and Sammons, P. (2013) *Effective Teaching: A Review of Research and Evidence*. Reading: Centre for British Teachers. (http://cdn.cfbt.com/~/media/cfbtcorporate/files/research/2013/r-effective-teaching-2013.pdf)

Palmer, S. and Corbett, P. (2003) *Literacy: what works?* Cheltenham: Nelson Thornes.

Wray, D. and Medwell, J. (2002) *Teaching Literacy Effectively*. Abingdon: RoutledgeFalmer.

4
Speaking and listening: developing talk in the primary classroom

TEACHERS' STANDARDS

A teacher must:

3. **Demonstrate good subject and curriculum knowledge**

   - have a secure knowledge of the relevant subject(s) and curriculum areas, foster and maintain pupils' interest in the subject, and address misunderstandings
   - demonstrate a critical understanding of developments in the subject and curriculum areas, and promote the value of scholarship
   - demonstrate an understanding of and take responsibility for promoting high standards of literacy, articulacy and the correct use of standard English, whatever the teacher's specialist subject
   - if teaching early reading, demonstrate a clear understanding of systematic synthetic phonics

4. **Plan and teach well structured lessons**

   - impart knowledge and develop understanding through effective use of lesson time
   - promote a love of learning and children's intellectual curiosity
   - contribute to the design and provision of an engaging curriculum within the relevant subject area(s).

5. **Adapt teaching to respond to the strengths and needs of all pupils**

   - have a secure understanding of how a range of factors can inhibit pupils' ability to learn, and how best to overcome these
   - have a clear understanding of the needs of all pupils, including those with special educational needs; those of high ability; those with English as an additional language; those with disabilities; and be able to use and evaluate distinctive teaching approaches to engage and support them.

8. **Fulfil wider professional responsibilities**

   - take responsibility for improving teaching through appropriate professional development

Introduction

Talk is central to the primary curriculum and particularly important in English. Encouraging children to listen carefully and become confident speakers in a wide range of different contexts will provide them with a strong foundation for communication in the broadest sense, as well as establishing a framework for the teaching of reading and writing. The ability to communicate clearly and directly in Standard English underpins all effective teaching, so it is vital that beginning teachers learn to develop a clear speaking voice.

This chapter suggests some detailed ideas for developing effective talk in the classroom from the Early Years onwards. Many of the activities draw on drama techniques. Above all, well-planned oral work in the classroom can be enjoyable, interesting and imaginative, and can extend pupils' experience and understanding in a number of ways.

Encouraging talk in the Early Years

It is not always realised how much talking young children do at home, for instance while playing on their own or with each other, and with adults at mealtimes, bath time and bedtime.

RESEARCH SUMMARY RESEARCH SUMMARY **RESEARCH SUMMARY** RESEARCH SUMMARY

Gordon Wells' (1987) research in the 1980s showed that young children talked far more at home than at school, and that talk at home was often child-led, whereas talk at school was more likely to be teacher-led.

Cathy Nutbrown's (2012) report on qualifications and career pathways in the Early Years, suggested that 'children learn much in sustained interaction with other children, as well as adults who are attuned to children's learning and development needs who can support their play and foster early interactions between young children' (p. 12). The concept of 'Sustained Shared Thinking' has become widely used to describe this kind of teacher–child spoken interaction which can lead to sustained cognitive development (Siraj-Blatchford *et al.,* 2002). Sustained shared thinking has been defined as: 'An episode in which two or more individuals "work together" in an intellectual way to solve a problem, clarify a concept, evaluate activities, extend a narrative etc. Both parties must contribute to the thinking and it must develop and extend the understanding.' (Siraj-Blatchford *et al.,* 2002: p. 8)

While it is clearly important that children learn how to operate in different situations, it is also important for teachers to realise the effects that their own language may have on young children's language development.

There is no shortage of activities to do in Nursery and Reception classes which start from and extend young children's early language skills, as well as helping with early number and science work.

Rhymes

Children love rhymes of all kinds. As well as being fun, rhymes help to increase vocabulary and children's early reading and writing skills through developing phonemic awareness (see Chapter 5). There are many kinds of rhymes, the most common being nursery rhymes; there are also action, nonsense, finger and number rhymes which help children to develop rhythm and simple coordination as well as counting skills. The frequent repetition and use of refrains help to reinforce the vocabulary and rhymes, and young children enjoy being able to learn and recite the rhymes by heart. Plenty of rhymes can be found in *This Little Puffin*, Elizabeth Matterson's collection of children's playground games and rhymes, or Rosen and Steele's *Inky Pinky Ponky*. A simple example of an action rhyme is shown below, with actions in brackets:

Five little peas in a pea pod pressed.	(clench fist to represent pod)
First one grew, then another,	(hold up one then two fingers)
and so did all the rest.	(hold up other fingers in turn)
They grew and they grew	(move both hands away from
and they didn't stop,	each other as the pod grows)
until one day the pod went POP!	(clap hands to make a loud pop)

Rhymes like this are ideally spoken or sung in the carpeted area, with enough space for the children to make simple movements. For rhymes that demand more space (e.g. 'Five little speckled frogs' in which some children can be frogs in the pond), the children could sit in a circle.

Sensory play

Sensory play means play with sand and water, or with other materials such as clay, play-dough, etc. The children will usually talk among themselves about what they are doing and what the water or sand feels like. If the teacher or classroom assistant 'plays' along-side the children, plenty of opportunities for extended talking and questioning arise. For example, if a child is filling a bucket with water, you might say, 'Now try pouring the water on to the water wheel. What happens when you do that?' Simple vocabulary about capacity and weight such as 'full', 'empty', 'heavy' and 'light' can be introduced. The children can be encouraged to describe how the sand or water feels as they play with it. Introduce plenty of different-sized containers for comparison.

Here are some ideas for sensory activities for small groups:

- 'feely' bags with differently shaped objects (for example ball, cube, ring) – ask the children to describe the shapes;
- 'feely' bags with contrasting materials (for example satin and hessian, wood and metal) to introduce vocabulary like 'smooth' and 'rough';
- containers with foods of different textures (for example jelly, jam, peeled orange, hard boiled egg) to encourage descriptive responses;
- blindfold tasting to experience different flavours such as sweet and sour (for example apple juice, lemon juice).

The last two activities need careful planning and organisation to avoid possible mess (aprons and paper towels need to be on hand), and clear controls need to be established to avoid over-excitement. You also need to check any possible allergies or dietary habits if food tasting is involved. In spite of these caveats, these are rewarding activities that often encourage the shyest pupil to open up and talk.

Imaginative play

Imaginative play is a particularly effective way to encourage young children to talk. However, it will not happen by itself. Imaginative play needs careful organisation and thought, with sensitive teacher intervention in order to extend the children's language development. Nursery and Reception classes often have home corners for domestic play, but, if left unattended, this can lead to stereotyped play with limited gender roles. A more effective alternative is to set up varied role-play areas, which can be developed with the involvement of the children themselves, and which are changed regularly.

IN THE CLASSROOM

Books can be a useful starting point for role-play areas, which can also be related to topic work. For example, a topic on food in a Reception class involved reading Allan and Janet Ahlberg's *Mrs Wobble the Waitress*, and led to planning and making a café area in the classroom. The children discussed what they wanted in the café, planned and designed the menus and signs, and took on the roles of cook, waiter and waitress, receptionist and customers. As a culmination of the project, the children invited their parents into the café, and served them fruit drinks and cakes, which they had made themselves. In this case, the role-play developed from an activity for small groups into a more public event with a real purpose and audience.

Other role-play areas that have been used successfully include real-life situations such as a doctor's surgery, hospital, optician, travel agent, shop (for example a baker's, green-grocer's, clothes shop or newsagent), or imaginary/fairy story places, such as the three bears' house, a gingerbread cottage, the yellow submarine, or an underwater kingdom. The teacher can easily and naturally take on a role in these situations and enter into the role-play as and when it seems appropriate. However, it is important to be sensitive to the children's space and either wait to be invited or ask if you can join in.

Some other useful hints are listed below.

- Restrict numbers in the role-play area to three or four at a time. Keep a record of who has used it so that everyone can take a turn.
- Make role cards or labels for the different roles (doctor, nurse, patient) for easy identification and to ensure the children swap roles regularly. This helps to avoid gender stereotyping of roles and to alter power relations (for example to avoid the same child always being in charge).
- Introduce an event or challenge into the role-play in order to maintain motivation and interest (for example the shoe shop has a sale or the three bears hold a party).

These activities need much careful organisation and planning. However, at least some of the work can be built into the literacy lesson (stories as a starting point in shared reading or making notices in guided writing). Time in the area itself can also be one of the activities during group work or built into other times of the day as there may well be cross-curricular links (such as travel agent links to geography or optician links to science).

Storytelling and traditional stories

The use of traditional stories, storytelling and retelling have long been in the repertoire of experienced Early Years teachers (Grainger, 1997). You need to introduce a wide range of stories to the children, both in picture book format and through oral telling. This is a good opportunity to include traditional stories and folk tales from all around the world (such as Anansi stories from the Caribbean or Russian Baba Yaga stories) in order to broaden horizons from Hans Andersen and Grimm, and avoid race, gender and class stereotypes.

Many children will only be familiar with traditional stories from Walt Disney film versions; returning to the originals will broaden their experience. Many pre-recorded stories are now available for quiet listening, but nothing equals the power of the direct approach. Look out for local storytellers who will visit the school, or theatre-in-education companies who can bring stories to life in a vivid and immediate way.

In retelling stories in an interactive way, teachers can begin to reinforce traditional story openings ('Once upon a time') and endings, as well as story structure and narrative. This helps children when they are learning to read, as well as in writing their own stories later. Children's confidence can be developed through storytelling activities, as well as early cooperative skills. Using and telling stories in different languages can help bilingual children and those with English as an additional language to develop their new language as well as reinforcing skills in their first language.

IN THE CLASSROOM

Most children already know the story of Goldilocks and the three bears, but it has plenty of potential for development and oral work. In a Nursery class, the teacher told the story to the children and then asked them to retell it with her. They drew pictures of their favourite part of the story. They made porridge, added different flavours (salt, sugar, honey, etc.) and talked about which they preferred. With the teacher's help, they turned the home corner into the three bears' cottage and re-enacted the story through role-play. They read and discussed Goldilocks' letter of apology to the three bears in Janet and Allan Ahlberg's *The Jolly Postman*. A parent helper dressed up as Baby Bear and appeared in the classroom lost and upset because her chair had been broken by Goldilocks. The children helped her by asking if she knew the way home, suggested phoning home or the police, and took her to the school office to make the call. This led to further discussion with the teacher about times when they had been lost or upset (QCA, 1999).

Puppets

Puppets are another valuable resource in the Early Years classroom, and can help oral work, story-making and manual dexterity. Simple finger puppets made from felt can be easily made with young children and shoeboxes can be transformed into puppet theatres. Many glove puppets, usually of animals, are also available commercially, and can be used effectively by the teacher and children alike. Often, children who have been reluctant to speak will talk through their puppets: it is a less immediate, and therefore sometimes less threatening, means of encouraging talk than role-play. Many of the features of storytelling mentioned above can also be incorporated in work with puppets. Using puppets also helps to develop an early sense of audience and performance, and encourages co-operation and interaction with others.

Speaking and listening at Key Stage 1

Many of the ideas and strategies for oral work already introduced can be adapted and developed further at Key Stage 1, using group discussion and drama to develop imaginative responses as well as concentration and confidence in speaking.

RESEARCH SUMMARY RESEARCH SUMMARY **RESEARCH SUMMARY** RESEARCH SUMMARY

Neil Mercer and his colleagues carried out a number of very important research studies into the role of speaking and listening in learning. One study, for example, focused on the question, 'Does improving children's talk skills improve their participation in lessons?' This study involved Year 2 pupils and was part of the 'Talking for Success Project' (Wegerif *et al.,* 2004). The researchers argued that having poor communication skills would reduce children's participation in lessons, exclude them from learning activities and could result in lower levels of achievement. Their project was designed to improve children's access to education through teaching them how to interact and reason with each other. They found that the programme led to improved interactions and participation by the target group pupils. They asked more questions and gave reasons more often than the control group children. They also learned to involve each other, listen carefully to what each other said and respond constructively, even if their response was a challenge. In addition, target group children completed more puzzles correctly in a reasoning test after the programme than before.

Responding to texts

There are numerous possibilities at Key Stage 1 to develop oral responses to picture books, poems and rhymes, building on work already done in the Nursery and Reception classes. An extension of rhyming activities in the Early Years leads into action stories and the beginnings of movement and drama. A particularly effective example is *We're Going on a Bear Hunt* by Rosen and Oxenbury, which can be carried out sitting on the carpet or enacted in a larger space with the children moving around the room. The beginning of the story, with suggested actions for the carpeted area, is shown below, with capitals for spoken emphasis and actions in brackets.

	(start rhythm by slapping knees: 1-2, 1-2)
We're going on a bear hunt.	(continue rhythm to show walking)
We're going to catch a BIG one.	(emphasise 'big' with hands far apart)
It's a BEAUTIFUL day.	(hands make circle to show sun)
I'm not scared.	(shake head for extra emphasis)
Uh-oh! Grass! Long wavy grass.	(hands up and down to show grass)
Refrain:	
We can't go OVER it.	(lift hands to show 'over')
We can't go UNDER it.	(lower hands to show 'under')
We can't go ROUND it.	(move hands round)
We'll have to go THROUGH it.	(move hands forward or 'through')
Swishy-swashy! Swishy-swashy!	(move hands from side to side)

The action builds up with a succession of obstacles, which the children have to overcome (useful for introducing prepositions of place). The refrain is repeated at each obstacle, with a different sound and action, and the adventure ends with a quick retreat home with the actions in reverse order when a large bear is finally found. It is great fun, and children in Key Stage 1 enjoy this kind of activity as much as those in the Early Years. For Year 1 children, you will need to build up to this after practice with simpler action rhymes, and accompanying stories with actions or sounds. Associated activities include hearing and making up riddles, tongue twisters and nonsense rhymes, which develop and extend children's phonemic awareness in enjoyable ways.

Role-play and role-play areas can also provide enriching language experiences at Key Stage 1 and are particularly effective with stories as a stimulus.

IN THE CLASSROOM

A topic on communication in a Year 1 class, including a post office role-play, was sparked off by reading the Ahlbergs' *The Jolly Postman* and led to the setting up of a post office in the activity area outside the classroom. The teacher arranged for a parent who was a postman to talk to the children about his job. They also visited the local post office to see what they would need to include. After this preparation, the children made a large postbox, designed and made forms and wrote out notices. They took turns to serve in the post office and be customers. The teacher also set aside a writing corner in the classroom and encouraged the children to write letters to her or each other, which they posted in the postbox. Although the children's writing was at an early stage, the motivation that was generated by the project led many children to make dramatic improvements in their ability to write simple sentences as well as in their oral work.

Storytelling can also be extended at Key Stage 1, and can be linked to simple drama techniques. The example below uses the traditional story of Goldilocks and the three bears again, but shows how it can be extended in different ways at Key Stage 1.

IN THE CLASSROOM

The teacher of a Year 1 class started with an indirect way into the story by taking on the role of Goldilocks' mother. She enacted a short breakfast time scene where she discovered Goldilocks was missing ('Goldilocks! Your porridge is getting cold') and then enlisted the children's help to find her. This involved recounting the main events of the story, drawing a map showing the route from Goldilocks' house to the three bears' cottage in the woods, a police investigation including 'hot seating' where the three bears were interviewed about their reactions to events, and a 'freeze frame' where groups of children made tableaux or still photographs of the main events for the local newspaper. They also discussed and wrote news flashes for radio or television and short accounts for the newspaper. ICT was involved in tape recording the interviews and word processing the news items. Finally, Goldilocks was tracked down and interviewed or 'hot seated' to find out what had made her run away to the woods.

There are many other ways of developing oral work in response to texts at Key Stage 1. Aidan Chambers (1993) suggests some ways into discussion, through his 'tell me' techniques, which he argues are more direct and concrete than the often off-putting question 'why?' Through the 'tell me' approach, children are encouraged to talk about what they first noticed about a book or story, what they liked and disliked, and to point out any puzzles and patterns. This can lead into detailed work on a story in order to share ideas, and find clues and evidence to support a particular view. The techniques are very useful in promoting high-quality group discussion work, and can also lead into writing through the keeping of reading journals. Although Chambers' work predates the literacy lesson, the suggested activities can easily be adapted to fit shared and particularly guided reading sessions.

Story-making and talking about writing

As in the Early Years work, many of the oral activities about books and poems described above, especially storytelling and drama, link to children's own writing at Key Stage 1. As well as discussing story structures, characters and actions in relation to texts, children can be encouraged to create their own stories orally in readiness for writing.

A story circle is an enjoyable way into story-making, and also enhances imagination, listening skills and turn-taking. It is best carried out in groups rather than with the whole class, and can be fitted easily into a group activity in a literacy lesson. Building on games like 'I went to market and I bought a…', which are essentially listing and memory exercises, story circles can involve more complex sequencing of ideas and events. For example, the teacher or a child can start a story with a simple opening, for example 'One morning, Sally went to see her friend Ahmed'. The story is passed round the circle, with each person starting their contribution with 'fortunately' or 'unfortunately', which can give rise to highly amusing results. An alternative is to use different words and phrases to link each person's turn, such as 'then', 'suddenly', 'meanwhile', 'after that', trying not to repeat the same ones.

Another variation is to place one or more objects (such as a hat, a ring and a box) in the centre of the circle: the group has to make up a short story in which the objects play an important part. A discussion about the objects, considering such factors as to whom they belong, what use or importance they have and where they were found, needs to precede the story itself. Once the ingredients are clear, then the group can begin to construct the story.

The teacher can introduce a particular focus, such as what the characters are like, who owns the objects, or what actions led to the finding of the objects.

IN THE CLASSROOM

After reading Michael Morpurgo's *The Wreck of the Zanzibar* to a Year 2 class, the teacher started a group story circle by showing them a bottle she had supposedly found washed up on the beach. It contained a message that was very old and torn, but which was partly legible and was from Richard Jenkins, who had been shipwrecked on a desert island and was asking for help. The group were asked to discuss who they thought Richard Jenkins was, when he lived (there was no date on the message) and why/how/by whom he might have been shipwrecked. They had to use the clues in the message and list all their ideas and unanswered questions on a large sheet of paper. The next day, with the teacher's help to review their work, they decided on the beginning of their story and built up the events and character profiles using the evidence and ideas they had gathered the previous day. At the teacher's suggestion, they 'hot seated' two of the group, who took on the roles of Richard's best friend and his sister. At this point, one of the group acted as scribe to start writing down the story, which was completed in extended writing time, word processed and illustrated with maps of the island to form a class book.

Other useful starting points for story-making are photographs. They can be collected from magazines and newspapers, but this may limit the images to film and pop stars or people in news stories, which can predetermine the direction of the children's ideas. It is better to use specially prepared collections – for example photographs of families – in which a range of people are presented, and there are accompanying guidelines for teachers. Discussions of photographs need to be handled sensitively in order to avoid reinforcing prejudices, for instance when looking at a family of travellers, but with careful intervention photos can broaden children's horizons and viewpoints and help to challenge gender, race and class stereotypes.

IN THE CLASSROOM

An able Year 2 class had been discussing families, following a reading of Judy Blume's *Superfudge*. The teacher used a family photopack to consider a range of family units before moving into some dramatic writing. First, she put up a selection of the photographs around the walls and asked the children to look carefully at them and put an initial beside the ones they liked best. Then she grouped them according to their choices, and gave each group one photograph. The photos were mounted on a large sheet of paper and the groups were asked to write down as many questions as they could think of, with arrows to the people concerned (for example 'Why is he wearing that funny hat?' and 'Why does she look so upset?') and then to fill in speech or thought bubbles which helped to explain or answer their questions ('This hat hurts but I wanted to look smart' and 'My brother just hit me because I took his sweets'). With the teacher's help, the children discussed the family relationships and related them to their own experiences where they could. The next stage was to record these phrases and then add some dialogue between the family members. The children eventually presented their recordings to each other.

EMBEDDING ICT EMBEDDING ICT **EMBEDDING ICT** EMBEDDING ICT **EMBEDDING ICT**

Tape recorders can be useful tools for recording story ideas, especially when children find writing difficult, and can be used to redraft and edit different versions of stories. They are also effective as a way to turn children's own experiences into oral stories. Recordings of stories can be used as starting points for children's story-making. Although consideration has to be given to noise levels when recording, tape recording can act as a control when space is limited and it is difficult to act out a scene or short play. Using the computer, children can then word process a transcript of their story or play to publish in a book or use in future drama sessions. Older children could use a basic editing program to add sound effects or music to the recording.

Speaking and listening at Key Stage 2

At Key Stage 2, oral work can be extended to involve more complex uses of language in discussion and drama, developing children's skills in reasoning, persuading, constructing an argument or viewpoint, problem solving and evaluating, as well as imaginative responses. Links with reading and writing can be made more extensively and at a higher level, as well as cross-curricular links. Direct work on language, Standard English, accent and dialect can also be carried out.

Responding to stories, poems and non-fiction texts will form a large part of oral work at Key Stage 2. Many of the ideas and techniques discussed at Key Stage 1 can be extended with appropriate texts; for example, the 'tell me' approach can be used with a range of relevant authors, such as Anne Fine, Dick King-Smith, William Mayne and Philippa Pearce. Rather than making this a separate section here, links to texts (both fiction and non-fiction) will be included as part of other oral work.

RESEARCH SUMMARY RESEARCH SUMMARY **RESEARCH SUMMARY** RESEARCH SUMMARY

Wolf *et al.* (2004) carried out a study in the US to explore the question of how classroom talk supported reading comprehension. They built on previous research, which found that the use of collaborative talk during reading lessons was positively associated with gains in comprehension. Their study examined the quality of teachers' and children's talk in ten different schools. It found that effective classroom talk was linked to a high level of pupil thinking and active use of knowledge. Discussion-based activities, in combination with academically challenging tasks, were positively related to children's development of literacy skills. These activities were found to have a positive impact on children's achievement when teachers:

- initiated discussion by using an open-ended query, e.g. 'What's going on here?', and extended the discussion by asking a follow-up query, 'That is what the author said, but what did she mean?'; and
- used a significant number of describing and explaining questions, e.g. 'tell me how you solved the problem'.

Reading, writing and drama

As at Key Stage 1, starting points for imaginative and dramatic writing at Key Stage 2 can be a discussion of stories, poems, objects or photographs (see examples in Key Stage 1 section). Cross-curricular links can also be made, as illustrated in the next example, which uses story, role-play and drama as ways into the development of empathy in a history topic.

IN THE CLASSROOM

A Year 3 class was working on the Victorians, and their teacher read parts of Dorothy Edwards's *A Strong and Willing Girl*, in which a parlour maid tells stories about her life in service. In preparation for a visit to a local Victorian manor house, which included an 'upstairs-downstairs' role-play, a visiting drama teacher took on the role of Lizzy the servant girl, and enacted a short scene about her work. The children were asked to think about who the character was, what she was doing, and what she was feeling (the scene had shown Lizzy upset and angry about an event in the house), and then to decide on questions to ask her in a 'hot seating' session. This led on to the children devising plans about what Lizzy should do next to solve her problem, and improvising short scenes around their ideas. They then wrote imaginary letters home to Lizzy's Mum (as if Lizzy could write), describing events and feelings. After the outing to the manor house, the drama teacher returned to lead a whole-class simulation exercise in the hall in which the children set up a Victorian household. Role cards and instruction sheets were written by the children to denote the different roles and jobs they had seen and tried out on their visit, and the drama teacher took on the role of housekeeper, using a bell as a control device to call the household together for important meetings.

Much useful and enjoyable oral work at Key Stage 2 can be undertaken about the process of drafting and redrafting children's writing. For factual writing, everyday instructional texts such as recipes and timetables or persuasive texts such as advertisements and letters to the press can form the stimulus for group discussion and writing. Once a first draft of the writing is produced, children can work with response partners in order to identify features for improvement.

For example, the children in a Year 4 class worked in pairs, using a work card to help. The children took it in turns to read their work aloud while their partner listened carefully. They were asked to consider and discuss the following kinds of questions about the writing.

- Do you think the writing is interesting/enjoyable?
- Is there anything missing in the piece?
- Can you suggest any helpful words or expressions?
- Can you suggest a more suitable beginning or ending to the piece?
- Do you think it is too long or too short?
- Can anything be missed out?
- Has the writer written what he/she was asked to write?

These questions can be altered according to the particular focus and purpose of the writing; for example, work on characters and story structure can emphasise questions about characterisation and the stages of the story. The activity encourages pupils to listen and express their views clearly, to work co-operatively and independently, and to develop their ideas about writing and responding to writing.

Response partners are a good way into more formal presentations to a large group, which can seem daunting without prior experience in a more protected setting. Once the children are used to pair work, they can move on to more complex oral activities such as 'jigsaws'. In this, the children are divided into 'home' groups in which each pupil is allocated a specific task (for example finding out about different aspects of life in Roman Britain). The children with the same tasks from each home group come together into 'expert' groups in which they pool information about their topic, either independently or guided by the teacher. Once they have completed their tasks, the children return to their home groups to report back their findings. The idea of the child as expert is related to Dorothy Heathcote's dramatic device 'the mantle of the expert' (Heathcote and Bolton, 1995), in which the roles are reversed in a drama and the children are more knowledgeable than the teacher; for example, the teacher is a town planner who wants to develop a site, and the children are archaeologists who know that a Roman villa is buried beneath it. An example is given in the next section.

Discussion groups can also be the basis of oral work that comes together in a class presentation. This could be through the scripting and performing of a short dialogue or play. It could also be in the preparation, writing and presenting of a radio or television documentary.

IN THE CLASSROOM

A small rural primary school was celebrating its centenary and used the opportunity to carry out a number of activities related to the school and its history. Years 5 and 6 did some research about this by reading the school log book and interviewing parents, grandparents and other older people in the village who were former pupils of the school. Out of this came the start of a television documentary.

The teacher divided the class into groups and each group worked on one item for the programme. There were two overall presenters who acted as continuity for the items, as well as presenters, interviewers or performers within each item. One group video recorded interviews with former pupils and with people who worked in the school (the headteacher, caretaker, secretary and dinner ladies). Two groups re-enacted events described in the log book or in interviews. Another group improvised a school scene from Laurie Lee's *Cider With Rosie*, set in a rural school in the early 1900s. The final group acted as collators, providing presenters, a linking script and footage of the current school, and camera crew for some groups. Story boards and cue cards were made, and the final script was word processed. The completed documentary, which took nearly half a term using some literacy lessons and topic time, was presented in a special assembly to the school and an invited audience.

Learning about language

Oral work at Key Stage 2 can address language and how it works directly through a range of activities. For example, in Years 4 and 5, simple pair exercises can be set up to explore accent, dialect and register, through comparing role-plays of informal telephone conversations with a friend to more formal communications with doctors, banks and businesses. In Year 6, detailed language investigations can be carried out through constructing language autobiographies, in which pupils talk to a partner about their own language background or analyse the language, accents and dialects used in a variety of television soap operas.

Differences in language and register can also be approached through drama (Clipson-Boyles, 1998). By taking on roles, children draw on their often unconscious knowledge about language to use different ways of speaking. The teacher can be helpful in modelling this through teacher-in-role. It is important to stress that neither the teacher nor children need to be good actors. In Dorothy Heathcote's words, it is more a question of 'donning an attitude' (Heathcote and Bolton, 1995), which teachers do all the time in the classroom. An example is shown below, which also brings in problem solving and listening to viewpoints.

IN THE CLASSROOM

A Year 4 class was studying volcanoes as part of a geography topic, and building on work done on map-making. They had read parts of William Mayne's *Low Tide*, in which the effects of a tidal wave on a community are vividly portrayed. The teacher set up a whole-class improvisation in which he took on the role of village elder (rather than leader) within a community that lived near a volcano. The crops were failing and there were warning signs that the volcano might erupt soon. The elder brought some evidence (pieces of rock, earth samples and plants) to a village meeting. Addressing the villagers in a formal way ('My friends, I have called this meeting to discuss an important matter'), he asked the children in role as village experts (farmers, geologists and plant specialists) to express their views as to whether they should stay and risk the volcano destroying them, or leave and find a safer place to rebuild their community. The children took it in turns to speak and express their point of view, echoing the formal register used by the elder ('I have lived in this village all my life and I know from the stories of my father and mother that these signs mean danger'). A lively discussion followed about the meaning of the signs and what this meant for the future of the community. The elder summed up the mood of the meeting and the views expressed. The villagers had decided to leave, and the drama ended with the villagers returning to family groups to make plans for their departure and decide what they should take with them. Following this problem-solving drama, the children were asked to reflect on their drama experience, and to write a diary entry to record their feelings about leaving the village.

THE BIGGER PICTURE   THE BIGGER PICTURE   THE BIGGER PICTURE   THE BIGGER PICTURE

When you are planning to develop children's speaking and listening skills at Key Stage 2, remember that talk is important in all areas of the curriculum. In addition to the classroom examples described here, think about planning opportunities for children to talk as they undertake investigations in maths and science, including formulating hypotheses, discussing how they can devise a fair test, deciding what data to collect and agreeing how these will be evaluated. In PE, children can work in pairs to comment on each other's performance and explain how this could be improved. When preparing to go on educational visits, give children opportunities to discuss the kinds of questions that they will ask while they are there and appropriate ways to talk to any people they are likely to meet.

Using language to formulate an argument and express different viewpoints can also be done through the more traditional channel of debates. These provide clear structures for teachers and children alike, and enable views to be prepared and scripted in advance. Children can practise the techniques of persuasion with pair work (e.g. marketing and phone calls) as well as letter writing. There are many variations on this theme, using a dramatic slant. For example, trial scenes also provide a framework within which different viewpoints and arguments can be put forward forcefully and persuasively. With a bit of imagination, trials can be set up to fit many topics (a Roman trial, a medieval trial or a Victorian trial), but obviously these all need researching in advance so that the structure and roles are appropriate to the period and setting. The structure of a formal meeting is also a good one to use in a variety of contexts, such as the volcano-threatened village discussed above, and enables the teacher to establish clear frameworks for behaviour.

IN THE CLASSROOM

The teacher of a Year 6 class used the real-life example of a nearby site due for demolition to combine work on persuasive argument with consideration of differing needs in the local community. The class visited the site, which consisted of some derelict land and a bingo hall that was up for sale. In groups, the pupils discussed and prepared questions arising from the visit, and then interviewed local shopkeepers and residents in order to obtain their views on the future of the site. Using the notes and recordings they had made, the pupils decided on roles that represented the different interest groups involved (developers, residents, shopkeepers, the media and councillors) and prepared arguments that those people could put forward at a community meeting. They also consulted local papers to see what kinds of articles or letters were written about local issues. After much preparation through discussion and writing, the class set up the meeting, which the teacher chaired in the role of a local councillor. The developers were asked to make a presentation about their proposals to turn the site into a leisure centre and then each person put forward his or her view. The discussion opened out into a heated debate about the issues, at the end of which a vote was taken, and the developers were asked to modify their plans in accord with the community's wishes.

The oral activities outlined during the chapter need to be planned carefully, and chosen to match the age, abilities and experience of the children. Some activities will need to be developed slowly after simpler preparatory exercises. For example, it is hard to expect a class or a teacher to embark on a full-scale drama simulation without building up slowly with prior pair or group role-plays. Choose approaches and styles that suit you and the children, and also fit in with other literacy work being planned that term.

Some of the work described above needs careful handling and a sensitive approach on the part of the teacher. Again, prior work on developing pupils' listening skills and respect for others' viewpoints can help when dealing with emotive issues. Be encouraging to pupils who are just beginning to have the confidence to talk in the classroom. There is nothing worse than saying that children's tentatively spoken words are wrong, but they may need help to improve how they express themselves. There is also nothing more rewarding than seeing children who have previously been withdrawn begin to express themselves with confidence. Through oral work and drama, many children who in other contexts lack the ability to express themselves (e.g. in written work) find a voice and an ability to work in an imaginative and often powerful way.

Teachers need to have the confidence to try out some of the drama ideas described. Many teachers are scared at the mention of drama, and yet they may tell and read stories with expression and meaning. It is only a small step further to take on a role within a drama situation or set up a group improvisation.

REFLECTIVE TASK

The 'In the Classroom' sections throughout this chapter have given you a number of examples to consider good teaching practice. Check through these again and choose one that particularly appeals to you. Think about how you might adapt the ideas in your chosen example to children you teach/have taught yourself.

A SUMMARY OF **KEY POINTS**

➢ **Talk is central to learning and particularly important in English.**

➢ **In the Early Years, the use of rhymes helps to increase children's vocabulary and develop phonemic awareness.**

➢ **Other helpful contexts for talk are included in sensory and imaginative play, through storytelling and the use of puppets.**

➢ **In Key Stage 1, these strategies can be further developed to include responding to a wider range of texts, story-making and talking about writing,**

➢ **At Key Stage 2, the opportunities to talk need to be ever widened, including through children's reading and writing and through a range of drama activities.**

➢ **Children can learn about and develop their spoken language skills through all areas of the curriculum.**

M-LEVEL EXTENSION > > M-LEVEL EXTENSION > > M-LEVEL EXTENSION

Look in more detail at the research conducted by Gordon Wells in the 1980s. Consider whether children still get talked to more at home than at school, or whether factors such as increased hours spent watching television or playing computer games has changed this. Find out about early intervention programmes such as the Big Wide Talk, schemes such as Books for Babies and Family Learning courses provided through Children's Centres. What does recent research suggest is the current situation about this issue?

FURTHER READING FURTHER READING FURTHER READING FURTHER READING

Chambers, A. (1993) *Tell Me: Children, Reading and Talk*. Stroud: Thimble Press.

Clipson-Boyles, S. (1998) *Drama in Primary English Teaching*. London: David Fulton.

DfE (2013) *Teachers' Standards*. London: DfE. (https://www.gov.uk/government/uploads/system/uploads/attachment_data/file/208682/Teachers__Standards_2013.pdf)

Grainger, T. (1997) *Traditional Storytelling in the Primary Classroom*. Leamington Spa: Scholastic.

Nutbrown, C. (2012) *Foundations for Quality: The Independent review of early education and child-care qualifications. Final Report*. Runcorn: DfE. (https://www.gov.uk/government/uploads/system/uploads/attachment_data/file/175463/Nutbrown-Review.pdf)

Siraj-Blatchford, I., Sylva, K., Muttock, S., Gilden, R. and Bell, D. (2002) *Researching Effective Pedagogy in the Early Years (REPEY) DfES Research Report 365*. Norwich: HMSO. (http://dera.ioe.ac.uk/4650/1/RR356.pdf)

Tickell, C. (2011) *The Early Years: Foundations for Life, Health and Learning. An Independent Report on the Early Years Foundation Stage to Her Majesty's Government*. London: DfE.

Wells, G. (2009) *The Meaning Makers: Learning to talk and talking to learn* (2nd edn). Bristol: Multilingual Matters.

5
Teaching reading at and before Key Stage 1

TEACHERS' STANDARDS

A teacher must:

3. **Demonstrate good subject and curriculum knowledge**

   - have a secure knowledge of the relevant subject(s) and curriculum areas, foster and maintain pupils' interest in the subject, and address misunderstandings
   - demonstrate a critical understanding of developments in the subject and curriculum areas, and promote the value of scholarship
   - demonstrate an understanding of and take responsibility for promoting high standards of literacy, articulacy and the correct use of standard English, whatever the teacher's specialist subject
   - if teaching early reading, demonstrate a clear understanding of systematic synthetic phonics

4. **Plan and teach well-structured lessons**

   - impart knowledge and develop understanding through effective use of lesson time
   - promote a love of learning and children's intellectual curiosity
   - contribute to the design and provision of an engaging curriculum within the relevant subject area(s).

5. **Adapt teaching to respond to the strengths and needs of all pupils**

   - have a secure understanding of how a range of factors can inhibit pupils' ability to learn, and how best to overcome these
   - have a clear understanding of the needs of all pupils, including those with special educational needs; those of high ability; those with English as an additional language; those with disabilities; and be able to use and evaluate distinctive teaching approaches to engage and support them.

8. **Fulfil wider professional responsibilities**

   - take responsibility for improving teaching through appropriate professional development

Introduction

This section of the book introduces you to some key issues in early reading development. It discusses the kinds of knowledge children need so that they can learn to read written language, and focuses on the processes with which they have to become familiar in order to be able to translate written symbols into meaning.

RESEARCH SUMMARY   RESEARCH SUMMARY   **RESEARCH SUMMARY**   RESEARCH SUMMARY

Learning to read is a simple process – or is it? Researchers Myra Barrs and Anne Thomas (1996) explain:

It seems that people would prefer reading to be simple: a simple and easily definable activity with simple ways of learning how to do it. But reading is not a simple activity; it is one of the mind's most complex accomplishments. (p. 2)

The nature of the reading process has been widely researched, and researchers have discovered that readers employ a range of complex, subtle processes to get meaning from text, using a range of cues, involving knowledge of letters, words, grammar and the wider world.

Adults and children reading – the simple view

Research, and our own experience, tells us that when adults read, they tend to use, almost unconsciously, the full range of cue systems in an integrated way. We tend to know most words we read instantly, by sight, and those we do not recognise in this way, we decipher using a seamless mixture of phonic/graphic/grammatical/contextual clues. There is research, however, which suggests that beginning readers do not proceed in quite this way.

The simple view of reading (SVR) which identifies two dimensions of reading – 'word recognition' and 'language comprehension', is a way of representing reading which shows that, to become proficient readers and writers, children must develop both word recognition and language comprehension. This model was the basis of the *Independent Review of the Teaching of Early Reading* (Rose, 2006).

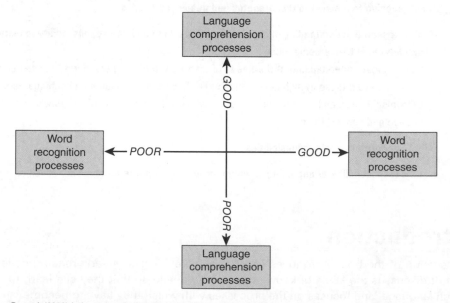

Source: Rose, J. (2006) *Independent Review of the Teaching of Early Reading: Final Report*, London: DfES, Figure 2, p. 77.

Reading is the act of making meaning from text. The simple view is useful as a way of thinking about key features of this very complex process. The SVR emphasises the need for children to learn both how to decode words and how to make meaning through comprehension. Both of these aspects of reading are necessary, but neither, on its own, is sufficient. The child who can segment a word into phonemes but does not know what it means is not reading, because he or she is not making meaning.

Reading is a secondary symbolic system, which represents language on paper. The first prerequisite for reading for young children is language. In the early stages of reading young children need to develop their awareness of aspects of spoken language and how spoken language can be encoded and decoded. This involves developing phonological awareness and learning sound–symbol correspondences through phonics. In Chapter 6 we discuss phonics teaching in more detail but it is important to recognise that it is a time-limited activity, and that children need to learn how to use sound–symbol correspondences relatively early, so that this use becomes automatic. Comprehension is a more complex activity and reading comprehension develops in complexity throughout the school years. In Chapter 9 we focus on the nature and development of comprehension.

RESEARCH SUMMARY RESEARCH SUMMARY **RESEARCH SUMMARY** RESEARCH SUMMARY

The 'interactive-compensatory model'

Keith Stanovich (1984) proposed what he calls an 'interactive-compensatory model' of the reading process. He argues that the process of reading involves the reader in making various interactions with the text. Experienced readers who have good word recognition skills are able to concentrate more on the meaning, while inexperienced readers who have more difficulty reading individual words and phrases have to use more graphophonic cues, leaving less mental space for understanding the meaning of the text. Crucially, Stanovich argues that young readers who have little difficulty in learning sight vocabulary and in using phonic strategies often go on to be successful in their education generally, because the act of reading gives them access to a range of educational programmes that increase their general knowledge base. Those who fail in reading in the Early Years, conversely, lack the important knowledge that reading might have given to them. This has been termed the 'Matthew effect', in reference to St Matthew's gospel, whereby 'unto those who have is given…'. This has been the basis of ensuring that young readers get early intervention if they struggle with reading, as failure to offer the support they need can have a serious effect on all aspects of learning.

Decoding and comprehension are dimensions of reading which are based on a much wider network of experiences, feelings and understandings about reading for each child, and make a huge difference to whether and how children learn. Children who have positive experiences of early reading at home, know about the importance of reading, enjoy stories and are confident that they can become readers are likely to do so. Teaching reading in early years settings involves teaching in ways which convey these messages to children, about reading and about themselves. The activities you choose need to teach the key features of texts like stories and non-fiction texts, show children how the codes of reading work and make the whole experience motivating. This chapter concentrates on activities which show children how you and other children read, which engage them in reading themselves and which promote enjoyment of reading.

Using large texts – big books, and electronic texts

We cannot assume that all young children will necessarily understand what is involved in learning to read a book. Some children will have grown up surrounded by books; others might have no experience of seeing adults reading at home, and will therefore not know how to open a book in order to find the beginning of the story. Neither will they understand that print, in English, runs from left to right horizontally along the page and is usually read from top to bottom. Furthermore, children might have no notion that the printed words that you read to them from the page of text are the same as the words that are coming from your mouth.

Reading books and stories to young children is vital so that they understand what is enjoyable and informative about reading. However, as well as reading to very young children, you will also want to share readings with them. This gives you an opportunity to help young readers like this develop concepts of print and engagement with books and stories. Here is some general advice that you can adapt to suit the needs of particular children.

Book awareness and book handling

- Show the children the title and the cover of the book. Ask them to predict what it might be about, using the title and the cover illustration as clues.
- Talk about the author. Have you read anything else by this person?
- Talk about the illustrator. Have you read other books illustrated by this person?
- Model page turning and left-right sequencing by finger-pointing for the children.
- Encourage children to follow the text by using a pointer. If appropriate, pause before the final word as you read aloud, and invite the children, by your tone of voice, to take over the reading at this point.
- Run your finger over the letters of a word you are focusing on while you say the word slowly. Ask the children to say the whole word several times, following your finger movement. Ask the children to trace the shapes of the letters in the air with their finger.

Using context

- Encourage children to respond to the illustrations by drawing attention to them and talking about their meaning in the context of the story.
- Pause in your reading and talk about what's happening, and about what might happen next.
- Focus on one particular page of the book. Encourage children to observe and talk about each character and event, using both text and illustrations.
- Encourage children to retell the story in their own words, to you and to other children.
- Encourage children to use the story in the context of imaginative role-play.

Learning about words

- Point to particular words you want to draw attention to. Ask: 'What does this say?' or 'Whose name is this?' and 'Does anyone remember this word from our phonics session?'
- Use a laminated sheet over the text and ask children to underline all the words on the page they know. Talk about these particular words and about any other words they are unsure of. Does the word appear elsewhere on the page? What is the initial or final sound? Are there any syllables that you can read? What does the word mean? How can we find out?

- Select a 'word of the day' from the text and encourage children to recognise and read this word in different parts of the classroom.
- Extract a longer word from the text and find any shorter words within the long word, so that the children become aware of specific letter sequences inside words.

Learning about sounds during reading

- Finger-point to initial sounds or blends in words that you want to draw children's attention to.
- Run your finger, or a pointer, under the line of print as the children read alongside you. This will develop their experience of reading aloud and help them to keep together, as well as demonstrating left-right sequencing.

Guided reading

The group activity known as **guided reading** is a time to help children to read and interpret the text, and take the opportunity of working with a small group to show them how to identify new or unfamiliar words using the sound symbol (grapheme–phoneme) correspondences (GPCs) they already know and the sight words they know. Guided reading is a very important time for explicit teaching. Here are some suggestions for how you might use it.

- Model page turning and left-right sequencing by finger-pointing for children.
- Encourage children to handle books, giving them responsibility for page-turning.
- Encourage the children to follow the text with their finger as you read together. Guide the child's finger if necessary.
- Identify words which they are unlikely to have encountered before you read the book. Discuss the meaning and form of these words to help with comprehension and decoding.
- Give the children time to read to you, so that they feel a sense of accomplishment.

To get the most from a guided reading session the following structure supports your questioning and children's interactions with the book.

Book introduction

- Identify your teaching objective.
- Establish what type of text it is, because it makes a difference to how it is read.
- Encourage the children to make links to existing knowledge and experience using prediction and speculation.
- Recall recently introduced strategies (focusing on phonics for early readers).
- Identify points of potential difficulty.
- Generate questions for resolution during independent reading.

Strategy check

- Phonics as a first-call strategy for non-fluent readers.
- Help fluent pupils to recall a range of comprehension and decoding strategies.

Independent reading

- Sample reading, provide appropriate prompts and specific praise.
- Monitor for accuracy, phrasing, fluency and comprehension.

Returning to the text

- Summarise.
- Praise use of reading strategies.
- Generate questions to develop and assess understanding at word/sentence/text level.

Responding to the text

- Prompt for personal response to text.
- Return to teaching objectives.

Which texts shall I use for shared and guided reading at Key Stage 1?

There are many texts and types of texts that are suitable for use for these activities. Here are a few criteria that might help you to make appropriate choices.

- Texts that are decodable given the phonic knowledge that children in the class have been taught. Successful decoding develops confidence and also helps the child to understand what they are reading.
- Texts with repeated words, phrases and sentences to encourage prediction and give children the confidence to join in and follow.
- Texts with a flowing rhythm and a language structure that helps children to predict what might happen next.
- Texts that help children to enter the world of their imagination, so there is plenty of opportunity for them to talk about the story, to predict what will happen next, and to be excited when re-reading.
- Texts that encourage children to become literary critics as soon as they start reading so that they get into characters' heads and judge their actions against what they themselves might have done.
- Texts that extend children's knowledge of the world.
- Texts with complex pictures for children to examine closely and where smaller details support the main picture and promote discussion.
- Texts with interesting dialogue that can be read using different voices or accents, for example *The Bad-Tempered Ladybird* by Eric Carle.

REFLECTIVE TASK

Think about the range of texts that you have used with beginning readers or have seen used.

- Can you match this range to the list given above?
- Were there any gaps in the range you used or saw used?
- What might you do to try to fill any such gaps?

Using environmental print to support reading in literacy lessons

Public print always has a clear purpose, whether in the form of road signs, DANGER notices, bus destinations or advertisements. Drawing children's attention to the environmental texts around them helps them to understand that print carries a message – a crucial reading lesson in itself. We have all met children who understand very little written text in books but who can read a burger chain sign and point out a toy store with no difficulty. By using the children's own experiences as a basis for developing their awareness of public print, you can help them to become aware of words and phrases and of the sounds within words. Here are some ideas.

- Make your own book of signs around the school using a digital camera (street names, school signs, 'Way in', 'Exit', and so on). Read these regularly as your shared text and encourage children to identify particular words and phrases.
- Use carefully mounted food wrappers as an alphabet frieze round the room.
- Encourage children to make their own versions of alphabets, using everyday print such as food labels or advertisements for toys.
- Invite children to make their own advertisements for the classroom shop, or for a bring-and-buy sale. Help children to design versions of their own favourite products, using the word processor to experiment with different fonts and print sizes.
- Make a collection of local tickets and put these into a transparent photograph wallet so that children can read both sides of the tickets and talk about them together.

EMBEDDING ICT   EMBEDDING ICT   **EMBEDDING ICT**   EMBEDDING ICT   **EMBEDDING ICT**

Don't collect all of the examples of environmental print yourself. Get the children involved too. There are plenty of basic digital cameras on the market that can be used even by very young children. Give them opportunities to take part in identifying notices and signs that they want to include, taking the photographs, including checking the previews, uploading the pictures to the computer and printing them out to make their own group or class book or display.

RESEARCH SUMMARY   RESEARCH SUMMARY   **RESEARCH SUMMARY**   RESEARCH SUMMARY

The importance of environmental print in young children's reading lives

Children are familiar with a great deal of print that they see around them at home and in their community before they come to school. Margaret Meek (1982) argued:

> *Public print has an important place in the lives of many young children before they come to school because it is interwoven in the daily transactions with family and community. Many a non-reader has failed just because he did not link the way he looked at advertisements on his way to school with what he has to look at on the school notice board. It is so easy for us to take all public print for granted that we often forget our part in pointing it out as something to be looked at. One of the paradoxes of being literate is that we know so well what notices and signs are, and what they say, that we no longer look at them. The learner, on the other hand, can make good use of such things. (p. 41)*

Hilary Minns (1990), in her study of five pre-school children, noted that they were conscious of various uses of public print: food labels, newspapers, shopping catalogues, calendars (in more than one language), advertisements, birthday cards, invitations, letters, bills, crosswords, the writing on coins and bank notes, football pools coupons, diet sheets, tickets, appointments, number plates and maps.

Ann Ketch (1991) created an alphabet for her early readers based on the different sweets, drinks and savouries the children in her class chose to eat. She photographed the wrappers and put these in alphabetical order in a homemade book, which she called 'The Delicious Alphabet'. By reading the book together, the children extended their knowledge of:

- initial sounds and letters and GPCs and alphabetical order;
- print styles (upper and lower case, italics, joined, etc.);
- book handling and page turning;
- word recognition;
- prediction, and the meanings that are attached to words.

THE BIGGER PICTURE THE BIGGER PICTURE **THE BIGGER PICTURE** THE BIGGER PICTURE

When you are planning to use environmental print to support reading, of course you will use examples from around the school, but think more widely than this. Are there any educational visits planned, for example to the local library or supermarket, fire station or place of worship? These can all be rich in environmental print and you could collect photographs of signs and notices and samples of leaflets and posters. You could also use this as an opportunity for a home–school activity and get parents involved in collecting examples when they are out with their children or sending in items such as food packaging. Use children's home–school diaries to alert them or put an article in the next class newsletter.

Helping children who are 'stuck': strategies to use in shared and guided reading

In shared and guided reading sessions, you will meet situations where children cannot recognise particular words. Here are some strategies to help you.

Problem	Solution
Children cannot recognise a word, even though you have read it together less than five minutes ago.	Say to the children: 'We've already read that word on page 2. Let's look at it again. Can you find where it is?' (Turn back to page 2.) Read page 2 again with the children, and finger-point as you go along, pausing at the word you want to highlight. Ask the children to say the word to you if they can, and then read the whole of page 2 again. Point to the word again and say it aloud together. Talk about anything that might help the children to remember the word – the known GPCs, a double-letter sound in the middle, an initial letter they recognise – take your cue from them. Now return to the page you were reading and ask the children to show you where the word appears. Read the whole page, so that the word is seen and understood in context.

Problem	Solution
The children still cannot recognise or remember the word.	Stay silent for a while to give the children time to think and sort it out. (If you help too soon, the children might begin to rely on this help and not use strategies they already have in place.)
The children still do not seem able to read the word and are getting frustrated.	Tell the children what the word is (and make a note of their difficulty and what the likely cause might be).
The children read a word incorrectly but the **miscue** does not interfere with the meaning (e.g. I went to my *home* instead of I went to my *house*).	Ignore the miscue *for the time being* if you are reading a story together. The children are clearly making sense of the text and reading with meaning. At the end of the story, point out the miscue and talk about why the children might have misread the word, and then focusing on 'm' and 'ou'.
The children read a word incorrectly and the miscue interferes with the meaning, e.g. I went to see my *house* instead of I went to see my *horse*.	Give the children time to self-correct. If they read on without self-correcting (even though the text makes no sense with the substitution of 'house' for 'horse') talk to the children about the miscue, pointing out the significant difference between 'ou' and 'or'. (Make a note to reinforce the learning of these two digraphs.) Re-read the whole of the sentence together. If reading 'house' rather than 'horse' changes the meaning of the text to the point of nonsense, you might want to draw the children's attention to the whole sentence or paragraph in order to help to reinforce their semantic or contextual understanding.
The children apparently read fluently, but on checking you find that they have not really understood much on the page.	Pause at the end of each page and focus on the meaning in both text and pictures. Ask questions like: What is happening here? What do you expect Meera will say on the next page? What do you think will happen in the end? Why is she looking so sad in this picture? What do you think she might be thinking? What might happen after the story ends? This will support their contextual understanding.
The children have quite a good sight vocabulary, and understand a lot of what they read, but they have very limited experience of word-building strategies.	Use the segmenting and blending skills the children are learning in their phonics sessions. Focus on the initial or the final sound of the word that is causing difficulty: *c-a-t*. Break the word into syllables: *gar-den*. Focus on the part of the word that is causing trouble: diff-i-*cult*. Focus on the part of the word that the children already know: green*house*; this might help the children to guess the complete word by using the context. Make a note of which sounds and blends are causing the trouble. Teach them separately.

Problem	Solution
The children recognise the words on the page and understand the meaning, but read aloud in a flat monotone.	Model expressive reading for the children. Read alternate pages of the text so they can hear 'the tune on the page'.
	Read the first sentence or paragraph on each page to give an indication of the expressive mood of the text, then invite the children to take over the reading at this point.
	If there is dialogue in the text, read it with the children as though you are reading a play.
	Give the children playscripts to read aloud in guided reading sessions. Encourage children to listen to recorded stories read by experienced readers.
	Invite children to tape stories and to listen to themselves on tape. Talk to them about their presentation. Could they improve it? How?

IN THE CLASSROOM

The Reception lesson plan on the next two pages is based on the picture-story book *The Very Hungry Caterpillar* by Eric Carle. The children already know the story because they have read it with the student several times. They have helped to make a wall frieze, painting the caterpillar, the butterfly, and all the different kinds of food it eats over the week. The student has made labels for each item of food and the children have read these on the frieze on several occasions. Now, the student is ready to attempt a more detailed analysis of some of the words in the story, matching words and pictures and focusing on initial sounds. The lesson plan was written by this student. As you read this lesson plan you will notice that the student has incorporated many features. Overall, the lesson has pace and a variety of stimulating and differentiated activities. Note, too, that the student builds in the use of a teaching assistant.

Lesson: Literacy

Focus: *The Very Hungry Caterpillar* by Eric Carle

Timing	Teacher activity	Pupil activity	Reading processes and reading knowledge
Shared text work: 15 mins.	Show the front cover of *The Very Hungry Caterpillar*. Ask the children to join in as I read the title. Ask who the author is. Do they know anything else he has written? (Show *The Bad-Tempered Ladybird*.)	Children read title together and respond to questioning.	Knowledge and understanding of texts. Developing knowledge of an author and authorship in general.

Timing	Teacher activity	Pupil activity	Reading processes and reading knowledge
	Explain that the 'phoneme thief' has struck again. The children have got to find the missing phonemes.	Children listen to instructions.	
	Read through the book and encourage the children to join in as I finger-point.	Children read together.	Reading text together. Following left-right sequence.
	Encourage the children to read the days of the week, following my finger-pointing.	Children read together, following finger-pointing.	Reading aloud with expression. Left-right sequencing, word recognition.
	When we come to a missing phoneme, read the word as it appears, without the initial sound. Ask the children what the word should be and then what phoneme they can hear at the beginning of the word. Ask a child to uncover the phoneme – were they correct?	Children identify the word and then say what phoneme they can hear at the beginning of it. They uncover the phoneme in the book.	Listening for initial sounds. Identifying initial sounds.
Focused word work: 15 mins.	Tell the children that we are going to play *The Very Hungry Caterpillar* Words and Pictures game. Arrange the children in two lines on the carpet, facing each other.	Children listen to instructions and sit on the carpet in two teams.	
	Give each child in one line a word representing an item of food the caterpillar ate. Ask each child to read it. Give the children in the opposite line a picture of the food item. Tell them that when you call out a word the child with that word has to stand up and give it to the child holding the matching picture.	Children in one team hold a picture of something that the caterpillar ate. Children in the other team hold a word that matches the picture.	Visual discrimination and word recognition. Matching words to pictures.

Timing	Teacher activity	Pupil activity	Reading processes and reading knowledge
	Call out the name of each item of food, one at a time. After saying the word ask the child to say what phoneme they can hear at the beginning of the word.	When children hear their word they identify its initial phoneme and match it to its picture.	Phonological awareness.
Activity: 20 mins.	Show Yellow and Blue groups' activity sheet. Tell the children that they have got to find the word that begins with the initial phoneme in the picture and then cut it out and stick it in the box by the picture. Ask what the picture is and then what phoneme they hear at the beginning of 'apple'. Ask a child to find which word begins with 'a' and then cut it out and stick it in the box. Identify the other foods. Remind children to be careful when using scissors and tell them not to use too much glue.	Children listen to instructions.	Phonological awareness.
	Dismiss Yellow group and then Blue group. Accompany Red Group to their table.	Yellow group and then Blue group go to their tables and begin their activity.	
	Give children in Red group their own worksheet. Encourage them to read their own sentence. Tell them they have got to find a word to match their picture to complete their sentence. Ask children to identify the initial phoneme of their picture and then find a word that begins with that sound. Then tell them to copy the sentence underneath.	Red group read their sentence one at a time, then children identify the initial phoneme of their picture and find a word that begins with that sound. Then they copy the sentence.	Reading aloud. Identifying phonemes.

Timing	Teacher activity	Pupil activity	Reading processes and reading knowledge
	Work with Blue group. Ensure they can identify the correct word to match each picture. Ask them to say what phoneme they can hear at the beginning of each word. Then tell them to copy each word underneath.	Blue group matches their words and pictures then copies each word. Yellow group matches their words and pictures with help from TA.	Word and picture matching. Word recognition.
Plenary: 10 mins.	Tell the children in Red group to read through their sentences. Ask children what phoneme they hear at the beginning of the food words. Ensure that Red group are standing in the wrong order. Ask the other children 'What did the caterpillar eat first, second', etc. Line up Red group in the correct order.	Red group read their sentences to the class. Children identify the food words and initial phonemes. Then the children remember what the caterpillar ate and Red group line up in the correct order.	Making a presentation to the class.

A SUMMARY OF **KEY POINTS**

➤ Reading is not a simple process.

➤ Adult reading involves the use of graphic, phonic, syntactic and semantic cues.

➤ Young children need to learn a good deal about texts and reading as well as phonics.

➤ Sharing large-format texts and group guided reading are effective strategies for teaching the use of phonics and other strategies for reading

➤ The use of environmental print helps children to make connections between reading in school and in the world outside.

➤ There are a number of strategies you can use to help children who are stuck on particular aspects in their reading.

M-LEVEL EXTENSION > > M-LEVEL EXTENSION > > M-LEVEL EXTENSION

Compare the approach to, and organisation of, the teaching of early reading in schools in which you have worked. Think particularly about the ways in which the teachers you have observed managed to integrate their use of various teaching strategies such as shared reading, guided reading, independent work, etc.

In the light of your observations, and of your reading of this chapter (and the following chapter), try to plan what you would consider to be some 'ideal' sequences of early reading lessons. You might find it particularly useful to base these sequences around particular texts, in the same way as *The Very Hungry Caterpillar* example discussed earlier.

FURTHER READING   FURTHER READING   FURTHER READING   FURTHER READING

Barrs, M. and Thomas, A. (eds) (1996) *The Reading Book*. London: Centre for Language in Primary Education.

DfE (2013) *The National Curriculum in England*. London: DfE. (https://www.gov.uk/dfe/nationalcurriculum)

DfE (2013) *Teachers' Standards*. London: DfE. (https://www.gov.uk/government/uploads/system/uploads/attachment_data/file/208682/Teachers__Standards_2013.pdf)

DfES (2006) *Independent Review of the Teaching of Early Reading*. London: DfES.

Ketch, A. (1991) 'The Delicious Alphabet', *English in Education*, vol. 25(1), pp. 1–4.

Meek, M. (1982) *Learning to Read*. London: Bodley Head.

Minns, H. (1990) *Read it to me Now! Learning at Home and at School*. London: Virago.

6
The teaching and learning of phonics

TEACHERS' STANDARDS

A teacher must:

2. **Promote good progress and outcomes by pupils**

   - be accountable for pupils' attainment, progress and outcomes
   - plan teaching to build on pupils' capabilities and prior knowledge
   - guide pupils to reflect on the progress they have made and their emerging needs
   - demonstrate knowledge and understanding of how pupils learn and how this impacts on teaching
   - encourage pupils to take a responsible and conscientious attitude to their own work and study.

3. **Demonstrate good subject and curriculum knowledge**

   - have a secure knowledge of the relevant subject(s) and curriculum areas, foster and maintain pupils' interest in the subject, and address misunderstandings
   - demonstrate a critical understanding of developments in the subject and curriculum areas, and promote the value of scholarship
   - demonstrate an understanding of and take responsibility for promoting high standards of literacy, articulacy and the correct use of standard English, whatever the teacher's specialist subject
   - if teaching early reading, demonstrate a clear understanding of systematic synthetic phonics

4. **Plan and teach well structured lessons**

   - impart knowledge and develop understanding through effective use of lesson time
   - reflect systematically on the effectiveness of lessons and approaches to teaching
   - contribute to the design and provision of an engaging curriculum within the relevant subject area(s).

5. **Adapt teaching to respond to the strengths and needs of all pupils**

   - know when and how to differentiate appropriately, using approaches which enable pupils to be taught effectively
   - have a secure understanding of how a range of factors can inhibit pupils' ability to learn, and how best to overcome these

6. **Make accurate and productive use of assessment**

   - know and understand how to assess the relevant subject and curriculum areas, including statutory assessment requirements
   - make use of formative and summative assessment to secure pupils' progress
   - use relevant data to monitor progress, set targets, and plan subsequent lessons
   - give pupils regular feedback, both orally and through accurate marking, and encourage pupils to respond to the feedback.

ıction

the spelling system in the English language means that children have
the relationship between the sound system and the writing system in
order to read and write. Adults read using a range of cueing systems to guide their
automatic word recognition: predicting meaning from what has gone before (using
semantic knowledge), paying attention to the grammatical structure of the sentence
(using syntactic knowledge) and learning to recognise particular words on sight
(using lexical knowledge). In addition, the appearance and layout of a text gives readers clues about how it should be read (using bibliographic knowledge). However,
early readers and writers cannot co-ordinate all these systems and may rely much
more heavily on the sound–symbol correspondences through which English is
decoded and encoded. Phonics teaching aims to help children learn to decode and
encode these correspondences automatically and can be seen as a 'leg up' to the processes of reading and writing.

The alphabetic nature of the English language makes it sensible to use a phonic-based
approach that helps young children to crack the code quickly and then render its use
automatic, freeing up the child's attention for the challenges presented by comprehension. Children who are taught patterns of sounds and letters can see how the spelling
systems of English work and build up a foundation of knowledge for reading and writing
new words for themselves. This ability gives them strategies that they can begin to use
independently and it therefore builds their confidence.

RESEARCH SUMMARY RESEARCH SUMMARY **RESEARCH SUMMARY** RESEARCH SUMMARY

Effective readers can recognise words very quickly and accurately, seemingly without effort. How do
they do this and how has this capacity been developed? Stanovich (1993: p. 282) asserts that 'the
word recognition processes of skilled readers [are] so rapid and automatic that they [do] not need
to rely on contextual information'. He refutes the view that effective readers recognise words largely
through context and that their focus on meaning reduces the need to attend to other features of print,
feeling that this slows down the process. According to Adams (1990: p. 146), '…deep and thorough
knowledge of letters, spelling patterns and words, and of the phonological translations of all three, are
of inescapable importance to both skilful reading and its acquisition'.

Effective phonics teaching

Children need a strong speaking and listening foundation and a rich background of literacy opportunities, including play, stories and rhymes, before beginning phonics work.
Building on sound (phonological) awareness, children can develop 'phonemic awareness
and phonic knowledge'. The Rose Review of Early Reading (2006) asserted that pupils
should be taught to:

- name, write and sound the letters of the alphabet;
- hear, identify, segment and blend phonemes in words;
- link sound and letter patterns, exploring rhyme, alliteration and other sound patterns;
- identify syllables in words;

- use their knowledge of sound–symbol relationships and phonological patterns (for example, adjacent consonants and vowel phonemes);
- learn some irregular words by sight;
- recognise that the same sounds may have different spellings and that the same spellings may relate to different sounds.

The key features of the synthetic approach to phonics are to teach beginner readers:

- about grapheme/phoneme (letter/sound) correspondences (the alphabetic principle) in a clearly defined, incremental sequence;
- to apply the skill of blending (synthesising) phonemes in order, all through a word to read it;
- to apply the skills of segmenting words into their constituent phonemes to spell;
- that blending and segmenting are reversible processes.

The Rose Review established discrete phonics teaching in daily sessions as the prime approach to teaching reading. Successful phonic work for word recognition is a time-limited activity that is eventually overtaken by work that develops comprehension. If children do not have automatic phonic skills by the end of Year 2 it is very much more difficult for them to learn, because there are competing systems, such as the visual patterns of spelling.

Phonics teaching must be well paced and engage children in multisensory activity. By listening, pronouncing, manipulating letters and creating letter shapes, children learn with enjoyment and engagement. A good deal of phonics teaching involves interactive whiteboards but this is accompanied by children moving, manipulating magnetic letters, writing on individual whiteboards and making shapes. Teachers use short, fast-paced activities and games to make phonics sessions fun.

EMBEDDING ICT EMBEDDING ICT **EMBEDDING ICT** EMBEDDING ICT **EMBEDDING ICT**

There are many programs available, both for use on the interactive whiteboard (IWB) and for children to use individually on the class computer, that will make phonics fun. Make sure that you know what is available in school and on the school virtual learning environment (VLE). However, it is important for you to realise that just because a program is on the IWB it is not interactive for all the children. You can use whiteboards and games with the electronic content to offer children a well-planned, enjoyable and effective phonics experience.

When teaching phonics, it is very important to be clear about what you are discussing. Most schools now use the following terms:

- **sound** – a sound that is not a speech sound, such as a rattle or squeak;
- **letter** – one of the 26 letters of the alphabet;
- **phoneme** – the smallest unit of sound in a spoken word. In cat there are three phonemes /c/ /a/ /t/ (in this book we will use slashes to indicate phonemes);
- **grapheme** – the letters used to represent a phoneme in writing. Some graphemes have one letter, some have two or three (c a t – three graphemes, ch o p – three graphemes, f i ght – three graphemes);
- **digraph** – a grapheme with two letters (ch, sh, th, etc.);
- **trigraph** – a grapheme with three letters (-igh);

- **blend** – the skill of blending individual phonemes together to produce a syllable (/c/ /a/ /t/ pronounced as cat)
- **segment** – the skill of identifying individual phonemes in a syllable (/cat broken down to /c/ /a/ /t/)

Check these terms in your school and make sure you use, and understand, the same vocabulary for phonics as everyone else in school.

It is important for you to remember that an estimated 15–25 per cent of children suffer from intermittent or temporary hearing impairment as a normal part of early childhood. This can make phonological awareness, and so phonics, more difficult and cause delay. It is important to identify these children, seek advice from a doctor or audiologist and to make sure the children are seated so that they can hear as well as possible. It is also helpful for teachers to enunciate words and phonemes carefully and clearly.

RESEARCH SUMMARY RESEARCH SUMMARY **RESEARCH SUMMARY** RESEARCH SUMMARY

Marilyn Jager Adams (1990) carried out a major review of all the aspects of phonics and early reading instruction for the US Department of Education, and she argues forcibly for the inclusion of phonic teaching alongside other forms of reading instruction. She argues that 'approaches in which systematic code instruction is included alongside meaning emphasis, language instruction, and connected reading are found to result in superior reading achievement overall' (p. 49).

Phonics schemes

There is a wide range of phonics schemes available in schools and there is no evidence to show that one scheme is more effective than another. However, the use of a well-structured programme in a systematic and rigorous way is an important factor in successful phonics teaching, because enthusiastic and systematic teaching is the key to children learning to use phonic skills effectively. The school phonics scheme can help all teachers and teaching assistants to teach in consistent ways and ensure there is a clear progression. The phonics scheme in your school is likely to address the order of introduction of the elements of phonics contained in the National Curriculum. Everyone in the school, including pupils, teachers, teaching assistants and parents, will share the same language about phonics.

Criteria published by the DfES for phonics programmes proposed, suggesting they should:

- present high quality systematic phonic work, as defined by the Rose *Review of the Teaching of Early Reading* (2006), as the prime approach to decoding print;
- be designed for the teaching of discrete, daily sessions progressing from simple to more complex phonic knowledge and skills and covering the major grapheme–phoneme correspondences;
- enable children's progress to be assessed;
- use a multi-sensory approach so that children learn variously from simultaneous visual, auditory and kinaesthetic activities which are designed to secure essential phonic knowledge and skills;
- demonstrate that phonemes should be blended, in order, from left to right, 'all through the word' for reading;
- demonstrate how words can be segmented into their constituent phonemes for spelling and that this is the reverse of blending phonemes to read words;

- ensure children apply phonic knowledge and skills as their first approach to reading and spelling even if a word is not completely phonically regular;
- ensure that children are taught high frequency words that do not conform completely to grapheme–phoneme correspondence rules;
- ensure that, as early as possible, children have opportunities to read texts (and spell words) that are within the reach of their phonic knowledge and skills even though every single word in the text may not be entirely decodable by the children unaided.

Most commercial phonics schemes and *Letters and Sounds* (2007), the pack of phonics teaching materials produced by the former Department for Education and Skills (DfES) which is used in many schools as the basis of their phonics scheme, meet these criteria and also use the sequence of phonics teaching in the 2014 National Curriculum, including Appendix 1 Spelling.

The first steps towards phonics is the promotion of speaking and listening skills, which are seen as crucially important skills in their own right as well as paving the way for high quality phonic work. The very earliest steps in phonics learning take place in the nursery and reception class, and are about developing the vocabulary and **phonological awareness** of young children so that they are ready for phonics teaching and learning.

The start of systematic phonic work begins, usually in the Reception year, with the rapid teaching of **grapheme–phoneme correspondences** (GPCs) so that children learn a spelling (grapheme) for each speech sound (phoneme). Decoding for reading and encoding for spelling are taught as reversible processes through the teaching of blending and segmenting at every opportunity. As soon as the first correspondences have been learned, children are taught to blend and segment with them, usually as using **consonant vowel consonant** (CVC) words. Blending means merging individual phonemes together into whole words; segmenting is the reverse process of splitting up whole spoken words into individual phonemes. By learning one representation for each of at least 42 of the 44 phonemes generally recognised as those of British Received Pronunciation (RP) children can write most words (although not spell correctly). At the same time, children learn a range of sight words which enable them to read and write sentences.

When they can securely blend and segment CVC words, children learn to read and spell words containing adjacent consonants including CCVC (e.g. flat, black) and CVCC (e.g. bank, gasp) words, as well as a wider range of vowel graphemes. Children also need to continue to learn more sight words and to recognise and spell common suffixes. If there were a perfect one-to-one mapping between graphemes and phonemes just knowing the basic GPC would be enough. However, English is unlike most other languages because many of the mappings are one-to-several in both directions: that is to say, most phonemes can be spelled in more than one way, and most graphemes can represent more than one phoneme, so children learn more than one spelling (grapheme) for phonemes and that one spelling (grapheme) can represent more than one phoneme.

Most phonics schemes include the teaching of aspects of morphology – suffixes and prefixes as well as inflected endings for plurals, past tenses and common spelling patterns. By the end of Key Stage 1, children should have developed fluent word reading skills and have a good foundation in spelling.

The beginnings of literacy learning

The teaching of phonics cannot happen in isolation – it must be based on children's experience of speaking and listening and on rich literacy experiences which teach children why they should engage with the whole process of reading and writing. Much of this happens in the home, but you should also create a classroom environment that supports children's knowledge of, and interest in, literacy, so that a print-rich classroom provides a sound basis for learning. Here are some suggestions.

- Create a classroom environment that is full of exciting reading material, beautifully displayed – books, posters, labels, advertisements, dictionaries, captions, notices and instructions.
- Use every opportunity to develop children's knowledge of the relationship between spoken and written language in real contexts (e.g. lists of children's names to do classroom jobs, displays of children's stories 'published' in the classroom for everyone to read, and labels that communicate important messages, such as 'Please close the door quietly or you will wake up the hamster.')
- Choose books and other texts that support children's developing knowledge of sounds and letters, for example *The Cat in the Hat* by Dr Seuss.
- Demonstrate writing for the children and take opportunities to write down their own words, so they begin to understand that what they say can become words on the page, and that their words are now permanent, and can be read by other people.
- Make a collection of rhymes and songs that help children to develop an 'ear' for rhythmic patterns.
- Engage in regular story reading and telling with groups of children and encourage browsing and exploration of reading and writing.

RESEARCH SUMMARY   RESEARCH SUMMARY   **RESEARCH SUMMARY**   RESEARCH SUMMARY

The debate about the nature of the reading process has always interested teachers of reading. Recent research has been sparked off by the current debate about the role of phonics in the teaching and learning of reading, and this has led to a revised model of effective reading instruction. The premise underlying this model is that reading instruction should target the various elements of skilled performance: comprehension, composition, vocabulary development, word identification, rate, fluency, spelling and grammar (Lipson and Wixson, 1997). Furthermore, if the effects of phonics instruction are going to transfer to reading and writing performance, then we must teach skills and strategies in the context of authentic reading and writing activities (Adams, 1990). The process of reading involves co-ordinating information from three cueing systems: graphophonic cues (the letters), syntactic cues (the grammar) and semantic cues (the meaning). Exemplary literacy programmes encourage readers to develop their abilities to use information from all three of these cueing systems, in the context of real reading and writing (Lipson and Wixson, 1997). These cueing systems work together to bring comprehension from text (Purcell-Gates, 1997). Many researchers believe that reading and writing development go hand in hand (Lipson and Wixson, 1997). Early writing activities serve to promote reading development. The implication is that teachers should systematically integrate phonics instruction into a total literacy programme (Stahl and McKenna, 2006). This means it is important that teachers should point out the purpose of phonics instruction and show young readers how they can *use* sound–symbol knowledge as part of the teaching, rather than just teaching sound–symbol correspondences as an end in themselves. Likewise, one of the most important 'phonic' activities at Key Stage 1 will be writing using invented spelling – a task that involves very young children in sophisticated analysis of sounds in words.

Learning phonological awareness – the first step towards phonics

Children move from speaking and listening to reading and writing. It is important for children to develop the necessary listening skills and phonological awareness.

Pre-school children are not experienced at explicit analysis of the sounds they hear and say. Early Years settings are usually the first places that children are asked to analyse sounds and begin to understand the patterns of sound. This is called **phonological awareness** and it is a basic requirement for children to learn phonics. It is important to know what to expect of them and why they find this detailed listening challenging.

Attending to particular sounds and matching them to their sources, or to particular events, is part of **sound discrimination** activities, which do not include words at all. You can easily offer real practice of this sort of activity by using a range of instruments under a cloth or screen then asking children to identify the source of the sounds, or have a 'sound table' where children can experiment with instruments. This sort of exploratory activity is ideal for developing sound listening.

The ability to discriminate words in a stream of speech is, probably, the easiest form of aural discrimination. However, **word discrimination** is not as obvious as it seems. There are no pauses between words in speech. Re-read the last sentence out loud with pauses between each word and you will notice how artificial it sounds. In speech, we know about word breaks because we know the meanings of words and hear the intonation. Young children learn to discriminate words gradually.

The next unit of sound that children seem able to discriminate is the **syllable**. This is really the rhythm of speech. Each syllable is made up from a number of sounds (usually a main vowel, with other sounds before and/or after) and represents a 'beat' in the pattern of sounds that make up speech. The best way to help children to develop their syllabification is by using clapping games.

- Ask children to clap their names to each other in a circle (my name is Caroline – my/name/is/Ca/ro/line – six claps. My/name/is/Shah – 4 claps).
- Introduce children to songs or poems where they have to clap each syllable to maintain the beat (Jack/and/Jill/went/up/the/hill, Ma/ry/Ma/ry/quite/con/tra/ry)
- Make up new verses to familiar songs and clap the beats.

As an educator, it is important to assess when children can participate effectively in these games, can recognise the syllables in words and can begin to sustain rhythms, because this needs to happen before phonemic analysis.

When children can syllabify, they can begin to analyse the sounds within syllables. They are generally able to identify beginning consonants of a syllable and 'the rest' (often a vowel and final consonant) known as the **onset** and **rime** of a syllable. These are very technical terms, which children do not need to know. However, for educators, it is important to watch out for children developing the ability to use common **rhyme**. Doing plenty of action rhymes and rhyme games allows you to assess who can identify rhymes at the ends of words.

RESEARCH SUMMARY RESEARCH SUMMARY **RESEARCH SUMMARY** RESEARCH SUMMARY

Researchers tell us that children who have an early grounding in phonological awareness are more likely to become early successful readers. It is now well established that there is a strong connection between children's ability to detect and manipulate the sounds making up spoken words and their reading development. Phonological ability in pre-school children is one of the biggest predictors of later success in reading ability (Goswami and Bryant, 1990).

THE BIGGER PICTURE THE BIGGER PICTURE **THE BIGGER PICTURE** THE BIGGER PICTURE

When you are planning work on phonics and phonological awareness, you need to plan suitable activities that will include all children and ensure that every child makes progress. You are likely to have children in your class or group who have additional and special educational needs. You may also have in the same group or class children who are able, gifted and talented in English. Talk to class teacher colleagues, take advice from the inclusion leader or teacher responsible for children with special needs and discuss the children with any teaching or learning support assistants who know them well to see what they suggest will help. See also Chapter 12 on including all children.

In Early Years settings, you will find it very helpful to make sets of rhyming words. Here are some examples of the kinds of rhyming sets that it would be useful to compile:

ch-ip	d-ip	h-ip	sh-ip
cl-uck	l-uck	d-uck	m-uck
ch-ew	dr-ew	fl-ew	thr-ew
f-ound	r-ound	gr-ound	s-ound

Use these words (spoken, not written) in short group sessions so that children have experience of listening to rhymes and predicting them. Other suggestions are:

- Complete rhyming couplets (Jack Sprat would eat no ____).
- Change the words of well-known rhymes, songs or stories so that children 'hear' different sounds and identify where they sound 'wrong', for example

  Mack and Bill went up the hill
  Goldisocks and The Three Hairs

- Ask children to listen to the words below and to tell you which rhyme and which are the odd ones out. Make up other sets of words.

bell	shell	bat	well
ball	fall	fill	wall
ring	bang	sing	wing
coat	boat	mat	goat

- Ask children to select items from a box or feelie bag and to say the word for the item aloud and then find another word that rhymes (dog, cat, ball, pen, car, bike).
- Choose engaging rhyming stories to help children to become aware of rhyming words, repeating couplets, alliteration and rhythm. Some of these are:

  Hairy Maclary from Donaldson's Dairy, by Lynley Dodd
  Each Peach Pear Plum, by Janet and Allan Ahlberg
  We're Going on a Bear Hunt, by Michael Rosen
  This is the Bear and the Scary Night, by Sarah Hayes
  The Cat in the Hat, by Dr Seuss
  Green Eggs and Ham, by Dr Seuss

RESEARCH SUMMARY RESEARCH SUMMARY **RESEARCH SUMMARY** RESEARCH SUMMARY

We know from the work of Goswami and Bryant (1990) that children who are sensitive to rhyme do much better at reading. A knowledge of nursery rhymes in pre-school children is strongly associated with success in reading. We also know that children who are taught about rhyme are more successful at reading than those who are not given this teaching. Rhyme, then, has to be central to any programme of phonics teaching.

Bryant and Bradley (1985) argue that children need to have lots of experience with nursery rhymes, and verses and word-games before they go to school. This will help them to understand how spoken words can be broken up into syllables and phonemes.

Phonemic awareness and phonics

When children are able to rhyme, they will probably be able to begin to develop **phonemic awareness** – the ability to discriminate the smallest units of sound in speech – phonemes. This is trickier than you think! For example, how many phonemes can you identify in the word mummy? (There are four, but many adults are led astray by thinking about the spelling.) This is not a 'natural' ability: it is one we learn as part of learning literacy, so it is important to give children the experiences they need early on. All these steps in phonological awareness are about listening and sounds. They are not written skills. When children show the first signs of phonemic awareness, they can move towards **phonics**, which is about teaching the relationships between sound and writing in English.

Here are some ideas that will help children to focus on listening to initial phonemes in words:

- Model the learning process for the child, e.g. 'Your name is Harry. Can you hear the 'h' sound at the beginning of your name? Let's say it together.'
- Reinforce the child's knowledge, e.g. 'Do you know any other names that begin with 'h'?
- Have some fun with sentences based on alliteration:

  Peter Piper picked a peck of pickled peppers.
  Harry the Hedgehog has holes in his hat.
  Gertie the Goldfish has glue on her gills.
  Peter the Puma has paint on his paws.

- Play I-spy.
- Use classroom objects to reinforce understanding:

    Point to the window and say: 'I can see something and it begins with wi…'
    Point to the table and say: 'I can see something and it begins with ta…'

- Use riddles:

    You sleep in it and it begins with 'b'.
    You watch it and it begins with 't'.
    You drink out of it and it begins with 'c'.

- Read out a set of four words and ask the question: 'Which word begins with the same sound as "mat"?'

    cat   chair   man   pot

- Introduce the words 'letter' and 'word'. Children need to know these because they will give them a consistent way of talking about a particular sound when they are reading or writing a word.
- Use the alliterative sentences above (Peter Piper, etc.) to highlight initial sounds with their letters. Make the sentences into posters and ask the children to illustrate them or write them on the board and then circle all the words that contain, for example, a letter 'p'. Read the words in each sentence together, finger-pointing to each initial letter.
- Make collections of objects and/or words beginning with the sound you are introducing and display these. Make labels for each name and read these together, finger-pointing to the initial sound and its letter.
- Draw children's attention to individual letters in the course of sharing books, e.g. draw attention to the letter 'b' if you are reading *The Three Bears*. Ask the children to bring their teddy bears to school to show everyone. Make a large bear from boxes and fabrics and mount it on the display board. Ask the children to paint and then cut out (with assistance if necessary) several large letter 'b's to put round the bear. They can trace around each letter shape with their finger or in the air. Make the home corner into a Three Bears' cottage, with labels emphasising 'b's. Share stories and rhymes about bears and make a display of books about bears.
- Use easily recognised food wrappers to reinforce knowledge of initial sounds and letters. Then prepare a list of well-known brands with their initial letters missing (-ars, -ounty, -itkat, and so on). Point to each word and ask the children to name the missing letter. Write this in the space and read the word again with the children, pointing to the initial letter, emphasising it as you read the word together.
- Ask children to listen to the words below and to say which is the odd one out this time (note the position of the crucial sound which varies in the words).

bun	hut	gun	sun	the critical sound is at the end of the word
hug	pig	dig	wig	the critical sound is in the middle of the word
bud	bun	bus	rug	the critical sound is at the beginning of the word

Learning the main grapheme–phoneme correspondences (GPCs)

Children who can hear that 'dog', 'duck' and 'dinosaur' all start with the same sound (the phoneme /d/) and that 'hat', 'rabbit' and 'pot' all end in the same sound (the phoneme /t/) are obviously developing an 'ear' for sounds – phonemic awareness. This is the time to teach them that these words, when written down for them to see, have letters in common. Writing and spelling introduce children to the alphabetical principle. By sharing writing and reading, you have an opportunity to focus children's attention on letter order, letter sounds and letter shapes in order to identify letter–sound correspondences. This can be picked up in direct phonics instruction so that children who have gained this insight make fast progress at learning GPCs. The aim of this will be to teach children:

- the 44 main phonemes of English and the most common graphemes that represent them;
- to blend phonemes and graphemes to make words;
- to segment graphemes and phonemes to decode words;
- that blending and segmenting are reversible processes.

This phase of phonics teaching is quite intense and will teach all 44 GPCs over a surprisingly short time. Children will learn some consonants and some vowels each week so that they can blend and segment consonant-vowel-consonant (CVC) words right from the beginning. There is no 'correct' order of teaching the GPCs but an example of the sort of weekly progression you might expect in this sort of programme is given below. However, you must know the order used in your school, so that you can select appropriate words for blending and segmenting.

Week	Graphemes/phonemes to be taught
1	a t s p
2	c/k o m g
3	h l n r
4	e d u f
5	b l j w
6	sh ai oa ee
7	ch or y ng
8	v oo OO z
9	x th TH ie
10	qu ou oi er
11	ue ar nk ck

You can see that the short vowels and consonants spelt with a single letter grapheme are generally taught first.

PRACTICAL TASK PRACTICAL TASK **PRACTICAL TASK** PRACTICAL TASK **PRACTICAL TASK**

You can only teach phonics well if your subject knowledge is good. Try these questions (answers given at the end of the chapter). If you do not get them all right, consider looking at our companion volume, *Primary English: Knowledge and Understanding* (Learning Matters SAGE, 2014).

1. How many syllables are there in each of these words?
   Sarah   telephone gooseberry

2. Which words rhyme with these?
   hair   care   lair   her   wear   pain
   jumped   bumped   walked   thumped   threaded held
   telephone   groan   bone   one
   Notice that rhyme is not dependent on spelling.

3. Identify the numbers of phonemes, graphemes and letters in the following words. The first one has been done for you.

Word	Number of phonemes	Number of graphemes	Number of letters
three	3	3	5
lady			
present			
laugh			
machine			
photograph			

4. The consonant sound /f/ can be spelt using several different graphemes, e.g. as in:
   *f*oal, *ph*oto, lau*gh* (and think in some English accents!). Think of ways to spell the following consonant sounds:
   /n/ /k/ /sh/

5. The long vowel sound /ee/ can be spelt using several different graphemes, as in: sw*ee*t, h*ea*t, th*ie*f, th*e*se. Think of ways to spell the following vowel sounds:
   /ae/ /ie/ /oe/

Learning to blend and segment longer words

When children have learnt the main GPCs and can blend and segment CVC words, it is important to build up longer words, which may have a number of adjacent consonants. This will involve lessons of a similar format to the one discussed above but which will focus on CCVC or CVCC (even CCVCC) words.

Learning alternate ways of pronouncing phonemes and alternate ways of spelling phonemes

The most difficult aspect of phonics is the recognition that the alphabetic principle in English is not simply one phoneme to one grapheme. Children will learn the different ways of spelling phonemes, such as the long vowels. The split digraphs (two letters, which work as a pair, split, to represent one sound, e.g. a-e as in *make* or i-e as in *site*) are an additional complication but also a matter of great interest for children. Mastering these patterns in reading and spelling gives young readers great flexibility. Some examples of graphemes that may be learnt at this stage of phonics teaching are given below:

Long vowels

/ae/ pain
/ee/ sweet
/ie/ tried
/oe/ road
/ue/ blue
/oo/ look
/OO/ zoo
/ar/ car (there may be regional variation)
/ur/ burn
/or/ for
/er/ sister
/ow/ down
/oi/ coin
/air/ stairs
/ear/ fear

Split digraphs

/o-e/ hole
/a-e/ make
/u-e/ tune
/i-e/ time

As you teach, you will need to be careful to take account of the predominant accents of the children you are teaching and select your example words accordingly. In some accents, for example, the long vowel phoneme in 'cone' will not sound at all like that in 'boat', and if you insist to children that these are the same phonemes, you risk confusing them completely.

Learning the common spelling patterns of English

Many words can be spelt in several phonically plausible ways. For instance, we spell *fish* with a /f/, but not a /ff/ or a /ph/ and we learn that the spelling -*el* is much less common at the end of a word than -*le*, but occurs after m, n, r, s, v and w. Experience tells us that certain spellings appear in certain positions and occur with greater frequency than others, and this knowledge guides us to make the correct choice. When children have learnt the very common GPCs there is a range of patterns of use that they need to learn in order to be able to spell correctly. Your phonics teaching will include teaching these patterns, even though many of them are not simply about sound–symbol correspondences. These are summarised in Annex 1 of the National Curriculum (DfE, 2013a) but it is very important that you teach them in the order agreed in your school, often based on a particular teaching scheme.

LIVERPOOL JOHN MOORES UNIVERSITY
LEARNING SERVICES

RESEARCH SUMMARY RESEARCH SUMMARY **RESEARCH SUMMARY** RESEARCH SUMMARY

A small seven-year longitudinal study in Clackmannanshire (Johnston and Watson, 2005) reported that the synthetic approach to phonics had achieved impressive results. At the end of Primary 7 (Year 6 in England), word reading was 3 years 6 months ahead of chronological age, spelling was 1 year 8 months ahead, and reading comprehension was 3.5 months ahead. Key features of the teaching were:

- short teaching sessions (15–20 minutes), broken up by a move from the carpet area to tables part-way through;
- a consistent structure for each session so that the children knew how the teacher would approach each part of their learning;
- revision of previously learnt letter–sound knowledge before the introduction of new work;
- a well-judged pace to the teaching;
- multisensory approaches;
- demonstration of the 'reversibility' of reading and spelling.

The 'reversibility' of decoding letters to read words and choosing letters to spell (encoding) meant that children were applying their phonic knowledge and the skills of blending and segmenting in two contexts: reading and writing. Since they were successful in this, building on firmly established knowledge and skills, they paved the way for further work and developed their confidence and self-esteem as readers and writers.

What will a discrete phonics teaching session involve?

EMBEDDING ICT EMBEDDING ICT **EMBEDDING ICT** EMBEDDING ICT **EMBEDDING ICT**

A phonics lesson will usually involve the teacher (or practitioner) and the whole class and often uses an interactive whiteboard (IWB) to focus the children's attention. Teachers help children to practise pronunciation by using the speech facility of an interactive whiteboard, whereby phonemes and words can be read aloud by the board, supplemented by using magnetic letters on magnetic boards (often in pairs), writing on individual whiteboards and pronouncing phonemes and words themselves. These activities may take place seated by the IWB or at desks. However, remember that just using an interactive whiteboard is not necessarily an interactive experience for children – you have to make sure they are active and engaged.

A phonics lesson will usually involve the following.

Revision of known GPCs

The children will recognise graphemes on the IWB or cards and pronounce the associated phonemes. They may also do it the other way round – suggesting ways to represent phonemes pronounced by the teacher or written on the IWB. To do this effectively, you must know which GPCs the children have already learnt.

Introduction of a new GPC or spelling rule

This might be a single letter grapheme or a digraph or trigraph. Children will look at how it is formed and may well 'air-write' the shape with their whole arm to help fix it in memory. They will pronounce the phoneme and then look at some words containing that grapheme so that they engage in segmenting and blending. Some schemes will introduce mnemonics, such as an action or story, associated with each grapheme. In phonics lessons for older children spelling the patterns listed in the National Curriculum Annex 1 (Spelling) may be taught.

Blending and segmenting

In this part of the lesson, children will blend and segment some known GPCs (including the new one) to make simple CVC words, as a whole class, or practice one of the spelling patterns which are part of their progression. The use of an IWB (or magnetic letters on a large board) lets the teacher do this process both visually and aurally so that children can see and hear blending and segmenting in action. Teachers may have a range of blending and segmenting games for children to play.

The children will practise blending and segmenting tasks, often in pairs, using magnetic letters, game cards or individual whiteboards. This involves them not only in seeing and hearing but also in manipulating, so that the lesson is a multisensory experience. In some classes, children will do this at desks or tables.

Reading and writing

As part of a phonics lesson, the teacher will engage children in reading a phonically decodable sentence, a short rhyme or story containing the target GPC. The children will use blending and segmenting and their knowledge of common spellings to read the text. They may also write a short text.

In this section of the lesson, they may use the words they have been learning by sight. These words are common but are not phonically regular. Children are taught to recognise these words by sight so that they become automatic.

During the phonics session, the teacher will be making careful assessment of which children are succeeding at the recognition, pronunciation, blending and segmenting. On the basis of these assessments, some children will follow the whole-class lesson with independent or group activities such as writing, reading or computer phonics games.

This is far from the only phonics teaching that children will experience. Teachers will use shared and group reading and writing to demonstrate and engage children in the use of phonics. Experimental literacy-play activities play an important part in helping early writers to learn about the letter–sound relationships in words, and parents, as long as they are well informed about the system, will help children to learn and use these early phonics skills.

Assessing phonics

All teachers and teaching assistants who teach phonics assess the children's achievement and keep records which inform their planning of lessons. A large part of this assessment is done through observation of both knowledge and skills. Children need secure knowledge of the GPCs and spelling conventions. They also need the skills of blending and segmenting phonemes and use of spelling conventions. It is important that the knowledge and skills be assessed during their phonics lessons, but also during their guided reading and writing activities. It is not enough to know phonics as a decontextualised trick, because it is the ability to use it to read and write that counts. For these reasons, most assessment will be done during normal teaching. However, there is also a national Phonics Screening Check, which is administered by teachers to all children currently in Year 1. This tests children's knowledge of GPCs and ability to blend and segment words and non-words. It is very important to look at and understand this test and to discuss with your teacher how the children are prepared for it, because unless they understand the test goals, fluent readers may use non-phonic strategies which depress their scores on this test.

PRACTICAL TASK PRACTICAL TASK **PRACTICAL TASK** PRACTICAL TASK **PRACTICAL TASK**

The accurate assessment of children's performance at all stages of phonics and phonological awareness is vital in planning for effective learning and teaching. Discuss this aspect of the school phonics programme with your class teacher or literacy co-ordinator.

- How is children's phonological awareness assessed so that practitioners know when to start systematic phonics instruction?
- What record of phonics achievement is kept?
- How does the teacher decide which children in the class need more work on a particular aspect of phonics?

Pronouncing phonemes

If **phonemes** are pronounced correctly ('p' – not 'puh'), they are easier to blend together. If they are 'stretched' by adding extra vowels, they are really difficult to blend. Phonics lessons judged by HMI to be at least good were characterised by adults' excellent knowledge of the phonic content to be taught and their skills in teaching it, including clear and precise pronunciation of phonemes which provided a good model for pupils and supported their blending skills (Rose, 2006).

This problem arises because not all sounds are easy to pronounce alone. **Consonants** can be particularly hard to pronounce, as they are rarely pronounced in speech without a vowel. There is always the temptation to add the unstressed vowel known in English as 'schwa' (a sort of /-uh/), especially when trying to say a phoneme loudly. This is particularly true when the sounds are very similar, such as /b/ and /p/, which are different only in the position of the vocal chords!

Letter names or phonemes or graphemes – which should we use?

Children should learn the phonemes and the letter names, and are capable of doing both without confusion. Research indicates that children often learn letter names earlier than they learn letter sounds and that five-year-olds who know more letter names also know more letter sounds. As children will meet many instances outside their settings and schools where letter names are used, it makes sense to teach them within the programme of early phonic work. They are then able to discuss graphemes precisely, without confusion.

RESEARCH SUMMARY RESEARCH SUMMARY **RESEARCH SUMMARY** RESEARCH SUMMARY

The Rose Review (2006) asserts that the distinction between a letter name and a letter sound is easily understood by the majority of children. Stuart (2006) has observed that it seems 'sensible to teach both names and sounds of letters. Names may be easier to learn because, being syllables rather than phonemes, they are more perceptible, and also because children expect things to have names and are accustomed to rapidly acquiring the names of things' (p. 22).

It is useful to teach the letters of the alphabet and alphabetical order, very early, before children begin to do synthetic phonics. Children can easily learn letter names through the 'alphabet song' – a mnemonic! Many children learn the alphabet to the tune of 'Twinkle, Twinkle, Little Star'.

In your phonics teaching, it is important to be precise when referring to phonemes and **graphemes**. Refer to the phoneme by sound (the word apple starts with the phoneme /a/). Refer to the graphemes by letter name (the word apple begins with the grapheme a). Children can cope with the fact that some graphemes have more than one letter but represent only one phoneme.

A SUMMARY OF **KEY POINTS**

- ➢ **Adults read using a range of cueing systems to guide their word recognition.**
- ➢ **Early readers rely much more heavily on sound–symbol correspondences.**
- ➢ **Phonics teaching aims to help children learn to decode these correspondences automatically and give them a 'leg-up to reading and writing'.**
- ➢ **It is recommended that phonics be taught discretely in daily lessons as the prime approach to establishing word recognition.**

M-LEVEL EXTENSION > > M-LEVEL EXTENSION > > M-LEVEL EXTENSION

One of your tasks as a teacher is to use resources effectively. In teaching phonics, there are many schemes available and you should be able to evaluate them.

An appropriate programme will:

- be fully compatible with a broad and rich curriculum;
- make clear the importance of speaking and listening as the foundation for embarking on a systematic phonics programme and for acquiring the skills of reading and writing;
- be systematic, with a clearly defined and structured progression for learning all the major GPCs: digraphs, trigraphs, adjacent consonants and alternative graphemes for the same sound;

- be delivered in discrete daily sessions at a brisk pace that is well matched to children's developing abilities;
- be underpinned by a synthetic approach to blending phonemes in order all through a word to read it, and segmenting words into their constituent phonemes to spell them;
- make clear that blending and segmenting are reversible processes;
- be multisensory, encompassing various visual, auditory and kinaesthetic activities that actively engage children (for example, manipulating magnetic or other solid letters to build words or activities involving physical movement to copy letter shapes);
- offer clear guidance on how to assess progress and use this to inform the next steps of learning;
- offer guidance about adapting the programme for children with special educational needs or who have missed earlier elements.

Look at your phonics scheme (paper and electronic resources, including the guidance offered by the scheme handbooks and websites) and identify the ways in which it meets these criteria.

Use the grid below to identify the key features of your school's approach to teaching phonics. To get this information you need to talk to the teachers, examine resources and scheme support materials and look at the school policy and guidance for parents.

Features of a systematic synthetic phonics programme	Your school's programme
1. **Rate at which grapheme–phoneme correspondences (GPCs) are introduced** GPCs introduced at the rate of about three to five a week, starting with single letters and a sound for each, then going on to the sounds represented by digraphs (e.g. sh and oo) and larger grapheme units (e.g. air, igh, eigh).	
2. **Point at which blending and segmenting phonemes is taught** Blending of phonemes for reading, starting after the first few GPCs have been taught and working with more GPCs as they are taught. Segmenting of phonemes for spelling, again starting after the first few GPCs have been taught and working with more GPCs as they are taught.	
3. **Activities and games used for teaching blending and segmenting** In the daily phonics session how are these activities used?	
4. **Approach to teaching most common and less common spellings for sounds** Introduction of the most common spellings for sounds first and then introduce alternative sounds for spellings and alternative spellings for sounds.	
5. **Approach to teaching high frequency words** Introduction of strategies for reading and spelling common high frequency words containing unusual GPCs.	
6. **Approach to teaching morphemes** Introduction of prefixes, suffixes, plural and past tense endings.	
7. **Use of reading schemes to support developing phonic knowledge** Provision of opportunities for the application of word-reading skills in reading books which are closely matched to children's developing skills – level appropriate decodable texts – to support children in using their phonemic strategies as a first approach to reading and spelling and to experiencing success.	

FURTHER READING   FURTHER READING   **FURTHER READING**   FURTHER READING

Bryant, P. and Bradley, L. (1985) *Children's Reading Problems*. Oxford: Basil Blackwell.

DfE (2013) *The National Curriculum in England*. London: DfE. (https://www.gov.uk/dfe/nationalcurriculum)

DfE (2013) *Teachers' Standards*. London: DfE. (https://www.gov.uk/government/uploads/system/uploads/attachment_data/file/208682/Teachers__Standards_2013.pdf)

DfES (2007) *Letters and Sounds: Principles and Practice of High Quality Phonics*. London: DfES.

Jolliffe, W., Waugh, D. and Carss, L. (2012) *Teaching Systematic Synthetic Phonics in Primary Schools*. London: Learning Matters SAGE.

Lipson, M.Y. and Wixon, K.K. (2002) *Assessment and Instruction of Reading and Writing Difficulty: an interactive approach* (3rd edn). Needham Heights, MA: Allyn and Bacon.

Masterson, J., Stuart, M., Dixon, M. and Lovejoy, S. (2003) *Children's Printed Word Database*. Swindon: Economic and Social Research Council.

Purcell-Gates, V. (1997) *Other People's Words: Cycle of Low Literacy*. Cambridge, MA: Harvard University Press.

Rose, J. (2006) *Independent Review of the Teaching of Early Reading: Final Report*. London: DfES.

Stahl, K.A. and McKenna, M.C. (2006) *Reading Research at Work: Foundations of Effective Practice*. London: Guilford.

Stuart, M. (2005) 'Phonemic analysis and reading development: some current issues', *Journal of Research in Reading*, vol. 28, pp. 39–49.

Answers to the Practical Task on p. 68

1. Sarah (2); telephone (3) – but it depends how you pronounce it.

   These words underline some key points about syllables.

   - Syllables are SOUNDS, not written units. So, gooseberry (3) has five letters we call vowels, but actually only the /oo/, /e/ and /y/ act as syllable nuclei, and even then the unstressed sound /y/ is difficult to hear.
   - Pronunciation can make a difference. Some words are pronounced in different ways and neither variant is wrong – just different.

2. Which words rhyme with these?

   hair   care   fair   her   wear   pain

   There are a number of ways to spell the last vowel and it is the last vowel and consonant (the end of the syllable) that rhyme here. Rhyme is about sound – not spelling.

   jumped   bumped   walked   thumped   threaded   held

   Walked doesn't rhyme because the last two sounds you can hear in jumped are /p/ /d/. So you listen for these in a rhyme.

   telephone   groan   bone   one

3.

Word	Number of phonemes	Number of graphemes	Number of letters
three	3	3	5
lady	4	4	4
present	7	7	7

laugh	3	3	5
machine	5	5	7
photograph	8	8	10

You should notice that the number of graphemes and phonemes in a word should always correspond, but that there will often be no correspondence at all with the number of letters.

4. /n/ – **kn**ight, **n**ight, **gn**ome, **pn**eumonia, di**nn**er, **mn**emonic
   /k/ – coo**k**, **q**ui**ck**, mi**x**, **ch**aos, **c**at
   /sh/ – **sh**ip, mi**ssi**on, **ch**ef, ma**ch**ine, sta**ti**on

5. /ae/ – pain, day, gate, station
   /ie/ – tried, light, my, shine, mind
   /oe/ – road, blow, bone, cold

This phonic unpredictability is the very reason why English is a difficult language in which to read using phonics alone. Other languages (e.g. Finnish, Spanish) are much more regular in the ways their phonemes and graphemes relate.

7
Teaching early writing

TEACHERS' STANDARDS

A teacher must:

2. **Promote good progress and outcomes by pupils**

   - **be accountable for pupils' attainment, progress and outcomes**
   - **plan teaching to build on pupils' capabilities and prior knowledge**
   - **guide pupils to reflect on the progress they have made and their emerging needs**
   - **demonstrate knowledge and understanding of how pupils learn and how this impacts on teaching**
   - **encourage pupils to take a responsible and conscientious attitude to their own work and study.**

3. **Demonstrate good subject and curriculum knowledge**

   - **have a secure knowledge of the relevant subject(s) and curriculum areas, foster and maintain pupils' interest in the subject, and address misunderstandings**
   - **demonstrate a critical understanding of developments in the subject and curriculum areas, and promote the value of scholarship**
   - **demonstrate an understanding of and take responsibility for promoting high standards of literacy, articulacy and the correct use of standard English, whatever the teacher's specialist subject**
   - **if teaching early reading, demonstrate a clear understanding of systematic synthetic phonics**

4. **Plan and teach well structured lessons**

   - **impart knowledge and develop understanding through effective use of lesson time**

Introduction

This chapter focuses mainly on the development of compositional skills in writing: that is, recognising who is to be written for, planning what is to be written, and choosing, arranging and modifying words so that the message is conveyed appropriately. These are complex processes and yet develop at the same time as the transcription skills of spelling and handwriting. These transcription skills have their own chapter. In this chapter, we will concentrate on how teachers can best support the development of writing in young children so that they become aware of the many aspects of writing and are able to manipulate written language effectively.

Development in writing

The early learning of language has been discussed in Chapter 2, but it is important to emphasise again that writing does not begin at school and cannot develop in isolation from reading and talk.

There is a great deal of knowledge about writing that experienced writers take for granted but that young children must learn. For example:

- adults write for lots of reasons;
- other adults read what is written;
- what is written is the same every time it is read;
- words that are spoken can be written down;
- what is written down can be spoken;
- what a word is (because there are no spaces in speech, what we refer to as a word is a unit of meaning);
- print and pictures are different;
- print moves from left to right in English.

These seem like basic concepts, but the degree of each child's understanding and ability when they enter school will vary. When asked what writing was, two four-year-old children, just going into school, gave quite different answers. According to Manjit, 'Writing is when you say something on paper. If someone's not there, you do a letter.' For Alexander, 'Writing is when you put the numbers in the right order to make your name.'

One of the most important issues in teaching early writing is to recognise exactly what children coming into your class know and can do. This allows you to present learning to write as a continuous experience and avoid children having to cope with discontinuities of expectation. Baseline assessment will enable Reception teachers to look closely at children's performance through observation and discussion. In other year groups, class records and samples of work will be passed on to give teachers a good idea of a child's development as a writer.

Children's earliest understandings about writing will be based on the experiences they have had, not just of writing, but also of speaking and listening and reading. Most children are effective speakers, although not always of English, before they come to school and it is this implicit knowledge of language they will use to develop as writers. Children whose parents read signs to them, hold them up to see the cashpoint machine, or play on the computer with them, will have given them insights into the meaning of those types of writing – signs and screen text. However, they will also have helped children make the link between the spoken and written word. When children come into school, they are able to see and hear teachers writing – doing shared writing, putting up lists, playing with children – but they are also able to talk about writing with teachers and develop a more explicit knowledge about language.

Teaching writing

The teaching of writing, building on children's existing knowledge about language, needs to:

- engage children in purposeful writing;
- show children how writing works;
- engage children in responding to writing;

- encourage children to practise, explore, experiment and play with writing;
- give children the chance to use writing and get a response.

Children in the Early Years will work in flexible, play-orientated ways, moving towards a literacy lesson as they enter Key Stage 1. At Key Stage 1, much teaching of writing will take place in the literacy lessons through shared reading and writing, guided reading and writing, independent investigations, practice activity and play. However, at both Foundation Stage and Key Stage 1, writing is a cross-curricular skill, which allows children to express and explore other subjects. Much of children's purposeful use of writing and practice will take place outside specific literacy lessons.

Shared reading and writing

Shared reading is an important demonstration, not only of the mechanics of reading, but also a chance to engage children with the ways in which forms of writing achieve their purpose. When children have read a number of traditional tales, they will be able to say that stories begin with 'Once upon a time', or 'Long ago' and end 'happily ever after'. Learning these conventions and linking them to the enjoyment of a traditional tale is the first step towards learning the structures and language use of traditional tales. Similarly, if children learn that instructions contain a number of steps to tell you what to do, they are beginning to understand how language meets its purpose. In practice, such shared reading experiences will be supported by shared writing experiences on other days. So, if children have read a traditional tale on Monday and Tuesday, they may well go on to write a similar tale about a character of their own later in the week.

Shared writing involves the teacher using a flipchart, overhead projector or interactive whiteboard to plan, write, explore and discuss a text in co-operation with the children. Working with the whole class means that children cannot only hear the teacher's views, but they can also hear other children's contributions and evaluate them. As you write for children you are, of course, also demonstrating basic transcription details like writing from left to right, letter formation, use of capital and lower-case letters, using spaces between words and working out how to spell words by sound. However, you are most importantly making the link between writing and reading and, by supporting the transcription details of writing, you are giving children the space to make language decisions such as choosing appropriate vocabulary, choosing sentence structures and word order and choosing text conventions and layout.

At the Foundation Stage, shared writing may involve a group of children or be shorter than 15 minutes. The text types will be linked to other topics in class – such as a shopping list, a description or a story. However, even at this stage, children need a wide range of texts and to see you, a more experienced author, making text decisions.

In Key Stage 1, you will be able to model a number of aspects of the writing process:

- *Planning writing* – This includes a discussion of what is involved and who the piece is for, as well as children's contributions to choosing characters or making concept maps. Teaching children to plan their writing, even if only mentally, is likely to help them organise their thoughts and structures. Too many children start to write and simply keep going without monitoring the structure and effect of their writing at regular intervals.
- *Drafting writing* – Drafting may involve using a text map or writing frame to help structure the piece. You should certainly refer to any planning notes made on a previous occasion. When drafting, it is important to model not only the transcribing but also the sort of thinking that takes place as you decide what to write. You can induct children into this by asking for their views, opinions and reasons.

- *Revising writing* – This involves looking at a piece of writing and considering its effect and how that effect is created. This is a good opportunity to evaluate the vocabulary, sentence types, sentence structures and text features to see whether they achieve the purpose intended. By making changes on a draft, you can show children that writing is provisional and can be improved. You are also showing them that there is not only one way of writing a certain text type. The editing of a piece of writing for transcription details is a very important skill, but is much less difficult for children to understand. They are usually able to look through a piece for capital letters and spelling errors quite early. They can then cope well with looking for appropriate sentence structures. Decisions about the effect of a vocabulary choice or a choice of sentence type may be more difficult, as they are required to see the text from a reader's point of view.

When undertaking any shared writing, there will always be a great many features to which you can usefully draw attention. Decide which objectives you will focus on and refer back to them during the shared reading. This helps you to make clear teaching points to the children. You may find it useful to have your objectives written on a wall poster so that you can check whether you have addressed them at the end of the shared writing. When starting a piece of shared writing, it is important to examine the problem – what type of text are you writing? What is this sort of text for? Who might read this type of text? What will the reader look for or expect? You may want to include this in your planning. Otherwise, planning may involve collecting and organising ideas. Planning may take a whole shared writing session and will usually involve writing notes and sentence fragments, although there will be times when you will list whole sentences. When discussing writing and language, use appropriate language terms and aim to be clear and accurate. It is, of course, essential that you understand fully the text type you are dealing with and the language features you will encounter.

When drafting in shared writing, you are aiming to engage and motivate all the children. It is very difficult to take contributions from a large number of children at the same time but there are a number of ways to increase participation. Some teachers use word cards or magnetic words and ask children to arrange them, which avoids the need to write at all. More usually, teachers write (or scribe) for the children. As well as scribing for a whole class, many teachers use small individual whiteboards for children to write words, sentences and longer passages on. They can then hold up their suggestions or show them to each other without shouting and becoming confused. Magnetic boards with letters or letter fans can be used in a similar way for spelling input. To encourage children to discuss ideas or make choices between two options, you can ask them to work with a partner to discuss a language choice, but do limit the discussion time and maintain the pace of the session. When taking suggestions from children, it is a good idea to ask them why they made their decision and always discuss and explain why one decision is better than another. This will help children learn how to become critical about their work as well as how to make decisions. When you are discussing issues with children, it is very easy to lose the 'flow' of a piece of writing. To prevent this, always re-read the preceding part of the passage when adding new material and re-read the text so far at regular intervals. It is a good idea to say any proposed sentence aloud as a rehearsal before adding it to a shared writing piece. These techniques ensure that all the children can follow the writing and do not become lost or bored.

EMBEDDING ICT EMBEDDING ICT **EMBEDDING ICT** EMBEDDING ICT **EMBEDDING ICT**

When planning and drafting shared writing and going on to develop it further through revising and editing, ICT can be integral in engaging and motivating children. The interactive whiteboard (IWB) can be used to record their contributions, give vocabulary choices, draft sentences and cut and paste them to re-sequence the piece, until everyone is happy with the result. The children can then move to working further on the same text or developing one of their own in groups on the classroom computer or in your school's ICT suite.

Any text type can be written collaboratively during a shared writing activity. It is particularly useful, however, in order to bring reading and writing closely together, to use shared reading texts as a starting point for shared writing. You might, for example:

- retell together a story you have recently read;
- extend or finish a story you have read;
- rework a story by substituting a character or by changing a setting;
- use the text you have read to 'scaffold' or 'frame' the writing, e.g. substitute new rhymes in a rhyming story (invent some new dogs to accompany Hairy Maclary or add some new animals to the story of the Grumpalump); use a simple poem to write another in the same pattern (Twinkle, twinkle, little cat…); write a recount using a simple writing frame (First we _____ then we _____ Next _____ When we arrived we _____ Finally we _____);
- use an extract from the text as a starting point, e.g. by carrying on from opening sentences or by finishing off a section of dialogue;
- write a new story round a familiar theme, e.g. new versions of fairy tales (read some of Roald Dahl's or Terry Jones's versions);
- find and record, in note form, information from the text you have read, then add further information to this.

Before writing
- Discuss the audience for the writing – who do we want to read this (ourselves, younger children, a character in the story, the local policeman, parents)?
- Discuss the tone of the writing – how should it sound (funny, scary, informative)?
- Discuss the purpose of the writing – is it to amuse, to tell a story, to recount an experience, to give instructions, to explain, to remind or to summarise?
- Collect and note down ideas for the writing.
- Discuss the sequence of the writing and how it can be made clear.

While writing
Demonstrate and discuss:

- the difference between spoken and written language;
- the direction and sequence of writing;
- how to form sentences;
- ways of joining sentences, e.g. and, also, before, when, so;
- agreement of tense, e.g. use of past tense for narratives;
- the use of punctuation to mark sentences, speech, questions and lists;
- layout: use of titles, headings, lists and paragraphs to organise meaning;
- use of appropriate technical vocabulary, e.g. noun, verb, adjective;
- spelling strategies, e.g. building words from known syllables and letter strings, spelling by analogy from known words or word parts, referring to words in text and using dictionaries and/or word banks;
- noting and investigating new spelling patterns;
- using new and alternative vocabulary for precision, to create effect, and to avoid dullness and repetition;

- using expressive and powerful language;
- letter formation and consistency, upper and lower case and the spacing between words;
- using other presentation features, e.g. capitals and underlining for emphasis;
- the features of different types of texts: style, grammar and language choices;
- changing writing as you work and using editing marks to indicate changes;
- adding, removing and reordering ideas;
- writing notes, asides and reminders for later inclusion or revision;
- checking for sense by re-reading as you write.

After writing
- Re-read the text with the class to discuss and improve its clarity, effect, suitability for purpose and audience.
- Edit to improve the text – use editing marks or rewrite as appropriate.
- Proofread, checking for accuracy in grammar, punctuation and spelling.
- Discuss the presentation of the writing, e.g. how might it be displayed and used subsequently?

Guided writing

Guided reading and writing also provide intensive teaching times. Each week, you will choose objectives for each group of children and some of these will be composing or sentence level objectives. Such tasks might include planning a story, character, or setting, drafting instructions or revising a text provided by the teacher. In guided writing, you can undertake more detailed discussion than in shared writing and differentiate the activity more closely through support and questioning. This means that in guided writing children can often produce work of a higher standard than they would independently. In guided writing, individual whiteboards and magnetic boards are also very useful for sharing ideas and contributions. In guided writing children can produce whole-group texts, plans or revisions but this requires a high level of co-operative skills and they usually produce writing in pairs or individually. In guided writing you may use strategies other than planning, drafting and revising, such as offering children sequencing passages to order or passages of writing to complete. These are useful to focus children's attention on specific aspects of language.

Independent writing

One aim of shared and guided writing is to offer children support in writing as a step towards independent writing. For every text type encountered, children need to do shared reading and writing of examples of the text type, do guided writing of selected aspects of the text and then write texts independently. This does not mean they should write a whole text in one session. In a single independent session, children might plan a piece of writing or draft part of a text. The difficulty of setting independent tasks is that they must be within the child's ability range and be clear enough for the child to carry out alone. At the same time the tasks should not lack challenge. Strategies to support independent writing and differentiate tasks to suit a range of children include:

- use of writing frames to give a writing structure;
- use of sentence starters;
- providing prompt posters for revision or text organisation;
- scaffolding a piece of writing by offering a range of vocabulary or ideas in the form of cards.

The aim of these teaching techniques is to move children through a process of experiences that will help them to write independently:

- discussing and understanding the writing task, purpose and audience;
- planning structures and ideas;
- seeing the teacher demonstrate writing;
- writing together with the teacher scribing;
- joining in composition using individual whiteboards;
- writing independently.

The literacy session may be the main focused teaching time for writing but a great deal of writing in the Early Years is done as part of school routine or through play activities. The use of written instructions and signs helps very young children to make the link between reading and writing. Simple routines such as asking every child to sign in as they enter the Reception class give children a purposeful writing task and, in this case, enable them to use their first secure written word – their name. Play activities are also some of the best opportunities for purposeful writing. In a role-play corner, for instance, children can take telephone messages, make shopping lists and write letters, cheques and signs. To do this, the appropriate materials must be available.

THE BIGGER PICTURE   THE BIGGER PICTURE   THE BIGGER PICTURE   THE BIGGER PICTURE

When you are planning early writing activities that are purposeful and that will help young children to understand the links between spoken language, reading and writing, you should consider how drama can be used. For example, you may be asked to devise and lead an assembly for a buddy class, year group, phase or for the whole school, or to put on a short performance for parents. Working in the ways described, you and the children could write a short play script based on a shared reading text, with the dialogue growing from the children's role-play or improvisation if the children are older.

It is also very important that children in the Early Years have access to writing as a free-play activity. This allows them to experiment with writing forms and conventions as well as choosing the purpose for their writing – such as notes to other children, pretend books or lists. Ideally, to allow children to experiment, a writing area will be provided, containing a variety of papers, pencils and pens as well as attractive writing formats such as note pads and yellow sticky notes. A good deal of children's experimental writing takes the form of notes and pretend letters. This will inevitably go home with the children and may not be easily accessible for you to make assessments of their understandings of writing.

Much of children's early writing is done in curriculum areas other than English. This has a number of advantages.

- Other curriculum areas provide a clear purpose for writing and a ready audience.
- In writing outside the literacy session there is less emphasis on children's writing.
- The content of writing in other areas of the curriculum is likely to be clear and may be interesting for children.

These advantages can be very motivating for children and they can produce a huge range of text types outside the literacy session, including maps, lists, reports, captions, posters, labels, diaries, word cards, instructions, accounts and many others.

EMBEDDING ICT   EMBEDDING ICT   EMBEDDING ICT   EMBEDDING ICT   EMBEDDING ICT

All of these text types, whether created within literacy sessions or in other areas of the curriculum, can be produced using a variety of writing media on paper. However, even the very youngest children can be supported to use ICT to create texts electronically, using basic word-processing programs, for example with a template that you have provided to help them to structure the particular text type required. You may set out a newspaper report with an inbuilt box for a photograph or illustration, or provide a sequence of pictures that tell a story with lines next to each for the children to label or write simple sentences to make a storyboard. See also Chapter 11 on teaching with electronic texts.

Responding to children's writing

In shared writing, children see the teacher as an experienced adult writer. However, the teacher is usually the child's writing audience and assessor as well.

The role of reader is very important in teaching writing because your response signals the success of the piece. It is usually possible to respond to a child's piece of writing as a reader by commenting, first of all, on the content or purpose of the writing. This is especially true of unsolicited or spontaneous writing. This gives the message that the child's writing is communicative and valued. Some teachers aim to write a comment about the content of a piece of writing on each piece of work they mark.

The teacher also has a role to play as a marker and assessor of the child's work. Not all pieces of work will be marked in the same way and it is very important to mark according to the clear task criteria you have set. When possible, this should be done alongside the child, as then feedback is immediate and useful. This is not always possible, of course, and a good quality comment at a later date is better than a hurried 'good', which signifies little about writing quality or whether the child has achieved an objective.

Children learn by experimenting, and this naturally involves them in making mistakes (we referred to these as 'approximations' in an earlier chapter). Mistakes should not be ignored or praised inappropriately. It is much more helpful to point out how the work can be changed and help the child to do this. When looking at a piece of work, it can be tempting to focus on what the child does not know, especially features such as spelling and use of punctuation. Of course, writing conventions must be learned, and teachers should not just ignore errors, but in many cases to correct every error would destroy the work. It is more productive to look for patterns of errors.

REFLECTIVE TASK

Look carefully at a piece of writing produced by a child you have taught. Examine it with the following questions in mind.

- Are there words or letter sequences that the child consistently spells wrongly?
- Do any of the spelling errors the child makes seem to follow a particular pattern, for example spelling by sounding words out?
- What is the likely explanation for a child making a particular punctuation error?

- Is the use of punctuation random, or does the child appear to be using a rule of some kind, even if this is not the conventional one?

Given the pattern of errors you have identified in this child's writing, what teaching would you now suggest as a way of taking this child forward?

Where error patterns like these are detected, targets can be set and children can improve their writing. Many teachers aim to mark one piece of writing in real detail for each half term or text type studied, then discuss it with the child in a writing conference. Some guidelines for this detailed marking will be found later in the book. Conferencing then allows the teacher to probe the child's understanding about the writing processes, text types and work. It is a good time to discuss progress and review targets, which might be kept in a writing book, target file or in a home-school book. The conference also gives the teacher a much fuller picture of the child's abilities, which will contribute to record-keeping and assessment, and the piece of work and conference notes can form part of a child's portfolio of work.

RESEARCH SUMMARY   RESEARCH SUMMARY   **RESEARCH SUMMARY**   RESEARCH SUMMARY

The 1980s saw a number of seminal studies of young children becoming writers, notable among these being the work of Bissex (1980) and Harste *et al.* (1984). The messages from these studies are still relevant in today's classrooms and can be summarised as follows.

- Given access to adult models of how writing is done, many children figure out lots of the rules for themselves.
- Adults can deliberately speed up this 'figuring out' by direct teaching, but must never lose sight of the fact that children engage in writing because it does something for them – they have the human need to communicate, and writing is just one more medium for this.
- Looking closely at what young children write can give teachers great insight into the writing rules the children have constructed for themselves, with consequent implications for what teaching they might then need.

A SUMMARY OF **KEY POINTS**

- ➢ **Writing does not begin at school and most young children have ideas about it before they arrive in school.**
- ➢ **Shared writing is a powerful way of teaching all aspects of the writing process.**
- ➢ **Guided writing can provide a transition between shared and independent writing.**
- ➢ **Teachers' responses to children's writing can be a crucial factor in their engagement with the process.**

M-LEVEL EXTENSION   > >   M-LEVEL EXTENSION   > >   M-LEVEL EXTENSION

Plan some teaching sessions in which you use the shared writing technique. Use the Before writing/During writing/After writing model to help you plan these sessions in detail. Think about the indicators you will use, against which you would judge the success of any of these teaching sessions. What is the role of ICT in your plans? What should be the role of ICT in shared writing generally?

FURTHER READING   FURTHER READING   **FURTHER READING**   FURTHER READING

Bissex, G.L. (1980) *Gnys at Wrk: A child learns to write*. Cambridge, MA: Harvard University Press.

Browne, A. (1999) *Teaching Writing at Key Stage 1 and Before*. London: Thomas Nelson.

DfE (2013) *Teachers' Standards*. London: DfE. (https://www.gov.uk/government/uploads/system/uploads/attachment_data/file/208682/Teachers__Standards_2013.pdf)

Harste, J.C., Woodward, V.A. and Burke, C.L. (1984) *Language Stories and Literacy Lessons*. Portsmouth, NH: Heinemann.

Hodson, P. and Jones, D. (2001) *Teaching Children to Write*. London: David Fulton.

8
Teaching handwriting and spelling

TEACHERS' STANDARDS

A teacher must:

2. **Promote good progress and outcomes by pupils**

    -   be accountable for pupils' attainment, progress and outcomes
    -   plan teaching to build on pupils' capabilities and prior knowledge
    -   guide pupils to reflect on the progress they have made and their emerging needs
    -   demonstrate knowledge and understanding of how pupils learn and how this impacts on teaching
    -   encourage pupils to take a responsible and conscientious attitude to their own work and study.

3. **Demonstrate good subject and curriculum knowledge**

    -   have a secure knowledge of the relevant subject(s) and curriculum areas, foster and maintain pupils' interest in the subject, and address misunderstandings
    -   demonstrate a critical understanding of developments in the subject and curriculum areas, and promote the value of scholarship
    -   demonstrate an understanding of and take responsibility for promoting high standards of literacy, articulacy and the correct use of standard English, whatever the teacher's specialist subject

4. **Plan and teach well structured lessons**

    -   impart knowledge and develop understanding through effective use of lesson time

Introduction

Handwriting and spelling, grouped as 'transcription' in the National Curriculum, are important parts of the complex processes of writing. One reason why these aspects of writing are so important is that they are very obvious indicators of progress. A child can easily see improvement in their own handwriting and will notice as spelling becomes easier. Developing fluency in both these areas of skill is very important as it frees attention for the other language decisions made in any act of composition. Handwriting is undoubtedly the simpler of the two skill domains and this chapter will deal with handwriting first. English spelling is complex and involves a wide range of strategies and knowledge.

Teaching handwriting

Children need to develop a number of types of handwriting:

- a fluent, joined-up, legible everyday script;
- a fast, less legible hand for note-taking and making;
- a best handwriting, which shows that they work with care and style.

Children do not develop good handwriting by accident and all children should be doing some structured, regular handwriting practice. Schools and teachers have to decide what to teach and how to teach it.

Firstly, all children need to develop a good pencil grip and writing position. Most three-fingered pencil grips are fine, with the exception of a simple 'fist', which is not sensitive enough for writing and should be discouraged as early as possible. Fat, soft, triangular pencils encourage the development of a good grip and left-handed children should be taught to hold the pencil slightly further up the shaft, away from the point to prevent smudging. Children with severe motor impairment, such as that caused by cerebral palsy, may push the pencil through a pencil grip or airflow ball to improve control. All writers benefit from sitting at the right height with feet flat on the ground, but left-handers really need to sit a little higher than right-handers to develop a good posture.

The next priority is to learn to form letters correctly so that when children start to join up letters, the hand movements they make will work smoothly. The letter shapes of most letters in the English language are, as Sassoon (1990) points out, based on ovals and vertical lines. There is some variation for different script styles – for instance, there are several ways of forming an *f*, *t*, *k*, or even a letter *a* – but most letters are very similar. Schools in England and Wales choose a school handwriting script with agreed letter formations and joins. You must make sure that you use your school's script when modelling writing to children and that you know the differences in letter formation for left-handed children.

REFLECTIVE TASK

Collect an example of your 'best' handwriting, your 'normal, legible' handwriting and your note-taking handwriting. How do the samples vary in terms of:

- consistency and regularity of letter formation and joins?
- orientation and consistency of spacing?
- proportions of letters (ascenders and descenders) and of spaces?

These are the criteria you would use for judging the handwriting in a child's piece of writing.

Look at your school script. How does your writing compare to it? What changes will you have to make, and practise, for use on placement? If you are not used to writing in large handwriting on boards and flipcharts, you will need to practise.

There are a number of ways to decide on the order of the introduction of letter shapes to young children. Some theorists (for example Sassoon, 1990) favour particular approaches such as the introduction of letters with a similar hand movement together. In practice, most teachers introduce letter formation of the letters studied in early phonics work so that children learn letter names, sounds and formation together, so most children learn initial consonants first, consonant blends and then formation of vowels. When teaching letter shapes, the emphasis should be firstly on the correct movement and only when this is achieved, on orientation, proportions relative to other letters and positioning on lines.

Ways of teaching letter formation include:

- tracing over sandpaper letters with a finger to feel the shapes;
- painting big letter shapes with a paintbrush;
- tracing letter shapes in trays of sand or jelly with the finger;
- using large letters to trace over repeatedly with crayons to form 'rainbow letters';
- tracing over rows of letters;
- using computer programs to trace letters and do letter-shaped puzzles;
- using a finger to make letter shapes in the air or on another child's back;
- tracing over letters made of dots;
- children writing their names or tracing them.

Some teachers use 'pencil play' activities to teach children to trace from left to right and to cross the mid-line but, in practice, very few children who have had normal use of crayons and paints for drawing need these activities. Using a computer mouse is a good way of developing fine motor control but does not generalise directly to letter formation – children will still need to practise.

All these activities can be done playfully and should not last for very long – they are not particularly imaginative or stimulating and little and often is preferable to letting them become boring. These activities seek to develop habits and so really benefit from close supervision. This is a type of task where an experienced teaching assistant or a willing parent helper can make a great difference.

When children can form letters correctly, they need to be taught the joins used in the school handwriting script. The order and timing of the introduction of joins is controversial. If the introduction of joins is left too late, some children have done so much printing they are unable to learn to join fluently and automatically. Some schools teach joined handwriting from the outset (as is done in France and Russia) but most schools in the UK introduce joining in Year 1 or 2. Several orders for introducing joins are found in commercially published handwriting schemes. It is perfectly acceptable to use any order the school has decided on, as long as it is taught consistently within the school. Again, the priority in learning to join letters is correct hand movements, then neatness and proportions. As with letter formation, correct joining requires regular practice and must be checked so that bad habits are not established. Although handwriting tasks can be done in the literacy session, they are usually quite short and do not require a 20-minute slot. Some teachers set a short handwriting task during registration and check a few children each day. Many teachers use children's drafted work as a focus for handwriting practice. Others use a commercial handwriting scheme containing exercises or passages they have prepared themselves. Interactive whiteboard-based schemes have been popular for teaching formation. Individual computer- or tablet-based handwriting resources, may not be a good use of limited computer time unless a child has a particular handwriting difficulty.

An important aspect of learning about handwriting comes when children have to choose how much attention to give to handwriting for a particular task. In modelling writing, you need to model using a fluent and legible script as well as modelling how you decide what level of neatness to use. As children become confident users of handwriting and can make decisions about font choice and presentational devices in IT, they may wish to slant their handwriting and give it a 'style'.

As children become more fluent, they will learn to use ink. Biro ink is very slippery and does not help good handwriting – fibre-tipped pens are much more controllable and produce a neater result. Most children will want to try a fountain pen – it is a messy (and enjoyable) experience for most. However, fountain pen is no 'better' than any other form of ink and is likely to disadvantage left-handers who tend to push the pen into the paper because of the letter formation demands of English. Older children may enjoy experimenting with calligraphy.

RESEARCH SUMMARY   RESEARCH SUMMARY   **RESEARCH SUMMARY**   RESEARCH SUMMARY

Automaticity in handwriting is now seen as of key importance in composing but UK policy and practice tends to have assumed that, by Year 6, handwriting is a matter of presentation, unrelated to composition processes. Recent research has been undertaken into the handwriting speed and orthographic motor integration of Year 6 pupils in relation to their composition (Medwell *et al.*, 2009) and into similar aspects of the writing of Year 2 children (Medwell *et al.*, 2007). These studies both suggest that handwriting is an important factor in composition, and that a proportion of children suffer from low levels of handwriting automaticity, which may be interfering with their composition. The teaching of handwriting is, it seems, not just important in improving children's presentation skills, but in their composition skills too.

EMBEDDING ICT   EMBEDDING ICT   **EMBEDDING ICT**   EMBEDDING ICT   **EMBEDDING ICT**

A final area of handwriting, which is not primarily about motor skill, is the use of word processors to present text. Even the youngest children can use a computer mouse and some parents may have a wide range of lap-ware for the under three-year-old! Children of three, four and five can pick out letters. All children need to be taught the layout of the computer keyboard, how to highlight, underline, embolden and change fonts by Year 2 and it has been suggested that we should aim to teach children to type by the age of 11.

As with any other area of skill, some children will find handwriting easier or more satisfying than others. Unfortunately, this means some have to practise more than others. Handwriting is only a very small part of writing, and does not give a reliable indicator of the quality of the content, so it must not always be the first criterion for marking, but remember to celebrate those who do particularly well at handwriting, as well as other parts of the writing process.

RESEARCH SUMMARY   RESEARCH SUMMARY   **RESEARCH SUMMARY**   RESEARCH SUMMARY

The changes in the teaching of handwriting and spelling in the last decade have been the subject of some unregulated or researched experiments in recent times. In almost all schools there has been the change from a sans serif script (abc) to a serif script with exit strokes (*abc*). Sassoon (1990) points out that, by using a script with exit strokes, children do not learn a 'stop' movement, which can lead to poor joining. The age at which children learn to join up has also changed. A decade ago it was usual for children to learn to join in junior school. Now, infant children routinely learn this. Peters (1985) theorised that this will facilitate good spelling because children learn to spell kinaesthetically – through habitual hand movements.

Teaching spelling

The spelling of English is complicated by the long, complex history of the language and the very flexibility of English. Spelling is primarily a word-level issue, but it is also partly dependent on knowing the grammar of English. For more information on spelling, see Chapters 4 and 5 in *Primary English: Knowledge and Understanding* (Learning Matters SAGE, 2014). The National Curriculum addresses this challenge under the headings of both 'Vocabulary, grammar, and punctuation' and 'Spelling'. There is also a discrete Appendix (1 – Spelling) which gives detailed guidance about which spelling items should be learnt at which year.

PRACTICAL TASK   PRACTICAL TASK   **PRACTICAL TASK**   PRACTICAL TASK   **PRACTICAL TASK**

Note down how you can remember to spell each word in this list correctly.

necessary	*separate*	*their*
there	*unkind*	*cat*
Wednesday	*monolingual*	*antebellum*
effect	*thought*	*weir*

These words use some of the strategies children must learn.

If you have completed the above task, you will probably have found that there are several ways to learn spellings and that different words require different strategies.

The most obvious strategy that children can use in spelling is the use of sound–symbol correspondences to spell words phonetically. A child who can discriminate onsets and rimes can use /c/ /at/ to form a whole range of other words – bat, mat, rat, hat, etc. A child who has the phonemic awareness to segment /c/ /a/ /t/ and relate these phonemes to the letters can form many more words – can, cap, cad, etc., as well as those mentioned above. This strategy may be obvious, but it is not simple. (For more information on this, see Chapter 4, *Primary English: Knowledge and Understanding*, Learning Matters SAGE, 2014)

RESEARCH SUMMARY   RESEARCH SUMMARY   **RESEARCH SUMMARY**   RESEARCH SUMMARY

Gentry (1982) identified a number of stages in the development of spelling in very young children. These stages, detailed below, all indicate different levels of understanding about the spelling of English.

The early stages demonstrate growing *phonological* and graphic *awareness*. Children then learn *phonemic* segmentation. Children who have reached the stage of transitional or correct spelling have developed the insight that sound–symbol correspondences are not enough to master English spelling and are looking at the other systems inherent in English.

Features of spelling development

1. Pre-communicative
   - Demonstrates knowledge of the alphabet by forming letters to represent the alphabet.
   - No knowledge of sound–symbol correspondences.
   - Uncertain of directionality.
   - May mix letters and numbers, lower and upper case letters.

2. Semi-phonetic
   - Begins to match letters to sounds.
   - Abbreviates words.
   - May use a letter name to represent the whole word.
   - Beginning to write left to right.
   - May understand word separation and division.

3. Phonetic
   - Almost total mapping of sound–symbol correspondences.
   - Systematically developing spellings of certain forms such as 'ed'.
   - Assigns letters on the basis of sound.
   - Evidence of word separation and spatial orientation.

4. Transitional
   - Adheres to basic traditions of the English spelling system.
   - Uses vowels or vowel digraphs in every syllable.
   - May reverse letters due to developing visual strategies.
   - Draws on an abundance of correctly spelled words.

5. Correct
   - Has basic knowledge of the English spelling system and rules.
   - Has knowledge of word structure, e.g. prefixes, suffixes, etc.
   - Has the ability to distinguish homonyms.
   - Has growing accuracy in use of double letters and silent consonants.
   - Tries out possible spelling and uses visual knowledge to select correct form.
   - Accumulates a large spelling vocabulary of learned words.

If you look at children's work, you will notice that their early spelling does not 'fit neatly into' one of Gentry's stages, but they are still very useful in helping you to infer what a child knows about spelling from what they do in their own, undirected writing.

EMBEDDING ICT   EMBEDDING ICT   EMBEDDING ICT   EMBEDDING ICT   EMBEDDING ICT

Find out what programs your school has available specifically to support the teaching of spelling, including those that promote the children's knowledge and understanding of sound–symbol correspondence.

These maybe for use in teacher-led sessions, for example using the IWB, or for children to use individually on the classroom computer or laptop, in order to practise and develop through the stages identified by Gentry above. Don't forget to check what is available on websites of resources, as other teachers and schools may add ideas for activities that they have found successful with groups similar to yours.

The teaching appropriate for children learning sound–symbol correspondences includes:

- phonics teaching in shared and guided reading;
- opportunities to experiment in independent work;
- clear, supportive, and very specific feedback from the teacher which must be based on the ability to look at a child's spelling and assess what they know about sound–symbol correspondences and what additional knowledge is necessary.

The teaching of sound–symbol correspondences in shared or guided reading could include:

- modelling and discussing children's contributions to spelling decisions;
- using letter fans to check which children can select letters;
- using individual whiteboards to see which children can identify letters, sequences and combinations of sounds;
- covering up parts of words and asking children to supply the words;
- highlighting letters and combinations of letters;
- sound rhymes and games.

In independent activities, children might develop their sound–symbol correspondences through:

- letter games;
- writing for other purposes;
- word puzzles;
- making word families;
- sound lotto.

As children develop as spellers, they learn to use other strategies. Peters (1985) suggests that the principal mode of adult spelling is visual. Adults remember visual letter patterns as well as using sound–symbol correspondences. She also suggests that we can learn visual patterns kinaesthetically so that our hands get the habit of writing certain patterns. This, it is suggested, is a good reason for teaching joined-up handwriting early on. Look at the following words, for instance:

- weir
- their
- eight
- weight
- height
- either

These words are *not* a regular phonic pattern – the 'ei' makes different sounds, but they do contain a visual pattern of letters, which can be learnt through repetition. It may be worth learning these words in conjunction with handwriting practice to get them firmly memorised. The most important strategy for memorising words, developed by Peters, is known as *look–cover–write–check*. Using a paper fan or exercise book, the child copies the word, looks at it to learn the visual pattern and segments it mentally, sometimes drawing over it with a pencil or 'visualising' it in the mind. The child then covers the word up and tries to write it. If correct, then the child goes on to the next word. If not, then the process is repeated. This simple, effective strategy should be learnt by all children from Year 1 and it is helpful if all parents also know it so they can help their children learn.

One important way of remembering spellings is to break them down into 'chunks' of either morphemes or syllables. Most people remember Wed-nes-day in this way. This sort of aural learning is closely related to sound–symbol correspondences. You need to demonstrate these words in shared writing. Another type of 'chunking' is the use of morphemic analysis. If children can understand the meaning and spelling rules associated with common **prefixes** and **suffixes**, they can use them flexibly. Ways to teach this include:

- identifying words with common prefixes or suffixes in shared or guided reading or writing and discussing the meaning and/or spelling conventions associated with them;
- introducing common prefixes in the whole-class session and using an IWB or OHP to involve children in manipulating them;
- setting children a word investigation task in independent time during the literacy session. This might include sorting words with common elements and deriving rules for their spelling and/or use.

(For more information on this, see Chapter 5 in *Primary English: Knowledge and Understanding*, Learning Matters SAGE, 2014.)

IN THE CLASSROOM

Mrs B wants the children in her class to:

1. know that the suffixes -ed, -ful, -al and -less can change words from nouns into adjectives;
2. know the common spelling conventions involved in adding suffixes that change words from nouns into adjectives.

To teach this, she uses a 15-minute section of her literacy session to generate lists of words which end in these suffixes. The children are then asked to focus on words that have a noun version. The class discuss the difference between 'blurred' and 'blur', 'point' and 'pointed', 'use' and 'useful' by putting each word into a sentence and comparing them.

In the independent work part of the session, Mrs B gives children a range of investigations to complete and report back to the class.

- One group has a set of cards with words ending in -ed. They have to identify the spelling rules for adding -ed to a word and identify which words use the suffix to make adjectives.
- A less able group is given two sets of words: those ending in two consonants and -ed and those ending in consonant, vowel and -ed. They have to identify the different spelling patterns.
- The rest of the class have similar activities with -ful, -al and -less.

At the end of the lesson, Mrs B asks the first two groups to report their findings and makes the teaching point through their examples and findings.

Another aspect of spelling that is particularly relevant to English is word origins, or etymology. By studying the origin of a word, children can learn how it is spelled. One way of finding out more about a word, and often of identifying the root of that word, is by using a large dictionary such as the *Concise Oxford Dictionary* which contains plenty of etymological information. There is also a wide range of online dictionaries and etymological dictionaries you could use. Children will also be very interested in dictionaries of place names and surnames. At a less sophisticated level, the use of root words, suffixes and prefixes has an etymological aspect. For instance, children who know bi- generally means two and the Greek word kyklos means 'circle, or wheel', are more likely to be able to spell bicycle correctly and generalise to related words.

There are some words we simply need to teach children to remember. Some memory aids are those we call **mnemonics**. These can help us to remember awkward words – such as 'there is **a rat** in separate' to help remember to spell it with an *a* rather than an *e*. Others include 'one **c**ollar and two **s**leeves' for necessary. These mnemonics can be taught to those children who have problems with particular words.

The literacy session is usually the main vehicle for spelling study, but there is also a range of enabling strategies teachers use to offer children practice and give them independence in spelling.

To offer practice, teachers sometimes set spelling tests. These can be a good learning tool or a real punishment, depending on how they are conducted.

- The words set should either have a spelling pattern (visual or morphological) or be a set of words identified by the child for study during other writing (possibly mistakes made that week).
- Words to be learnt should be checked, possibly by another child, to check they are accurate.
- Children and parents should know the *look–cover–write–check* strategy and use it.
- Children who learn their spellings should achieve high marks regularly. If they do not, you may need to change the words.
- Children can mark each other's spellings but you, as a teacher, should monitor achievement and intervene where a child is not succeeding.

Spelling tests are not the main vehicle of learning spelling but can support a useful homework task and are often part of class ritual.

Strategies teachers use to enable children to be more independent in spelling include:

- alphabet friezes and cards with pictures to help children make sound–symbol correspondences;
- alphabetically ordered wall 'pockets' with word cards in;
- word banks of topic words or common words (do make sure these are static, as mobiles are not easy to consult);
- a class word book in which unknown words can be written by the teacher for the child to do *look–cover–write–check* (not copy);
- use of an initial letter and 'magic line' to replace a word in writing so that spelling can be investigated later;
- a class convention whereby the child 'has a go' at a word and asks a friend before approaching the teacher;
- the use of dictionaries to look up spellings. This is not the primary function of dictionaries but children with some sound–symbol knowledge can use them effectively. As a teacher you should deliberately model the use of dictionaries to look up words, including the decisions you make about choices.

THE BIGGER PICTURE THE BIGGER PICTURE THE BIGGER PICTURE THE BIGGER PICTURE

When you are planning activities that are designed to encourage children to spell more independently, don't forget to include work based on other areas of learning and aspects of the wider curriculum as well as those met within literacy sessions. Specialised vocabulary needed for topics in subjects such as science, maths, history, geography and RE are sometimes learnt as 'one-offs' or irregular words, but they can often be chosen to highlight and reinforce particular spelling patterns that you are currently working on and added to that week's spelling test list. Even if the subject vocabulary seems to 'stand alone', why not include a batch of mathematical or history-related words instead of your usual word list and ask parents to help their children to learn both the spellings and meanings of the words?

As a teacher, your attitude to spelling will be evident in the way in which you mark it. At times, it will be a very important task criterion, at others it will not be the focus of marking. Some teachers mark all incorrect spellings in Year 2 and above; some only mark those they want children to learn. They feel that marking every spelling is demoralising. Each school will have a policy on this and you should adhere to it. When marking, identify words for children to learn but do not ask them to copy out the word a number of times. The best strategy is **look–cover–write–check**. When you do a detailed, thorough marking of a piece of a child's work for discussion with the child, you have a chance to look diagnostically at the spelling mistakes made. Ask yourself:

- is there a pattern to the errors?
- what is causing these errors?
- what strategy does this child need to learn?

In this way you can offer individual targets.

A SUMMARY OF **KEY POINTS**

➤ **Children need to develop a number of types of handwriting.**

➤ **They need to be taught correct pencil grip and correct movements.**

➤ **Teaching a joined writing style is now done much earlier in children's schooling than used to be the case.**

➤ **Fluent handwriting can assist correct spelling.**

➤ **There are many strategies that can be used to spell words, including phonological, morphological, etymological and letter string strategies.**

➤ **Systematic teaching of spelling can be interesting and empowering.**

➤ **Look–cover–write–check and the use of mnemonics can be very successful approaches to learning awkward spellings.**

M-LEVEL EXTENSION > > M-LEVEL EXTENSION > > M-LEVEL EXTENSION

There is a growing weight of research that suggests that we may have underestimated the importance of fluent handwriting to the overall quality of children's writing. Basically, the argument, which seems to be supported by current research, is that writing, as a complex mental activity, occupies the whole of a writer's working memory as they engage in it. If aspects of writing are automatic, the writer has to give no mental space to them and thus has more to spare to focus on other aspects of the process. If low-level tasks like letter production are not automatic (and for many young writers handwriting may well not be automatic) they may take up too much working memory, which leaves less for the other aspects such as composition.

You should read Medwell and Wray (2007, 2014) for a review of this research and a discussion of its implications for teachers.

FURTHER READING FURTHER READING FURTHER READING FURTHER READING

Bissex, G.L. (1980) *Gnys at Wrk: A child learns to write*. Cambridge, MA: Harvard University Press.

DfE (2013) *The National Curriculum in England*. London: DfE. (https://www.gov.uk/dfe/nationalcurriculum)

DfE (2013) *Teachers' Standards*. London: DfE. (https://www.gov.uk/government/uploads/system/uploads/attachment_data/file/208682/Teachers__Standards_2013.pdf)

DfES (2007) *Letters and Sounds*. London: DfES.

Medwell, J. and Wray, D. (2007) 'Handwriting: what we know and need to know', *Literacy*, vol. 41(1), pp. 10–15.

Medwell, J. and Wray, D. (2014) 'Handwriting automaticity: the search for performance thresholds', *Language and Education*, vol. 28(1), pp. 34–51. (http://www.tandfonline.com/doi/abs/10.1080/0950 0782.2013.763819)

Torbe, M. (1995) *Teaching and Learning Spelling*. London: Ward Lock Educational.

9
Developing reading at Key Stage 2

TEACHERS' STANDARDS

A teacher must:

2. **Promote good progress and outcomes by pupils**

   - be accountable for pupils' attainment, progress and outcomes
   - plan teaching to build on pupils' capabilities and prior knowledge
   - guide pupils to reflect on the progress they have made and their emerging needs
   - demonstrate knowledge and understanding of how pupils learn and how this impacts on teaching
   - encourage pupils to take a responsible and conscientious attitude to their own work and study.

3. **Demonstrate good subject and curriculum knowledge**

   - have a secure knowledge of the relevant subject(s) and curriculum areas, foster and maintain pupils' interest in the subject, and address misunderstandings
   - demonstrate a critical understanding of developments in the subject and curriculum areas, and promote the value of scholarship
   - demonstrate an understanding of and take responsibility for promoting high standards of literacy, articulacy and the correct use of standard English, whatever the teacher's specialist subject

4. **Plan and teach well structured lessons**

   - impart knowledge and develop understanding through effective use of lesson time

Introduction

Before the advent of the National Literacy Strategy in 1998, there was a good deal of long-standing evidence that the teaching of literacy to children at Key Stage 2 was, on the whole, not well done. In their 1978 survey of primary schools (DES, 1978), HMI found 'little evidence that more advanced reading skills were being taught' (para. 5.30). Their 1991 report on the teaching of reading in primary schools made an almost identical statement. There appeared to be two main problems concerning the development of reading at Key Stage 2.

There was a limited range and quality of junior children's interactions with reading material of all kinds. Narrative was very definitely the dominant **genre** both in children's reading and writing and, where efforts had been made to enhance and deepen children's responses to text, these seemed to have been confined to experiences with narratives of one kind or another. Yet it had been quite forcibly pointed out by Martin (1989), among several others, that the bulk of adult experiences with texts involved interactions with genres other than narrative. It was also the case that much of the reading done at Key Stage 2 tended to be at a surface level of understanding, rather than enhancing high-quality responses in the children.

The second problem was that children had difficulties in handling information, that is, in specifying, locating and effectively using sources of written information, for example in libraries. There had been a longstanding concern about children's acquisition of information skills, variously referred to as library skills, research skills and study skills (Wray, 1985). The most common teacher complaint arising from this concern was usually expressed as 'How can I stop my children copying from reference books?' Although most Key Stage 2 children seemed quite aware that they should not copy from reference books, and could give a cogent set of reasons why not, when they were actually engaged in the practical tasks of locating and selecting information in books they seemed to revert to copying behaviour with little demur.

Before exploring these areas, we need to look in a little more depth at the nature of what is usually referred to as **reading comprehension**.

Understanding: the nature of reading comprehension

Most teachers will see a large part of their role in developing reading as being concerned with developing children's abilities to understand and learn from written materials. Often, however, views of this role have not been helped by the terms used to describe these abilities. They have been described as 'higher-order' or 'advanced' reading skills, implying that these skills are relevant only to the oldest or the most able children (Wray, 1981). If, however, these skills are defined as those involved in the understanding of written material, it seems clear that it is impossible to do any teaching of reading without incorporating them in some way. Understanding is, after all, the whole point of reading.

Activities to develop the understanding of reading have traditionally occupied a large part of reading instruction at Key Stage 2 level. Chief among these activities has been the 'comprehension exercise', which usually consists of a passage of text followed by several questions. As an example of how the comprehension exercise works you might like to try the following activity.

REFLECTIVE TASK

Read the passage and try to answer the questions below.

The chanks vos blunging frewly bedeng the brudegan. Some chanks vos unred but the other chanks vos unredder. They vos all polket and rather chiglop so they did not mekle the spuler. A few were unstametick.

Questions:

1. What were the chanks doing?
2. How well did they blunge?

---

3. Where were they blunging?

4. In what ways were the chanks the same and in which ways were they different?

5. Were any chanks stametick?

You should have found it reasonably easy to provide acceptable answers to these questions, but you will certainly feel that you do not, even now, understand this passage. What is a chank, and what were they doing?

You are able to solve problems like this because you are a competent language user, and are able to apply your intuitive knowledge of language structures to the task. You know, for example, that the answer to a 'How well' question will usually be an adverb (even if you do not know the grammatical term), and you also know that most adverbs in English end in '-ly'. If you can solve problems like this, there must be a possibility that primary children also can, especially as it is reasonably well established that most children are competent language users by the age of seven. This casts grave doubt on the effectiveness of comprehension exercises as a means of developing or assessing children's abilities to understand their reading.

Fortunately, there are some alternative activities that can be used with children which are much more likely to involve real understanding. Some of these will be described later in the chapter, but at this point we need to look at the nature of understanding texts.

REFLECTIVE TASK

Read the following passage which, unless you have a background in nuclear physics, you are likely to find difficult to understand. Spend some time thinking about exactly what it is about the passage that makes it difficult to understand.

> *Ilya Prigogine has demonstrated that when an 'open system', one which exchanges matter and/or energy with its environment, has reached a state of maximum entropy, its molecules are in a state of equilibrium. Spontaneously, small fluctuations can increase in amplitude, bringing the system into a 'far from equilibrium' state. Perhaps it is the instability of sub-atomic particles (events) on the microscopic level that causes fluctuations on the so-called macroscopic level of molecules. At any rate, strongly fluctuating molecules in a far-from-equilibrium state are highly unstable. Responding to internal and/or external influences, they may either degenerate into chaos or reorganise at a higher level of complexity.*

You probably found it difficult to understand or remember much of this passage for the simple reason that it makes little sense to you. What is it that makes it difficult?

People commonly attribute difficulty in understanding texts to the difficult words used. This passage certainly has many obscure words that do cause difficulty. Understanding, however, relies on something a good deal deeper than just knowledge of vocabulary. To see this, try the next activity.

REFLECTIVE TASK
REFLECTIVE TASK

Read the following passage and try to make sense of it.

The procedure is actually quite simple. First you arrange things into different groups. Of course, one pile may be sufficient depending on how much there is to do. If you have to go somewhere else due to lack of facilities that is the next step, otherwise you are pretty well set. It is important not to overdo things. That is, it is better to do too few things at once than too many. In the short run this may not seem important but complications can easily arise. A mistake can be expensive as well. At first the whole procedure will seem complicated. Soon, however, it will become just another facet of life. It is difficult to foresee any end to the necessity for this task in the immediate future, but then one can never tell. After the procedure is completed one arranges the materials into different groups again. Then they can be put into their appropriate places. Eventually they will be used once more and the whole cycle will then have to be repeated. However, that is a part of life.

In this passage there are no difficult words, yet it is still very hard to understand. However, once you are told that the passage describes the procedure for washing clothes, you can understand it perfectly easily.

What really makes the difference in understanding text is the background knowledge of the reader. If you have adequate previous knowledge, and if you realise which particular knowledge the new passage links with, then understanding can take place. This background knowledge can be thought of in terms of structures of ideas, or schemata. Understanding becomes the process of fitting new information into these structures. This process is so crucial to understanding text that it is worthwhile spending a little time considering exactly how it works.

REFLECTIVE TASK
REFLECTIVE TASK

Look at the following story beginning:

The man was brought into the large white room. His eyes blinked in the bright light.

Try to picture in your mind the scene so far. Is the man sitting, lying or standing? Is he alone in the room? What sort of room is it? What might this story be going to be about?

Now read the next extract:

'Now, sit there,' said the nurse. 'And try to relax.'

Has this altered your picture of the man or of the room? What is this story going to be about?

After the first extract, you may have thought the story would be set in a hospital, or perhaps concern an interrogation. There are key words in the brief beginning which trigger off these expectations. After the second extract, the possibility of a dentist's surgery might enter your mind and the interrogation scenario may fade.

Each item you read sparks off an idea in your mind, each one of which has its own associated schema, or structure of underlying ideas. It is unlikely, for example, that your picture of the room after the first extract had a plush white carpet on the floor. You construct a great deal from very little information.

Understanding and, in fact, reading, is exactly like this. It is not simply a question of getting a meaning from what is on the page. When you read, you supply a good deal of the meaning to the page. The process is an interactive one, with the resultant learning being a combination of your previous ideas with new ones encountered in this text.

As another example of this, consider the following sentence:

Mary remembered her birthday money when she heard the ice-cream van coming.

Without trying too hard, you can supply a great deal of information to the meaning of this, chiefly to do with Mary's intentions and feelings, but also to do with the appearance of the van and its driver's intentions – you probably do not immediately suspect him as a potential child molester. Notice that most of this seems obvious and we barely give it much conscious thought. Our schemata for everyday events are so familiar, we do not notice when they are activated.

Now compare the picture you get from the following sentence:

Mary remembered her birthday money when she heard the bus coming.

What difference does this make to your picture of Mary, beyond the difference in her probable intentions? Most people say that she now seems rather older. Notice that this difference in understanding comes not so much from the words on the page as from the complex network of ideas these words make reference to. These networks have been referred to as schemata, and developments in our understanding of how they operate have had a great impact on our ideas about the nature and teaching of reading comprehension. If reading comprehension involves this kind of complex transaction between a reader's previous knowledge, ideas and attitudes, and the text, then the activities we use to develop comprehension need themselves to be interactive.

PRACTICAL TASK PRACTICAL TASK **PRACTICAL TASK** PRACTICAL TASK **PRACTICAL TASK**

You might want to try the above sentences about Mary on some Key Stage 2 children. Can they draw the same inferences? You might find they draw an even richer interpretation, given that they are closer to Mary in age than you are.

Experiment with varying small elements of the sentence to see what different schemata you can activate. For example:

Mary remembered her gun when she heard the ice-cream van coming.

Mary remembered her stomach when she heard the ice-cream van coming.

The Center for the Improvement of Early Reading Achievement (CIERA) at the University of Michigan was for a number of years a central base for research into reading comprehension. As CIERA argued, the purpose of reading is comprehension, and a key question concerns how we teach children to comprehend more difficult and varied texts. They claim that research has provided a general outline of how to teach reading comprehension effectively, and put forward some research-based principles for this teaching.

1. **Effective reading comprehension teaching is purposeful and explicit.** Effective teachers of reading are clear about their purposes. They know what they are trying to help a child achieve and how to accomplish their goal. They provide scaffolded instruction in research-tested strategies (predicting, thinking aloud, attending to text structure, constructing visual representations, generating questions and summarising). Scaffolded instruction includes explicit explanation and modelling of a strategy, discussion of why and when it is useful, and coaching in how to apply it to novel texts.

2. **Effective reading comprehension teaching requires classroom interactions that support the understanding of specific texts.** Effective teachers have a repertoire of techniques for enhancing children's comprehension of specific texts, including discussion, writing in response to reading, and multiple encounters with complex texts. They are clear about the purposes of teacher- and child-led discussions of texts, and include a balance of lower- and higher-level questions focusing on understanding and response.

3. **Effective reading comprehension teaching starts before children read conventionally.** Children in pre-school develop their comprehension skills through experiences that promote oral and written language skills, such as discussions, play activities, retellings, and emergent readings. Early childhood environments can be made literacy-rich through thoughtful inclusion of appropriate materials and practices. Reading and rereading a wide variety of texts contributes to both phonemic awareness and comprehension.

4. **Effective reading comprehension teaching focuses on the skills and strategies used by expert readers.** Expert readers are active readers who use text and their own knowledge to build a model of meaning, and then constantly revise that model as new information becomes available. They consider the author's intentions and style when judging a text's validity, and determine the purposes that the text can serve in their lives – how it can further their knowledge, deepen their enjoyment, and expand their ways of examining and communicating with the world. They also vary their reading strategy according to their purpose and the characteristics of the text they are reading, deciding whether to read carefully or impressionistically.

5. **Effective reading comprehension teaching requires careful analysis of text to determine its appropriateness for particular readers and strategies.** Teachers analyse each text to determine its potential challenges and match it with their goals. They consider the conceptual and decoding demands and apply strategies to meet those challenges. Interactions with texts requiring minimal teacher support help hold children accountable as independent readers. Scaffolded experiences ensure that all children are exposed to high-level text and interactions.

6. **Effective reading comprehension teaching builds on and results in knowledge, vocabulary, and advanced language development.** Children are better able to comprehend texts when they are taught to make connections between what they know and what they are reading. Good comprehension teaching helps them make these connections more effectively. Vocabulary knowledge is an important part of reading comprehension, and good vocabulary instruction involves children actively in learning word

meanings, as well as relating words to contexts and other known words. Teaching about words (including morphology) improves children's comprehension.

7. **Effective reading comprehension teaching pervades all genres and school subjects.** Children need to read in a wide variety of genres – not only narrative, but informational, procedural, biographical, persuasive, and poetic. They will only learn to do so through experience and instruction. Each school subject requires the ability to read in specific genres; therefore, comprehension should be taught in all subjects.

8. **Effective reading comprehension teaching actively engages children in text and motivates them to use strategies and skills.** Effective teachers create an environment in which children are actively involved in the reading process. In such an environment, children read more, which in turn improves their comprehension and knowledge. Children need to be motivated to learn and apply skills and strategies during reading.

9. **Effective reading comprehension teaching requires assessments that inform it and help monitor children's progress.** The use of multiple assessments provides specific and timely feedback to inform teaching and monitor children's progress. Good assessment identifies children's comprehension levels as they develop from pre-school to higher levels, and helps the teacher to evaluate each child's need for support in areas such as language development, strategy, and the application of knowledge. Effective assessment also enables teachers to reliably interpret data and communicate results to children, parents, and colleagues.

10. **Effective reading comprehension teaching requires continuous teacher learning** about the processes and techniques detailed in the previous nine principles, and ways to use such knowledge to develop the comprehension skills and strategies of all children. Working closely with their colleagues, effective teachers learn to use assessment data, reflections on their own practice, and moment-by-moment feedback from children to vary the support they provide to learners with different levels of expertise and confidence. (For further information, see www.ciera.org)

Interactive approaches to reading

Shared reading

At Key Stage 2, as at Key Stage 1, one key element in a literacy session is to work with the whole class on a shared text. This text may be a **big book** but you might use other sources of text as well. By Key Stage 2, these shared reading and writing sessions will need to look at a wide range of texts – poems, advertisements, newspaper articles, short extracts from novels, etc. Big books alone are not likely to meet the demand for such a wide range of reading material.

In any case, you might not be able to use big books because the physical constraints of your classroom will not enable all the children to sit together in an area where they can all have a good view of a big book. So you will probably need to have other strategies for sharing texts with your classes. There are a number of such strategies.

- You might be able to copy short straightforward texts by hand onto a chalkboard or IWB.
- You might also make each child a photocopy of the chosen text or extract.
- If you have access to an overhead projector, you can make OHP transparencies from the original text.
- You might be able to enlarge a text or extract on the photocopier.

- By typing a text into a word processor, you will be able to print it out with a font size of around 48 point – big enough for the class to read.
- You may use an electronic text enlarged on a screen or via the IWB.

Whatever strategies you use, it is important that all the children have sufficiently clear sight of the text to read it for themselves. It is not enough in these sessions for children only to have the text read aloud to them.

You might choose to work with the same text over several days or to move each day to something different, such as a text of a similar type or a further extract from the same text. The richer the text, the more likely you are to want to use it for several days in a row.

A typical sequence of shared reading sessions with a Year 4 class might be organised as follows:

Aim of the whole text/whole class session(s)
- To identify the author and title of the story.
- To examine the generic features of story openings: setting, characters and beginnings of plot (the who, where, when and what of the story) and consider why an author introduces these elements.
- To identify the use of nouns and proper nouns in stories.
- To identify written direct speech and speech marks.

Materials
- Poster or OHP of the introductory page from *The Hodgeheg* (Dick King-Smith).
- Highlighter pens.

Chapter 1

'Your Auntie Betty has copped it,' said Pa Hedgehog to Ma.
   'Oh no!' cried Ma. 'Where?'
   'Just down the road. Opposite the newsagent's. Bad place to cross, that.'
   'Everywhere's a bad place to cross nowadays,' said Ma. 'The traffic's dreadful. Do you realise, Pa, that's the third this year, and all on my side of the family too. First there was Grandfather, then my second cousin once removed and now poor old Auntie Betty...'
   They were sitting in a flower bed at their home, the garden of Number 5A of a row of semi-detached houses in a suburban street. On the other side of the road was a Park, very popular with the local hedgehogs on account of the good hunting it offered. As well as worms and slugs and snails, which they could find in their own gardens, there were special attractions in the park. Mice lived under the bandstand, feasting on the crumbs dropped from listeners' sandwiches; frogs dwelt in the Lily Pond, and in the Ornamental Gardens grass-snakes slithered through the shrubbery. All these creatures were regarded as great delicacies by the hedgehogs, and they could never resist the occasional night's sport in the Park. But to reach it, they had to cross the busy road.

Session 1: Introducing the text
- Introduce the text to the class and explain that you intend to look at how people use writing to entertain and that this is one of the roles of a novel.
- Pick out the title and author's name and ask the children to read these with you.
- Has anyone read the book? (Don't give the story away.)
- Does anyone know of other books by this author?

- If possible, show the children the actual book. Discuss the covers. Use the appropriate vocabulary – title, spine, author, illustration, blurb, ISBN, etc.
- Ask the children to predict what the book is going to be about, based on the title.
- Who might be in it? Where might it be set?
- Try to get children to say why they make the predictions they do.
- Read the extract aloud, pointing to the demonstration text, and ask the children to confirm or alter their predictions as you read.
- Check their understanding of the content:
  - Who is in the story?
  - Where is the story so far set?
  - What are the characters talking about?
  - Can children retell parts of the opening?
- Mark any unknown words with a highlighter pen and demonstrate how to look them up in a dictionary.

Session 2: Text-level work

Re-read the text with the class in an appropriate way. Either read it to the class or select children to read paragraphs.

- Ask the children how they know that this is the opening of a story/novel.
- Stories often try to get the reader 'hooked' straight away. Re-read and underline the first sentence. What does it tell you? Did it make you interested? How? Why?
- The beginnings of stories usually introduce characters. Who do they think is going to feature in this story? Highlight any references to characters.
- What do we know about the characters from this opening (characterisation)? What kinds of language do Pa and Ma use? What do we know about their family? What are their eating habits? Highlight the clues.
- The beginnings of stories often tell us where the story is going to take place – the setting.
- Where might the main part of this story take place? Highlight clues about the main setting. Does the author give us any details of the wider area (busy street, traffic, shops, etc.)?
- A story opening often establishes when the story takes place (time of day and/or era).
- Is this story happening a long time ago or nowadays? Highlight the clues, e.g. traffic, newsagents, semide-tached houses suggests twentieth/twenty-first century.
- A story opening also gives us some ideas about what might happen (the plot). Usually a problem arises and is solved as the story unfolds. What do we think the problem might be in this story? Highlight the clues, e.g. death of hedgehogs, nice food in park, busy road and especially the last sentence of the extract.

Session 3: Sentence-level and word-level work

- Re-read the text with the class in an appropriate way. Either select children to read paragraphs or ask the children to read silently.
- The story includes people, places and ideas that can be named. Pick out (and highlight) particular names (proper nouns). Note that they begin with capital letters.
- Do any of the characters speak? What, exactly, do they say? How is this indicated in the text? How do we know who has spoken? Highlight the speech marks and explain why they are called speech marks.
- Briefly recap the three sessions.
- The beginning of this story gains our attention, suggests the setting (time and place) the characters and the plot.
- Remind children of who, when, where, what.

Follow-up activities

- Ask the children to tell you the openings of well-known fairy stories that include who, where, when and what in the first few sentences. For example:

Once upon a time there lived a little girl called Red Riding Hood (who). One day her mother asked Red Riding Hood to visit her Granny (who, what). Her Granny lived in a cottage on the other side of the wood (where). 'Be careful going through the wood,' said her mother. 'Stay on the path and don't talk to any strangers.' (clue to plot, what)

Guided reading and group activities

Several activities that emphasise the interaction between the ideas brought to a text by the reader and the ideas expressed by the writer have the common title of DARTS: directed activities relating to texts. These include group cloze, group prediction, group sequencing, and text restructuring, and all these activities can be used across the curriculum, not just in literacy sessions.

Group cloze

The cloze exercise consists of a text with several deletions that children have to work together to complete. The following brief example will illustrate the activity.

John was a very lucky boy. He had been given lots of presents for his birthday and had had a _____ birthday party. He was still rather sad, though, because the thing he had wished for _____ all had not happened. He had wanted so much to have a real _____ of his own; perhaps a dog, or even a cat. But Mum and Dad had said that there was no room in the flat, and John knew they were _____. He was still disappointed, though.

The solution to these deletions lies in the combination and application of information found elsewhere in the text and in the reader's previous experiences. It also involves the application of understanding about syntactic structures. The reader has sometimes to read on past deleted words, and also to have some kind of affective response to the story. In attempting to complete the problem posed by the text, the reader has to give it detailed concentration and respond to its meaning. If the problem is tackled by a group of readers, then it is even more likely that learning will take place as each reader puts forward tentative solutions and these are affirmed, questioned or extended by other members of the group.

Cloze involves much more than simple guesswork. At best, it involves the systematic application of context cues, a sensitivity to nuances of meaning and to style, and the articulation of tentative hypotheses about texts. As will be seen later, it can also be a way of introducing content knowledge to children. There are a few guiding principles to its use which can help to ensure the maximum benefit.

- Choose deletions carefully. The activity seems to work best if words are deleted on the grounds that they are likely to cause discussion. There is little point in deleting words like 'the', 'but', etc. since these generally cause little debate. It is therefore not wise to delete words on a simple numerical basis, for example, every tenth word.
- Leave a lead-in paragraph free from deletions. This may give children the chance to develop some feel for the style of the passage they are working on.
- Get the children to work on the text in groups of at least three or four. They may try to complete it individually before discussing their solutions, or complete it as a group straightaway. In either case, they should be told to try to achieve an agreed version as this forces them to argue for or against particular suggestions.
- If the children have never used cloze before, they will benefit from working as a group with you. The teacher should not supply correct answers but should rather demonstrate the most useful process of working.

LIVERPOOL JOHN MOORES UNIVERSITY
LEARNING SERVICES

Procedures such as listening attentively to another's suggestions, justifying your own ideas and not being satisfied with the first solution that comes to mind can all be impressed on the children by the teacher's example.

Group prediction

The prediction activity involves a group of children discussing, together with you, a text of which they all have a copy. The discussion should be guided by three principles.

1. Establishing purposes for reading. The children should be reading to actually find something out, whether it be to confirm a guess as to what would happen in the text or to find evidence in the text for their opinions about events or characters.
2. Reasoning while reading. The readers should make reasoned deductions from the information presented in the text, balancing together various facts, statements, hints and possibilities, and checking them against their knowledge of the world and its likelihoods.
3. Testing predictions. The readers should test out predictions they make on the basis of what they read, by checking them against the actual information in the text.

In order to do these things, the group are given the text one instalment at a time. As they receive each instalment, they are asked to:

- explain what is happening;
- predict what may be going to happen next;
- predict how the text will end;
- revise their earlier predictions in the light of new reading.

Any comments or predictions they make have to be supported by reference to the text in front of them.

The process is thus one of shared hypothesis development and evaluation. The group are required to formulate hypotheses on the basis of what they have read and then to check these hypotheses by reference to later instalments of the text. They are involved in the anticipation/retrospection process that is at the heart of responsive reading.

Group sequencing

The group sequencing activity is based on the same principles as group prediction in that it involves a group of children formulating hypotheses about a text and evaluating these with reference to the information the text contains. It is also similar to the cloze procedure in that it involves children in checking the language they read against their own intuitive knowledge of language structure. The activity involves presenting a text to a group of children in sections, but giving them no overt clues about how the sections should ideally be arranged. The children have to rearrange the sections into an order that makes sense and which they can justify by reference to the conceptual or linguistic flow of the text. The text may be split into:

- paragraphs: which will focus readers' attention on the flow of meaning within a text;
- sentences: which will also concentrate attention on the flow of meaning, but will introduce the importance of linguistic cues, for example sequence words such as 'next', 'afterwards', or causal words such as 'therefore' and 'because';
- lines: which will shift attention to predominantly structural cues, especially punctuation and noun/pronoun relationships.

THE BIGGER PICTURE   THE BIGGER PICTURE   **THE BIGGER PICTURE**   THE BIGGER PICTURE

When you are planning activities for group sequencing, as well as re-sequencing paragraphs, sentences and lines, why not include the sequencing of graphic material, especially to ensure that your range of texts will engage all learners? In a report commissioned by the Canadian Council on Learning (2010), entitled *More than just funny books: Comics and prose literacy for boys*, a number of studies on gender differences in reading and reading preferences were reviewed. The report found that, far from replacing their reading of other genres, boys who read comic books regularly also tend to read more text-based materials and have higher levels of overall reading enjoyment than those who don't read comics. The report also concluded that using graphic materials in an educational setting can help all readers to develop visual literacy. The full report is available online (see www.ccl-cca.ca).

Text marking

Text-marking techniques, such as underlining, are used by many adults when they wish to note something in a text as being of significance. Of course, you cannot encourage children to write on school books but you can use text marking on teacher-prepared information sheets or on photocopies of pages from books. Use the strategy in a focused way with children. This can involve, for example, using different colours to mark the text in response to particular questions.

Children might also be asked to underline the sentence they think contains the main idea of a text. Different children may choose to underline different sentences and this can be used as a discussion point when children share and justify their decisions. They can also be asked to underline the most important sentence in each paragraph. Putting these sentences together should give them an outline summary of the whole passage.

Text can also be numbered to identify sequences of events. This is especially useful where steps in a process being described are separated by chunks of texts and children might lose the thread of the basic events.

Text restructuring

The essence of this strategy is to encourage children to read information and then show the information in some other way. In doing so, they have to pass the information through their brain – that is, work at understanding it. Restructuring can also give you access to children's levels of understanding and thus can be a useful assessment strategy.

There are many different ways of text restructuring. Figure 9.1 shows the work produced by a group of Year 5 children who had first read a text about the process of mummification in Ancient Egypt. They marked the text to show the stages of the process and then drew a series of pictures to represent these stages. The next day, and without further access to the original text, they wrote captions to accompany their pictures.

Text restructuring can also be used with quite young children. Five-year-old Kim, for example, having been read the big book *The Life of a Duck* by her teacher, showed the life cycle of a duck by means of a diagram (see Figure 9.2).

Her teacher was very pleased but then asked Kim to find out how long the whole process took. Kim consulted the book for herself and then added to her diagram (see Figure 9.3).

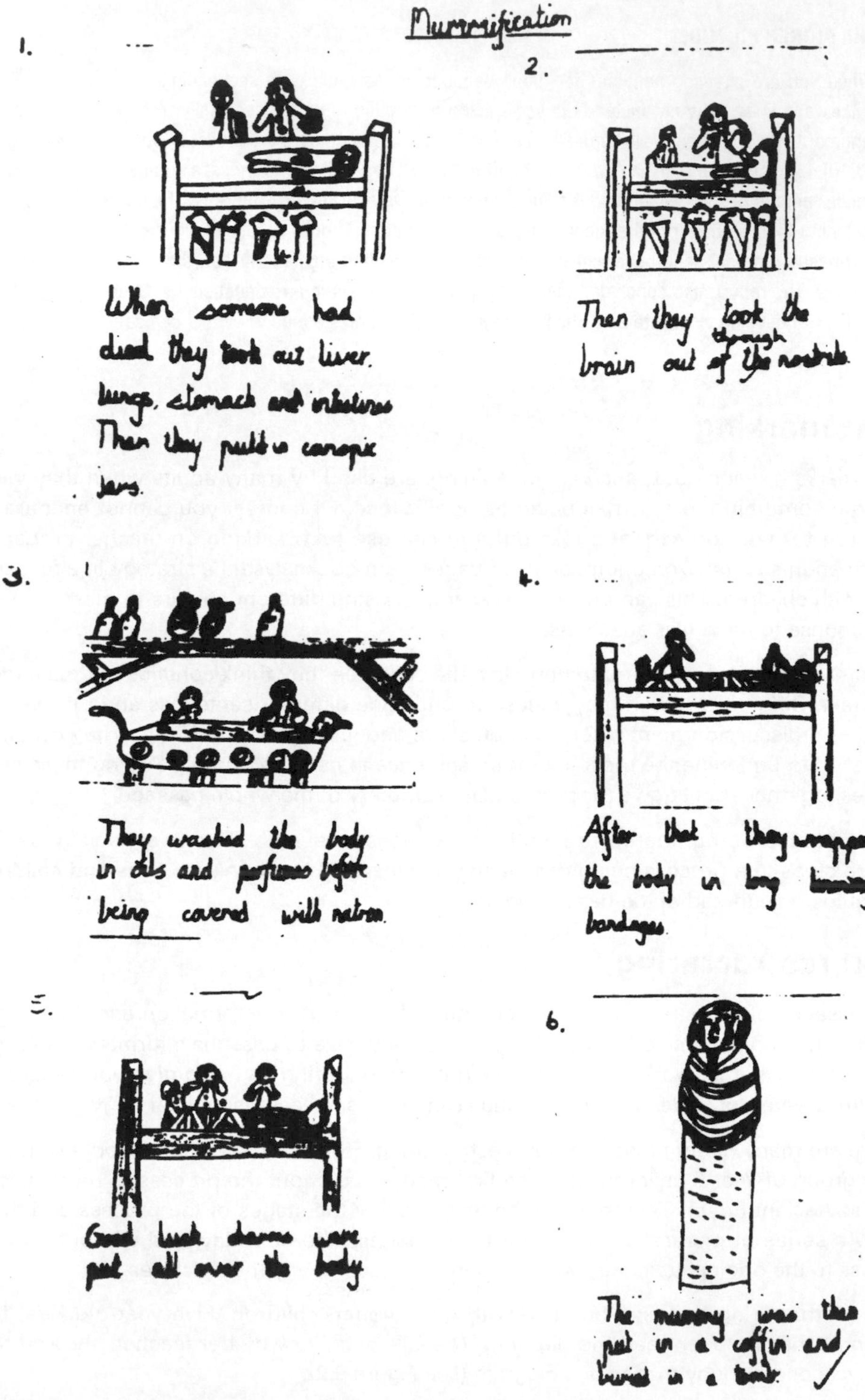

Mummification

1.

When someone had died they took out liver, lungs, stomach and intestines. Then they put in canopic jars.

2.

Then they took the brain out through of the nostrils.

3.

They washed the body in oils and perfumes before being covered with natron.

4.

After that they wrapped the body in long linning bandages.

5.

Good luck charms were put all over the body.

6.

The mummy was then put in a coffin and buried in a tomb.

Figure 9.1 Text restructuring – 'Mummification'

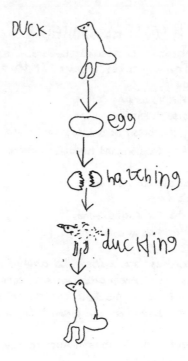

Figure 9.2   Kim's first diagram of the life of a duck

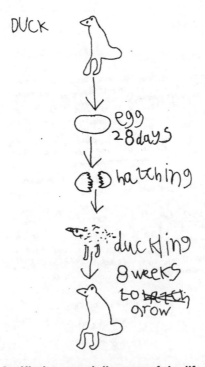

Figure 9.3   Kim's second diagram of the life of a duck

⚏ SCRIBES WANTED ⚏

Apprentices are needed to train as Scribes. Training takes 5 years. In that time you will

- learn the 700 writing signs
- practise writing
- copy letters, documents, accounts and stories
- pratise division and numberproblems

When qualified you will

- Collect taxes
- keep the records/taccounts
- record animals in tax counts

Sons of scribes are invited to apply for this job. Sons of farmers and workers cannot apply. Training will take place in the House of life. Apply to the Inspector of Accounts Scribes. Eygpt.

Figure 9.4   Scribes in Ancient Egypt

Greenwich
London
Sol0 5th
Mon 16 may
1547

Dear Jane

I am heartbroken at Henry Death. He was so good to me and his children. Before we were married I was a bit scared to marry him because he had divorced or killed 4 other wives before me. But he has proved me rong. I do feel sorry for Jane Seymour because People say it she had not died they would of saved together forever. She died because she was very weak after she had the baby. Someone made up a

Rime it gose like this divorced beheaded died divorced beheaded survived. I did love him so. The funeral is tomorrow would you like to come? I will tell you how he died. I came in to check his temperature. He was asleep so I tried to wake him but he did not. That was when I realised he was dead. Just lying there as pale as pale can be. Please write back

written by the
Royal hand of V hovely.

Catherine Parr

Figure 9.5   Catherine Parr's letter

Restructuring can also take place by asking children to transpose something from one written genre into another written genre. A group of ten-year-olds, for example, had read about scribes in Ancient Egypt. Normally, perhaps, they would simply have been asked to write about what they had read 'in your own words'. This would most likely have led to a good deal of copying of words and phrases from the original text. This time, however, they were asked to rewrite the information in the form of a job advertisement. They examined advertisements in newspapers and an example of their writing is shown in Figure 9.4. As can be seen, it is unlikely that this was directly copied; instead the children had had to read and understand the information.

This 'playing around' with genres not only forces children to reorganise their material, itself an aid to comprehension, but also gives them vital experience of the variety of genre forms and guides them away from straight copying of information they have read; this is familiar to many teachers – children using factual text to provide background details for fictional accounts. Figure 9.5 shows an example of this as one ten-year-old responds to her reading about the wives of Henry VIII.

RESEARCH SUMMARY   RESEARCH SUMMARY   **RESEARCH SUMMARY**   RESEARCH SUMMARY

Eric Lunzer and Keith Gardner (1979) carried out some seminal research into the use of reading among older pupils and found that the use of DARTs could significantly enhance these pupils' engagement with and understanding of texts. David Wray and Maureen Lewis (1997) extended these ideas and explored other approaches to developing reading comprehension.

Reading for information

IN THE CLASSROOM

Zoe is a ten-year-old with some learning difficulties. This half term, her class is studying 'Living Things' as their topic. For this lesson Zoe and her group have been asked to choose a particular living thing they are interested in and to 'find out about it'. Zoe and her friends have chosen dolphins and have picked out several information books from their class collection. For the next 45 minutes or so they work quietly and diligently with these books.

Towards the end of the lesson, Zoe's support teacher arrives and goes across to check on what the girls have done. In Zoe's book, she finds the piece of writing shown in Figure 9.6 below. She asks Zoe to read out what she has written but Zoe finds this nearly impossible to do. She also asks Zoe what she thinks she has learnt about dolphins, but Zoe cannot really think of much.

Most primary teachers will recognise what has happened here. Zoe has copied, word for word, from one or more information books. She has not processed what she has written beyond simply recognising that it is about dolphins. She has learnt very little from the lesson.

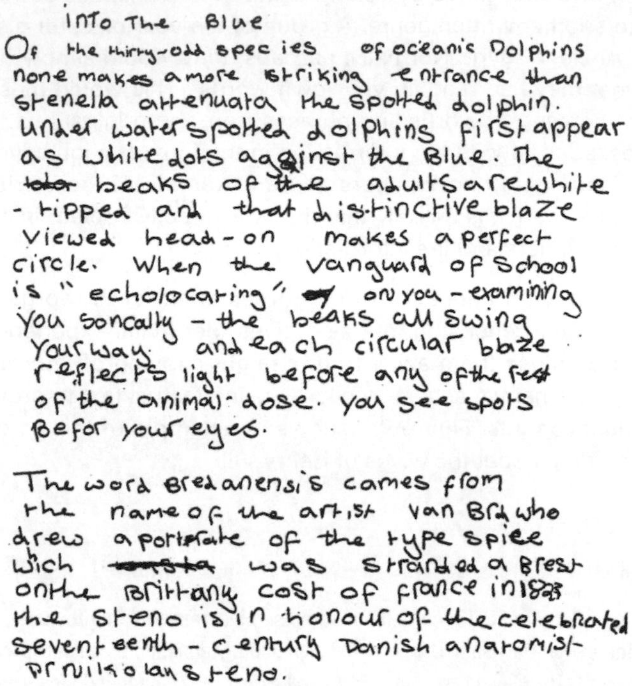

> Into The Blue
> Of the thirty-odd species of oceanic Dolphins
> none makes a more striking entrance than
> stenella attenuata the spotted dolphin.
> Under water spotted dolphins first appear
> as white dots against the Blue. The
> ~~tator~~ beaks of ~~the~~ adults are white
> - tipped and ~~that~~ distinctive blaze
> Viewed head-on makes a perfect
> circle. When the vanguard of School
> is "echolocating" ~~of~~ on you - examining
> You soncally - the beaks all swing
> Your way and each circular blaze
> reflects light before any of the rest
> of the animal-dose. you see spots
> Befor your eyes.
>
> The word Bredanensis comes from
> the name of the artist van Bred who
> drew a portraite of the type spiee
> wich ~~was sta~~ was stranded a Brest
> onthe Brittany cost of france in 1823
> the steno is in honour of the celebrated
> seventeenth-century Danish anatomist-
> Prnilsolans steno.

Figure 9.6   Zoe's writing about dolphins

RESEARCH SUMMARY   RESEARCH SUMMARY   **RESEARCH SUMMARY**   RESEARCH SUMMARY

David Wray and Maureen Lewis (1992) suggest, from their research, that most primary children know quite well that they should not copy directly from information books and many can give good reasons for this. Eight-year-old Anna, for example, told them that 'you learn a lot more if you write it in your own words'. Yet, faced with the activity of finding out from books, most children at some stage resort to copying. Why is this so common and how can teachers help children read for information more effectively?

One important part of the problem of copying seems to be the nature of the task children are often given when using information books. Zoe's task of 'finding out about' a topic is a common one but one which is not very helpful in focusing her on understanding what she finds. If the task is to find out about dolphins, then presumably any information about dolphins is acceptable. As Zoe discovers, there are whole books full of information about dolphins. How can she choose among all this information? She has no way of narrowing down the task and it becomes unmanageable. She really needs help before looking in the books in deciding what she wants to find out about dolphins.

Even if children manage to use 'information retrieval skills' well enough to locate material on the required topic, they still often find the text in that material difficult to deal with. Children in primary classrooms tend to lack experience of the different genres of non-fiction and their organisational structures (Littlefair, 1991). They find the linguistic features (vocabulary, connectives, cohesion, register) more difficult to comprehend than those of the more familiar narrative texts. Most children need support from teachers to enable them to cope more easily with the problems of factual text. There are a number of teaching strategies which can provide this support and make the activity of reading information a much more purposeful one.

What do I know and what do I want to know?

IN THE CLASSROOM

Zoe's support teacher did not leave things as they were. She was due to spend a lesson working with Zoe, so she decided to introduce a different way of approaching the task. At the end of the lesson, Zoe had produced a very different piece of writing about dolphins (see Figure 9.7).

How had the support teacher moved Zoe on from passive copying to undertaking her own research?

The first step was to close all the information books Zoe had been using. Zoe was then asked two of the most crucial questions in the process of reading for information:

- What do I know already about this topic?
- What do I want to know about it?

The teacher scribed what Zoe said (see Figure 9.8) and together they used these questions to guide their looking in the information books.

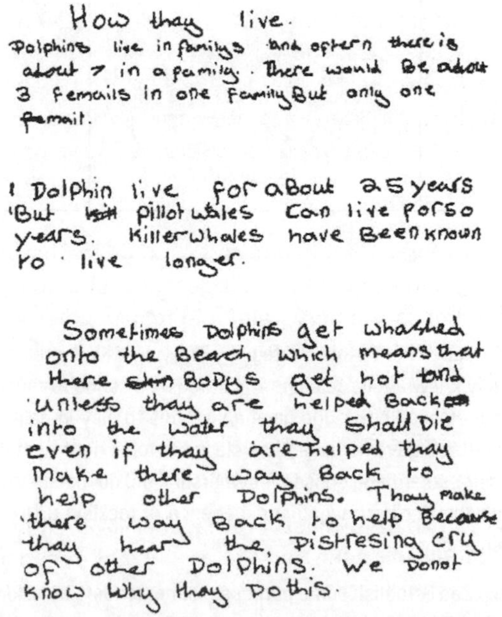

How they live.

Dolphins live in families and oftern there is about 7 in a family. There would be about 3 femails in one family But only one femail.

1 Dolphin live for about 25 years But pillot wales can live for 50 years. Killer whales have been known to live longer.

Sometimes Dolphins get whashed onto the Beach which means that there skin Bodys get hot and unless thay are helped Backe into the water thay shall die even if thay are helped thay make there way Back to help other Dolphins. Thay make there way Back to help Because thay hear the Distresing cry of other Dolphins. We Donot know why thay Do this.

Figure 9.7   Zoe's final writing about dolphins

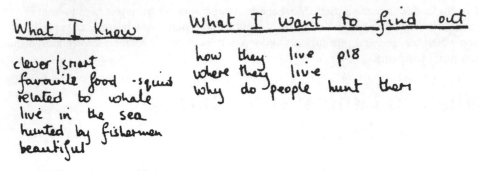

Figure 9.8   What Zoe knew and wanted to know

There is a great deal of research which suggests that children's previous knowledge in their understanding of new knowledge is important. It is also important that this previous knowledge is brought to the forefront of the learner's mind, in other words made explicit, if it is to be useful.

Many teachers already use discussion to activate previous knowledge but there are a range of other approaches to this which have the added advantage of giving the teacher some record of what children seem to know about a particular topic. One that you will find specially useful is the KWL grid. This is a simple but effective strategy that both takes children through the steps of the research process and also records their learning. A KWL grid consists of three columns:

What do I KNOW about this topic?	What do I WANT to know about it?	What did I LEARN?

IN THE CLASSROOM

Zoe's support teacher introduced her to this strategy by drawing a KWL grid in her notebook. She then asked Zoe what she already knew about dolphins and acted as a scribe to record Zoe's responses. Not only did this tapping into previous knowledge have a vital role to play in helping Zoe comprehend the texts she was to read, but it also gave her an active role in the topic right from the beginning. By asking her what she knew, her self-esteem and sense of 'ownership' of knowledge were enhanced instead of being faced instantly with the (for her) negative experience of tackling a text without knowing quite how she was to make sense of it.

The next stage was to help Zoe establish some purposes for her reading by asking her what she wanted to know now. This helped to focus the subsequent reading.

Extending the approach

Grids such as the KWL can not only provide a written record of children's approaches to the activity of reading for information but the format of the grid also acts as an organiser, helping children see more clearly the stages of their research. It gives children a logical structure for tackling research tasks in many areas of the curriculum and it is this combination of a simple but logical support scaffolding that seems to be so useful to children.

The grid can be extended by the addition of a fourth column so it becomes a KWFL grid – the F standing for 'Where will I FIND the information?' An example of this can be seen in Figure 9.9, which records some of the research of a Year 5 class into Kenya.

The grid shows that the children realised that there were more sources of useful information than merely information books and asking them to list some of these sources prompted their thinking about information. (Mrs Dingle was the fount of wisdom in the classroom who might be expected to know everything there was to know!)

EMBEDDING ICT   EMBEDDING ICT   **EMBEDDING ICT**   EMBEDDING ICT   **EMBEDDING ICT**

KWL and KWFL grids can be used by the children to make handwritten notes, as shown in Figure 9.9, but could also be pre-produced in several ways. You could lay out a standard grid and print out or make photocopies for use in class, the school library or attached to a clipboard when on an educational visit to record investigative findings. Alternatively, they could be used wholly electronically and completed on-screen as children undertake internet research. If you like to set information-gathering tasks for homework for older children, you could have a blank template on your class webpage so that it can be used at home.

Figure 9.9   A KWFL grid

Finding the answers

Locating information requires children to make decisions about where they might find the required information and then to use specific study skills such as using an index or searching a database for the details they need. The problems with this stage of the process lie not in the complexity of the skills involved but in the children's readiness to select and use the appropriate strategy to enable them to achieve their purpose most effectively. There are several ways to teach information-finding skills.

Using non-fiction big books

Key Stage 1 teachers are usually very aware of the advantages of using large versions of fiction texts, offering as they do the opportunity for groups of children to be able to see the text clearly, and providing the teacher with a vehicle to model how to use the features of that particular book and how to read it appropriately. Many publishers have brought out big versions of non-fiction books aimed at both Key Stage 1 and Key Stage 2 audiences and they provide a useful aid for teachers to model appropriate information-finding strategies and demonstrate a quick skim-read, scanning for a specific item of information/name and so on.

Using big books or working with a group as they undertake a research task, you can demonstrate what it is you actually do – not by merely telling but by showing and accompanying the showing with a monologue of your thought processes.

IN THE CLASSROOM

One group of children had asked 'How long does a chick stay a chick?' Using the big book version of *The Life of a Duck* (Magic Beans series, Heinemann, 1989) the teacher modelled for the group how they might use an information book to answer their question, but as she did so she talked about what she was doing and why. She made what is usually an internal monologue accessible to the children. The conversation went something like:

> *Now, Joanne asked about chicks growing into ducks. How can I see if this book has anything on chicks? What shall I do? Shall I read it from the beginning? No, that would take too long. I could look in the index – this list of words at the back that tells me what's in the book. Yes, I can look in the index. Let's look up chicks in the index. So I'm going to turn to the back of the book. Here it is. Index. Now. It's arranged alphabetically a… b… so c should be next… here it is. C. Can anybody see the word chick in this column…?*

This kind of modelling – making explicit to the children your thought processes as you read – gives the children some very important lessons on what an experienced reader does. Explicit vocalisation of the activity provides the children with a 'learning script' which they can 'parrot' when they are trying the task for themselves. For younger and/or inexperienced learners, the script often remains explicit – all teachers will have observed young children talking themselves through a task – but as they become more skilled the script becomes internalised and finally operates almost unconsciously.

Simple support strategies

Extra support strategies can be used by less skilled readers or younger children in the early stages of learning to use an index and contents. Children can be encouraged to write the word they are looking for on a piece of card, underlining the first letter. Turning to the index, they can then match the first letter with the appropriate alphabetical section before running the card down the section until they match the word. The page numbers can then be copied from the index onto the card. This helps the child recall which pages they need to visit (they can cross out the numbers as they do so) thus helping them hold that stage of the process in their mind without having constantly to turn back to the index. Having turned to the page, the children can be helped to scan for the word by running the card quickly over the print and looking to match the word they have written. After locating the word, the children can read the sentences immediately before and after the word to see if they contain the desired information.

A SUMMARY OF **KEY POINTS**

➢ **The teaching of reading does not stop at the end of Key Stage 1.**

➢ **The process of understanding in reading is one of interaction between what a reader knows and what the author has expressed.**

➢ **There are a number of strategies to develop this interaction, including cloze, sequencing, prediction, text marking and text restructuring.**

➢ **Shared reading also has an important role to play in developing interactive reading.**

➢ **Children need to be taught to pose questions and systematically answer them when using non-fiction material.**

M-LEVEL EXTENSION > > M-LEVEL EXTENSION > > M-LEVEL EXTENSION

You will have noticed that many of the examples given above of children reading are located in other areas of the curriculum than literacy. This is quite natural as children will need to read to learn in virtually all curriculum areas. How could they learn science, for example, without reading science texts?

This suggests that, in order to plan effectively for the development of reading at Key Stage 2, you will need to think more widely than just your literacy lessons. It would be very useful for you to reflect on some lessons or sequences of lessons you have planned in other subjects, and think about how you might plan for the development of children's reading in those lessons.

FURTHER READING FURTHER READING FURTHER READING FURTHER READING

Cairney, T. (1990) *Teaching Reading Comprehension*. Buckingham: Open University Press.

DfE (2013) *Teachers' Standards*. London: DfE. (https://www.gov.uk/government/uploads/system/uploads/attachment_data/file/208682/Teachers__Standards_2013.pdf)

Phinn, G. (2000) *Young Readers and Their Books*. London: David Fulton.

Phinn, G. (2009) *Teaching Poetry in the Primary Classroom*. Carmarthen: Crown House.

Wray, D. and Lewis, M. (1997) *Extending Literacy*. Abingdon: Routledge.

10
Teaching writing at Key Stage 2

TEACHERS' STANDARDS

A teacher must:

2. **Promote good progress and outcomes by pupils**

    - **be accountable for pupils' attainment, progress and outcomes**
    - **plan teaching to build on pupils' capabilities and prior knowledge**
    - **guide pupils to reflect on the progress they have made and their emerging needs**
    - **demonstrate knowledge and understanding of how pupils learn and how this impacts on teaching**
    - **encourage pupils to take a responsible and conscientious attitude to their own work and study.**

3. **Demonstrate good subject and curriculum knowledge**

    - **have a secure knowledge of the relevant subject(s) and curriculum areas, foster and maintain pupils' interest in the subject, and address misunderstandings**
    - **demonstrate a critical understanding of developments in the subject and curriculum areas, and promote the value of scholarship**
    - **demonstrate an understanding of and take responsibility for promoting high standards of literacy, articulacy and the correct use of standard English, whatever the teacher's specialist subject**

4. **Plan and teach well structured lessons**

    - **impart knowledge and develop understanding through effective use of lesson time**

Introduction

In Chapter 9, we explored the teaching of reading at Key Stage 2, and we made the point that before the advent of the National Literacy Strategy the teaching of literacy to children who had passed the basic stages was especially problematic. This was particularly true with regard to the teaching of writing. Many Key Stage 2 teachers 'taught' writing principally through giving their children more and more practice at doing it. Plenty of thought often went into providing suitable stimuli for starting children off with their writing – some teachers encouraged their children to draft and redraft their writing; most took care to provide feedback to children when they marked their written outcomes. Yet the teaching of writing skills was comparatively rare. Skills in this context refer, for example, to:

- being able to develop ideas into a form capable of being written;
- understanding the demands of a chosen writing form;
- being able to meet these demands in writing a particular form;

- being able to plan ahead in writing;
- being able to monitor, evaluate and revise what is being and has been written;
- understanding and meeting the demands of particular audiences for writing.

It will be helpful to clarify what we understand about the processes through which the writer has to go in order to compose effectively.

The writing process

Writing often seems a very mysterious process. When we write, somehow or other ideas in our heads, perhaps only in the very vaguest of forms, have to be shaped into coherent representations in language and transferred onto paper, screen or other media so they can be read by some other person. Although we vary greatly in the amount of writing that we do, we all have a tendency to take the process for granted. Even those who write a great deal will, when asked to describe the difficulties of writing, tend to focus on the original development of ideas rather than on the process of shaping these into language. The term we use to describe having difficulties in writing, 'writer's block', is understood by most people to mean having difficulty in getting ideas for writing rather than difficulty in transferring these to the page.

Yet the process of writing is not so simple. How exactly do we shape our ideas into writeable forms, and does the process then simply involve the transferring of these ideas to a page? Do we all follow the same process in writing or does the process vary according to how skilful we are at writing, how experienced we are, our individual styles or personalities, or on any other dimension?

You might begin a closer look at these questions by examining your own writing processes.

REFLECTIVE TASK

1. Think about the most recent piece of sustained writing you have done. Examples you might choose could be a personal letter to a friend or a policy document for your school. How did you actually set about this writing? Jot down, in note form, as much as you can remember about your approach to this task.

2. It would be very useful if you could compare your approach to this writing task with that of someone else. Are there similarities or differences in the ways you both tackled the task? If there are differences, how might you account for these? Are they merely the result of both of you engaging in slightly different writing tasks or are there more fundamental reasons for the differences?

You probably discerned several stages to the process of writing. The sequence below may not agree completely with your own description but might be useful as a starting point for discussion.

In order to produce a piece of writing, the writer needs to:

- have something worth saying;
- decide that writing is the most appropriate medium for saying this;
- have an audience in mind for what will be written;
- think about how ideas will be expressed;
- put these expressions down on paper;

- reconsider what has been written, and perhaps make alterations;
- pass on the writing to where it was intended to go.

These stages do not include the pencil sharpening, false starts, coffee making and various other activities that some writers find essential! Very few adults are able to produce a neat, accurate piece of writing that says all they want to say in the appropriate style and form at one short sitting. Interruptions and disruptions are normal in experiences of writing rather than exceptions.

Dimensions of the writing process

Our look above at the activities of an adult writer has revealed the multiple dimensions involved in the writing process. Let us look more closely at these dimensions.

In order to communicate ideas, the writer must compose and this involves:

- getting and evaluating information;
- evolving and synthesising ideas;
- shaping information and ideas into a form that can be expressed in writing.

This is essentially a creative act involving the moulding of ideas and the creation and ordering of knowledge. **Composition** is, therefore, a thoughtful activity. This view of composition, and writing in general, places emphasis on the role of language as a means of making sense of the world. As writers write, they shape their experiences and ideas in novel ways and, in the course of this, usually clarify what is in their minds. Some people claim writing to be 'epistemic', that is a creator of knowledge in its own right.

The writer must also transcribe the composition. This involves choosing an appropriate form and presenting a correct layout. **Transcription** also sometimes requires attention to accuracy in spelling, grammar, punctuation and handwriting. It is clear that transcription assumes different levels of importance, depending on the purpose of and **audience** for a piece of writing. A letter to a bank manager or an application for a job require much more care to be given to features such as spelling and handwriting than do shopping lists or the notes we take during a lecture. Yet transcription always takes place and always demands some of our attention in writing.

Ideally, the writer should be able to co-ordinate these two dimensions of writing, but this is often difficult. Composition and transcription may inhibit one another and orchestrating the two may be very difficult. Many adults find that they make more mistakes and changes when writing something important because their minds are so involved with composing the ideas. For children, who may have less than complete mastery of the processes involved, this orchestration is doubly difficult.

The result of this problem of co-ordination is sometimes that children come to believe that particular parts of the writing process are more important than others and should take the lion's share of their attention.

RESEARCH SUMMARY RESEARCH SUMMARY **RESEARCH SUMMARY** RESEARCH SUMMARY

As part of a study of children's ideas about writing in school, David Wray (1993) asked a large group of primary children, aged 7 to 11 years, to write a response to the following statement.

Someone in the class below yours has asked you what the writing will be like when he/she comes into your class. Write and tell him/her, and try to give him/her some useful advice about what he/she will have to do to do good writing in your class.

The children's responses were read and a record kept of their mentions of particular aspects of writing. The following list shows the aspects that were mentioned, in order of their popularity:

1. Spelling (mentioned 579 times, that is 19.88% of the total number of mentions of all features). It would usually be referred to by phrases such as, 'Make sure you get your spellings right', or 'Use a dictionary to spell words you don't know'.

2. Neatness (503 – 17.27%). This would be referred to by statements like, 'Do your best handwriting' or 'Make sure it is not messy'.

3. Length (372 – 12.77%). Many children stressed that the writing had to be 'long enough', although a significant number warned not to make it too long 'because Miss might get bored'.

4. Ideas (359 – 12.33%). There were several comments along the lines of: 'Try to have some funny bits', or 'Stories should be interesting and exciting'.

5. Punctuation (312 – 10.71%). Here were mentions of the need for full stops and capital letters, commas and speech marks.

6. Words (213 – 7.31%). Statements were used such as 'Don't use the same word over and over again'.

7. Tools (160 – 5.49%). There was surprisingly frequent mention of the materials with which to write, such as 'make sure your pencil is sharp', or 'Mr Ellis gets cross if you do not use a ruler to underline the title'.

8. Structure (132 – 4.53%). There was some mention of structural features such as 'A story needs a beginning, a middle and an end'.

9. Characters (100 – 3.43%). Some children gave advice such as 'Write about interesting people'.

10. Style (60 – 2.06%). Relatively few mentions were made of stylistic features such as 'In poems you can repeat words to make it sound good', or 'Don't begin sentences with "and"'.

11. Layout (46 – 1.58%). Some children referred to the drawing of a margin or the placing of the date, etc.

It seems that primary children on the whole do not value aspects of writing connected with composition but pay greater attention to transcription. This suggests that, when children are writing, they are likely to be giving so much attention to transcribing that they have little to spare for composition, which is arguably the most important dimension of writing. To develop fully as writers, children will need help in orchestrating the dimensions.

Breaking down the writing process

One way of overcoming the problem of orchestrating dimensions of writing is to approach composition and transcription separately with children. You might do this by introducing them to the drafting process, that is, to the idea that a piece of writing may go through several versions. This approach can allow the writer the freedom to concentrate firstly on composition and then later to deal with transcription. Drafting, however, implies more than just 'writing it in rough first'. It allows children to get to grips with three very important processes in writing: planning, revision and editing.

RESEARCH SUMMARY RESEARCH SUMMARY **RESEARCH SUMMARY** RESEARCH SUMMARY

Breaking down the writing process in this way is characteristic of the work of Donald Graves, whose 1983 book *Writing: Teachers and Children at Work* is widely regarded as having begun the 'process writing' movement. In the United Kingdom, Graves' work heavily influenced the National Writing Project (1987–90).

Planning

Many children have only vague notions about planning. Elizabeth (eight years old), when asked how she planned her writing, said, 'I write the first idea, then I get another one and I write it down, and I go on until I've run out, and that's the end.' While this may be appropriate in a few situations, it is not the way adult writers work, nor is it the ideal way for children to work. Planning can help children to generate ideas and formulate thoughts. Noting down their plans for writing can also help children remember all the ideas they want to work with. Eira (seven years old) commented, 'the plan sort of helps when it brings back the ideas I forget, and I get new ones then too.' If the burden of memory is alleviated, the child may be better able to reflect on and organise those ideas.

There are many ways to plan a piece of writing: a child may jot down a few key words from a class discussion session, he or she may create idea webs, or there may be a class 'formula' introduced by the teacher.

One teacher introduced her class of nine-year-olds to the idea of topic webs. They began with the topic for writing in the centre and then contributed connected ideas that were added to the web. This teacher taught her children that 'ideas are like butterflies; if you don't catch them quickly and write them down, they soon flutter away'.

Another teacher decided to introduce her class of seven-year-olds to planning by asking them to draw 'beginning', 'middle', and 'end' boxes and put key words into them. This focused their attention on the structure of their writing.

Another idea that has been successfully used by teachers is to give children frameworks around which to structure their writing (see Wray and Lewis, 1998 for more details of this approach). **Writing frames** provide children with sets of sentence starts and connectives into which they work their own ideas. The frame helps keep their writing coherent and can act as a plan and a set of prompts to writing.

Different frames can help children plan different types of writing. If, for example, they are reporting on research they have been carrying out using information books, they may use a frame like the following:

Although I already knew that..

I have learnt some new facts. I learnt that..

I also learnt that..

Another fact I learnt...

However, the most interesting thing I learnt was...

If, however, they are planning to write an argument in favour of a particular viewpoint, the frame may look like this:

Although not everybody would agree, I want to argue that...

I have several reasons for arguing for this point of view. My first reason is................

A further reason is...

Furthermore...

Therefore, although some people argue that...

I think I have shown that...

Many children will need this sort of help to get started, but it is important that through their school careers they experience planning in different ways, for two main reasons. Firstly, some types of planning, like the examples above, help develop certain features only of writing. More importantly, though, you are aiming to give children sufficient experience to enable them to choose a form of planning most suited to their needs. The form and amount of planning necessary depends on the child and on the task.

Revision

If children are allowed to draft work, they are more likely to see it as provisional, and therefore change and improve it. Children, and adults, may need to reflect on and revise their compositions several times.

It is important to realise the difference between **revision** and **editing**. Revision implies qualitative change of content, style or sequence. Although it is the most difficult aspect of the writing process to introduce, revision of drafted writing should naturally follow on from planning. The questions writers ask themselves during revision will depend on the piece of writing, but will include:

- Does it say what I want to say?
- Is it in the right order?
- Is the form right?

Many teachers offer their children sets of questions to get them started on revision, such as:

- Does everything make sense?
- Could I add something?
- Should I leave anything out?
- Are there any parts in the wrong order?

You might display these questions as posters or cards and children might use them independently, or with a partner. They may be the first step towards enabling children to look critically at their work without the prompting of the teacher.

Revision may involve minor adjustments, like insertions, crossings out, etc., or it may necessitate rewriting and moving blocks. Some of these strategies are more difficult than others and it is likely that children will need a great deal of support before they are able to use them independently. There are particular techniques to which they can be introduced, such as the use of scissors to physically cut out sections to re-sequence writing. They may also be fairly resistant to alterations such as crossing out sections of writing (perhaps because crossings out are often associated in children's minds with mistakes), and will need special reassurance that this kind of revision is approved of by their teachers.

Revising one's own writing can be quite difficult, even for adults. Writers are often too close to their own writing to be able to look at it with a properly critical eye. Because of this, it can often be useful to encourage children to work in small groups to help revise each other's writing. Fresh eyes can spot problems and also help the writer become more able to see them.

Editing

When the writing is at a stage where the author is starting to think about a final draft, then editing becomes necessary. Editing involves correcting the surface features of the text: spelling, grammar and punctuation, etc. Most children are familiar with this in the form of a teacher's 'marking'. Some teachers mark these surface features automatically, and so children set great store by them. This at least means that editing is the easiest part of the process to introduce. These features of language are important, and although you can correct them quickly and accurately, it is preferable for children to correct work themselves. This is not only a step towards independence, it also allows children to develop transferable strategies for future work.

To support the children in doing this, you might use wall charts and cards offering questions and advice. Such wall charts may even introduce children to professional proof-readers' codes and children usually enjoy using these. These charts can be used by individuals or, more often, pairs of children. Peer editing is helpful in that it offers the child support, advice and opinions, which can be accepted or rejected depending on the author's judgement. It also allows realistic organisation of your time as purposeful, task-orientated discussion can take place without your being present.

Publication and evaluation

Drafting is a very powerful process that allows children to concentrate on the various elements of writing separately. The emphasis is on producing a better quality product for an audience. This means, of course, that children need to publish and evaluate their writing. In this context, publish means simply 'to make public', and this can take many forms. Some work may be read out to a teacher, friend, group or class, perhaps in a designated 'sharing time'. Publication could also mean displaying work so that it becomes reading material in a real sense, from a single piece of writing on the wall to a book written for younger children by a group. In all cases, it is important that publication should have the appropriate form and that final decisions about content and so on should be made by the author. When the publication reaches its intended audience, then any sort of response can be used for evaluation. This may be between you and the child, among a small group, or more publicly. In any case, both you and the children need to understand the need for constructive criticism.

When publication is the perceived end-point of the writing, children are helped to develop their awareness of audience. This has an effect on both the composition and transcription processes which children need to begin to take account of early in their writing experience. They need, in general, to have experience of writing for a range of purposes.

EMBEDDING ICT   EMBEDDING ICT   **EMBEDDING ICT**   EMBEDDING ICT   **EMBEDDING ICT**

ICT can be used integrally in every part of the writing process at Key Stage 2. Your IWB provides an ideal medium for introductory teacher-led work on any shared reading texts used as exemplars, and for shared and guided writing activities. The children can use a word-processing program for every part of their writing process, including all elements of drafting – planning, revision and editing – and for publication and evaluation too. Writing frames and scaffolding approaches work well electronically, with less confident writers deriving comfort from the fact that any mistakes that they make can be easily corrected and need not appear in later drafts. Once finalised, the text can be published in a range of formats or uploaded onto the class webpage or the VLE. For more on teaching with electronic texts, see Chapter 11.

Planning for the process

The process of writing that we have just explored is not linear in operation in the sense of a series of steps through which writers proceed in order. Rather, the process is recursive and reflective, with several parts operating simultaneously.

This has several implications for the teaching of writing which you might consider. You need to allow for these things in organising your teaching of writing.

- Children need time to reflect on their writing.
- Allowance needs to be given for the erratic nature of the process.
- Children might benefit from discussing their approaches to writing with their classmates.

Teaching the writing process

There are a number of teaching strategies you might employ, both in and out of the literacy session, to teach writing to Key Stage 2 children. Some of these are described in this section, with some examples of how they might be employed.

Shared reading

No, you are not reading the wrong chapter! Shared reading is an essential step in the effective teaching of writing. In the course of reading a shared text with a class, you can, as well as focusing on teaching them how to read this text, also teach a good deal about how the text is structured. A highly developed familiarity with the structure of a text is necessary if children are subsequently to write texts like this themselves. Put crudely, you would not expect children to write very good poetry if they had never read any or had any read to them. The same is true of all text types. As an example, look at the following transcription of some writing produced by a seven-year-old who was asked to write a set of instructions for how to plant cress seeds.

Cress

We had some seeds and Mrs Lewis gave us some seeds in our hands then we sprinkled the seed on the plate. Then Mrs Lewis gave us a piece of paper to cover the seeds. We are going to leave them to grow. Every day we will check the seeds to see if they have grown.

This may be a fairly accurate account of what happened in the lesson, but it is not a set of instructions; it lacks basic features such as a statement of the goal ('How to plant cress seeds'), a list of materials and equipment needed, a sequence of steps to follow and the correct use of tense (the imperative would be more appropriate than simple past tense).

You can draw children's attention to these features by using texts such as instructions in shared reading sessions. The following is an example of how you might do this using an instructional text.

IN THE CLASSROOM

Miss R's Year 5 class was beginning some work on writing instructional texts. In a shared reading session, she introduced them to the recipe for making pizza shown in Figure 10.1. After reading the text together, they discussed the following points:

- How do you know this is a recipe? **(It tells you how to cook something. There's a list of ingredients.)**
- What kind of text is that? **(It tells you how to do something. Instructions.)**
- Can you think of any other texts that are like recipes and tell you how to do something? **(Rules for playing games. Instructions for fixing the computer.)**
- What does a recipe always begin with? **(There will always be a title. The title tells you what you are going to make.)**
- What does the first part of this recipe tell you? **(How big a pizza it will make. How long it takes.)**
- What does the next part tell you? **(The ingredients. What you need to make the pizza.)**
- How are the ingredients organised? **(A list. Measurements for each item.)**
- What follows the ingredients? **(What you have to do. The method.)**
- What do you notice about these directions? **(They are in the form of a numbered list. They use commands, or imperatives. They refer to time, either directly or by the use of chronological connectives, until, then, etc.)**

Making pizza

This recipe will make a 12 to 16 inch pizza
Preparation time: 15 minutes
Cooking time: 20 minutes

Ingredients	Directions
1 cup warm water	1. *Stir the sugar and yeast into the water until they are dissolved.*
1 tablespoon white sugar	2. *Add the olive oil and the salt and then stir.*
$2\frac{1}{4}$ teaspoons active dried yeast	3. *Stir in the flour until it is well blended.*
3 tablespoons olive oil	4. *Let the dough rest for 10 minutes.*
1 teaspoon salt	5. *Dip your fingers in olive oil and pat the dough into a flat pan or onto a pizza stone.*
$2\frac{1}{2}$ cups plain flour	6. *If you wish, you can sprinkle basil, thyme or other seasonings on top.*
	7. *Place your favourite pizza toppings on top. Use tomato paste and cheese as a base.*
	8. *Bake for 15 to 20 minutes in a preheated oven at 200°C.*

Figure 10.1   A recipe for making pizza

Through this shared reading, you can both familiarise your children with the key structural features of the text type they will be going on to write and focus their attention on crucial linguistic and grammatical features. This knowledge will later be applied when they come to write their own texts.

You might also want to involve your children in compiling a checklist of these crucial text type features. This is a learning activity in its own right as they now have to think abstractly about text features. It can also be used later as an aide-mémoire when they come to write. Miss R went on to do this with her Year 5 class. The questions she used to prompt them, together with some of their answers, are presented in Figure 10.2.

Thinking about recipes		
Questions the children were asked	**Things you might point out**	**Some of the children's responses**
What comes first in a recipe?	*The title of the dish. The goal of the recipe.*	*What you're going to make. The name of what you're making.*
What comes next?	*List of ingredients.*	*What you need. All your equipment and things.*
How are these laid out on the page?	*Vertical lists.*	*Lists.*
In what order are the ingredients listed?	*This is debatable.*	*The order in which you use them. The biggest things first.*
What comes next in the recipe?	*Directions for making the dish.*	*What you have to do.*
In what order are these listed?	*Chronological.*	*The right order.*
Why?	*Because that's how you use them.*	*You'd get mixed up.*
How are they laid out on the page?	*Usually a numbered list.*	*Number of steps. 1, 2, 3, 4...*
What tense are they written in?	*Imperative.*	*Do this...*
Do they use passive or active verbs?	*Active.*	*You have to do actions.*
Who is the audience for a recipe?	*There is an implied second person – an implied but not stated 'you'.*	*Anyone making the dish. The cook.*
What style of language would you expect?	*Unembellished, businesslike, formal.*	*Plain and simple.*
Why?	*Ease of use – you need instant reference.*	*It has to be quick to read.*

Figure 10.2 Key features of recipes

Shared writing

As well as ensuring that your children understand the key features of what they are going to write, you need to show them how to compose and transcribe such texts. Teacher demonstrations of this kind are crucial teaching opportunities for two main reasons:

1. They can draw children's attention to many of the invisible elements of a writer's craft, such as the thought processes during the production of the writing.
2. They can show the children that you are a writer too, not just someone who tells them to write.

Shared writing is a powerful teaching strategy and involves much more than just writing down what children say. Shared writing provides you with opportunities to:

- work with the whole class to model, explore and discuss the decisions that writers make when they are writing;
- make links between reading and writing explicit;
- demonstrate how writers use language to achieve particular effects;
- remove temporarily some of the problems of orchestrating writing skills by taking on the burden of some aspects, for example spelling and handwriting, thereby enabling the children to focus exclusively on how composition works;
- focus on particular aspects of the writing process, such as planning, composing, revising or editing;
- scaffold children in the use of appropriate technical language to discuss what writers do and think.

While you are doing a shared writing activity, you will need to think about the following aspects.

- Discuss with the children the audience and purpose of the writing task you are engaged in, and discuss how that will influence the content, structure and grammar of what is written.
- Rehearse sentences orally before you write them down. This offers an excellent model for children's own composition as it encourages thoughtfulness.
- Emphasise your use of punctuation, and verbalise your reasons for using particular marks.
- Re-read what you have written at regular intervals. This encourages children to think about the flow from one sentence to another.
- Hold debates with yourself as you decide between possible options in your writing. Verbalise the ways you decide what works best.
- You might want to make the occasional deliberate mistake in your writing. This will help keep the children's attention and will also allow you deliberately to focus on particular common errors.

Of course, not every shared writing session needs to be the same and there are three main teaching techniques you can use to help children gradually move towards independence.

Modelling writing

You will need to demonstrate how to write a text and while doing this you should think aloud, modelling the thought processes you use while writing. You might do such things as the following.

- Rehearse a sentence orally before writing it, make changes to it, explaining why you chose certain words and not others, and point out mistakes you have made or points on which you can improve.
- Show them what you do in writing when you run out of ideas (re-read what you have written, discuss it with another person, or refer back to your plan).
- Show them what you do when you need to write quickly (write in note form and use abbreviations).
- Show what you do when you don't know how a word is spelt (try it several ways to see what looks right, write what you think and mark it to check later or use a word with a similar meaning that you can spell!).

Scribing

Here, you invite the children to take part in the composition process, while you transcribe an agreed version of what they say. You might:

- Ask them to suggest a sentence at a time, which you respond to, expanding and modifying as you feel, but explaining why you are doing this.
- Take two or more suggestions and ask the class to give you reasons for preferring one or the other.
- Give them time to compose in writing, perhaps using jotter books, or small individual whiteboards, before asking for their suggestions.

Prompted writing

Here, you ask the children to write short sections with very clear guidelines from you. This will allow time for children to practise particular points in their writing. You might:

- ask them for a sentence that tells you one more thing about the main character in the story you are writing;
- ask for two more sentences, each containing at least one subordinate clause;
- ask them to write the next persuasive point in the argument you have already planned.

Guided writing

Guided writing is an additional supported step towards independent writing. Children can be offered clear support but the onus is on them to make decisions, compose and revise their own texts. There are three main purposes for guided writing.

1. *To help children plan and draft their independent work.* You can support this work by helping children to orchestrate all the decisions needed to draft their own text. This might involve children in such things as:

- retelling a story they have previously had read to them, where the content is predetermined and their task is to find a way of communicating that content;
- writing an explanatory paragraph following a model they have earlier discussed in shared reading;
- using the computer to rewrite a piece of formal or archaic writing to make it more conversational or modern.

2. *To help children revise and edit work already begun.* Encourage them to share their writing with the group and:

- re-read it to check its clarity;
- enhance the vocabulary choices they have made by responding to suggestions from other children;
- work on strengthening particular words, phrases or text sections such as introductions and endings;
- check their use of cohesion, such as consistent use of pronouns, use of connectives and consistency of tense.

3. *To provide differentiated support for particular children or groups.* Children will need greater levels of individual teaching than will be possible in whole-class work and you can use guided writing to:

- repeat a shared writing session with more support for the less confident writers;
- prepare certain children for a forthcoming shared writing session by previewing the key ideas they will be using;
- stretch more able writers in composing or editing activities;
- work intensively with less able writers.

THE BIGGER PICTURE THE BIGGER PICTURE **THE BIGGER PICTURE** THE BIGGER PICTURE

When you are planning guided writing activities as part of the process of developing children's independent writing, these need not always be traditional 'literacy' texts. Guided writing techniques can be part of many other areas of the children's learning. For example, you may want to introduce children to the correct way to write up a science experiment or present the findings of a maths investigation or technology project. The move from short pieces of writing to extended writing does not have to take place solely in English sessions, but can be developed in history, geography or RE. Similarly, writing frames, research-recording grids and other scaffolding methods can be useful in all subject areas, including when undertaking cross-curricular topics or theme work. Using guided writing in other parts of the curriculum reinforces the expectation that literacy skills are not just for use in English sessions, but are for all written work.

Scaffolding writing

Some children will learn most of what they need to know about writing a particular text type from their shared reading and writing sessions. For many, however, the jump from being shown how to write in a particular way to being able to write in that way independently is simply too big for them to make easily. They need more support as they begin to learn to be independent writers.

This phase involves scaffolded writing, during which you can offer children strategies to aid their writing, which they can use without an adult necessarily being alongside them. One popular such strategy is the use of writing frames, which were earlier considered as an aid to planning writing. They can also act both as a way of increasing a child's experience of a particular type of writing and as a substitute for the teacher's direct interventions which encourage children to extend their writing.

A writing frame consists of a skeleton outline to scaffold children's writing of a particular text type. The skeleton framework consists of different key words or phrases, according to the particular generic form. The template of starters, connectives and sentence modifiers which constitute a writing frame gives children a structure within which they can concentrate on communicating what they want to say, rather than getting lost in the form. However, by using the form, children become increasingly familiar with it.

Some example writing frames were given earlier in the chapter; further photocopiable examples can be found in Lewis and Wray (1997) and Wray and Lewis (1998), and downloadable versions at http://www.literacyworld.info/resources.html

Writing with this kind of frame scaffolds writing in a number of ways.

- It does not present writers with a blank page. There is comfort in the fact that there is already some writing on this page. This alone can be enough to encourage less confident writers to write at greater length.
- The frame provides a series of prompts to children's writing. Using the frame is rather like having a dialogue with the page and the prompts serve to model the register of that particular piece of writing.
- The frame deliberately includes connectives beyond the simple 'and then'. Extended use of frames can result in children spontaneously using these more elaborate connectives in other writing.
- The frame is designed around the typical structure of a particular genre. It gives children access to this structure and implicitly teaches them a way of writing this type of text.

You should always begin your use of a frame with shared writing, discussion and teacher modelling before moving on to collaborative writing (teacher and children together) and then to the child undertaking writing supported by the frame. This oral, teacher modelling, joint construction pattern of teaching is vital, for it not only models the generic form and teaches the words that signal connections and transitions, but it also provides opportunities for developing children's oral language and their thinking. Some children, especially those with learning difficulties, may need many oral sessions and sessions in which their teacher acts as a scribe before they are ready to attempt their own writing.

You may find it useful to make 'big' versions of the frames for use in shared writing. It is important that the children understand that the frame is a supportive draft and words may be crossed out or substituted. Extra sentences may be added or surplus starters crossed out. The frame should be treated as a flexible aid rather than as a rigid form.

When the children have a purpose for writing, you may decide to offer them a frame:

- when they first attempt independent writing in an unfamiliar text type and a scaffold might be helpful to them;
- when a child/group of children appears stuck in a particular mode of writing, e.g. constantly using 'and then...' 'and then' when writing an account;
- when they 'wander' between text types in a way that demonstrates a lack of understanding of a particular type, e.g. while writing an instructional text such as a recipe they start in the second person ('First you beat the egg') but then shift into a recount ('Next I stirred in the flour');
- when they have written something in one structure (often a personal recount) which would be more appropriate in a different form, e.g. writing up a science experiment as a non-chronological report.

Writing frames can be helpful to children of all ages and all abilities. You might, however, find them particularly useful with children of average writing ability and with those who find writing difficult. It would of course be unnecessary to use the frame with writers already confident and fluent in a particular text type but they can be used to introduce such writers to new types. The aim with all children is for them to reach the stage of assimilating the generic structures and language features into their independent writing repertoires. Children therefore need to use the frames less and less as their knowledge of a particular form increases. At this later stage, when children begin to show evidence of independent usage, you may need only to have a master copy of the frames available as help cards for those occasions when children need a prompt. A box of such help cards could be a part of the writing area in which children are encouraged to refer to many different aids to their writing. This is one way of encouraging children to begin to make independent decisions about their own learning.

Also, as children become familiar with the frame structures, a number of alternative support structures can be used, such as prompt sheets containing lists of possible ways of connecting ideas together. A number of these will be found in Lewis and Wray (1998).

A SUMMARY OF **KEY POINTS**

> **The process of writing needs to be taught directly.**
> **The process involves elements such as planning, composition, transcription, revision, editing and publication.**
> **Teaching the writing of a particular text type begins with familiarising children with the features of this text type, through shared reading and a progressive focus on key features.**
> **Shared writing, during which the teacher models how to compose a particular text, is a vital teaching strategy.**

> ➤ Guided writing gradually puts the onus more and more onto the children in writing.
>
> ➤ Many children will need their writing to be scaffolded, perhaps by the use of writing frames, as they move towards becoming independent writers of a range of text types.

M-LEVEL EXTENSION > > M-LEVEL EXTENSION > > M-LEVEL EXTENSION

David Wray has developed his work on writing frames, referred to earlier in this chapter, to encompass a fuller model of how to teach writing. A description of this model, together with several practical ideas for using it in the Key Stage 2 classroom can be found in Wray 2002. The model is outlined below.

Teaching sequence for a new text type		Possible activities
1. **What do I have to do?**	a) Familiarise pupils with the text type by providing examples.	• Make sure the classroom environment contains lots of examples of this text type.
	b) Focus their attention on the key features of the text type.	• Shared reading. • Sequencing.
	c) Define the conventions of this text.	• Draft lists of conventions. • Produce class posters.
2. **Show me how to do it.**	• Model the writing of a text.	• Shared writing. • Metacognitive modelling.
3. **Do it with me.**	• Get pupils to compose an example collaboratively with you or as a group.	• Group writing tasks. • Reciprocal teaching.
4. **Help me to do it.**	• Scaffold pupils' use of the text type.	• Planning frames. • Writing frames.
5. **I can do it!**	• Help pupils towards independence.	• Collaborative editing of each other's writing.

Try out some of the activities implicit in this model and reflect on how they work in the development of pupils' writing. Does this approach work with all your groups, including children in Key Stage 1? Does it work for some text types better than others?

FURTHER READING FURTHER READING FURTHER READING FURTHER READING

Corbett, P. (2001) *How to Teach Fiction Writing at Key Stage 2*. London: David Fulton.

DfE (2013) *Teachers' Standards*. London: DfE. (https://www.gov.uk/government/uploads/system/uploads/attachment_data/file/208682/Teachers__Standards_2013.pdf)

Lewis, M. and Wray, D. (1994) *Developing Children's Non-fiction Writing*. Leamington Spa: Scholastic.

Lewis, M. and Wray, D. (1997) *Writing Frames*. Reading: University of Reading, Reading and Language Information Centre.

Wray, D. (2002) *Practical Ways to Teach Writing*. Reading: National Centre for Language in Literacy.

Wray, D. and Lewis, M. (1998) *Writing across the Curriculum*. Reading: University of Reading, Reading and Language Information Centre.

11
Teaching with electronic texts

TEACHERS' STANDARDS

A teacher must:

1. **Set high expectations which inspire, motivate and challenge pupils**

    *   **establish a safe and stimulating environment for pupils, rooted in mutual respect**

3. **Demonstrate good subject and curriculum knowledge**

    *   **have a secure knowledge of the relevant subject(s) and curriculum areas, foster and maintain pupils' interest in the subject, and address misunderstandings**
    *   **demonstrate a critical understanding of developments in the subject and curriculum areas, and promote the value of scholarship**
    *   **demonstrate an understanding of and take responsibility for promoting high standards of literacy, articulacy and the correct use of standard English, whatever the teacher's specialist subject**

4. **Plan and teach well structured lessons**

    *   **contribute to the design and provision of an engaging curriculum within the relevant subject area(s).**

5. **Adapt teaching to respond to the strengths and needs of all pupils**

    *   **know when and how to differentiate appropriately, using approaches which enable pupils to be taught effectively**
    *   **have a secure understanding of how a range of factors can inhibit pupils' ability to learn, and how best to overcome these**

Introduction: expanding literacy

Traditionally, literacy has been simply defined as the condition of being able to read and write and for most people this definition is adequate. However, it is becoming increasingly apparent that we need to expand our definition of literacy to include the reading and writing not only of printed texts but of electronic texts. Computers are being used to create and revise texts, to send and receive mail electronically, to present texts of all kinds on-screen instead of in printed books, and to access large databases of texts. Clearly, teachers need to include electronic forms of reading and writing in the literacy experiences they offer children. This raises the question of how learners can be prepared to read and write electronically.

Reading electronically

Electronic books

Some of the earliest reading materials available electronically were adaptations of existing print texts. These included collections of books which had been converted to work from a CD-ROM. Of course, they were not just placed on a CD, but were enhanced to harness the power of the computer. Some contained a multimedia book, which was read aloud by the computer while sound effects and music complemented the story. These books presented many options, such as varying speeds of reading, explanations of words and even options to have the book read in a different language. The idea was that, as children's reading ability grew, they could use the computer just to say the words they could not read.

Later, companies such as Sherston Software began to produce much smaller 'Talking Books'. The simplicity of the Sherston system meant that these books had a major impact in UK schools, especially when the best-selling British reading scheme, Oxford Reading Tree, adopted the system to produce electronic versions of its books.

Most electronic books produced for school use have similar facilities. They all provide onscreen text, illustrated with pictures. By clicking on certain icons, the text is read aloud or the pictures are animated. They all also provide the facility for the reader to click on individual words or phrases to hear these read aloud.

RESEARCH SUMMARY RESEARCH SUMMARY **RESEARCH SUMMARY** RESEARCH SUMMARY

A number of research studies have investigated the impact of such electronic stories on children's reading. Medwell, for example (1996, 1998), explored whether talking books could help young children learn to read traditional print texts, and if so, how they supported children's reading. Reception/Year 1 children were studied as they used the Sherston *Naughty Stories* and the Oxford Reading Tree *Talking Stories*. The results suggested that talking books do help young children to learn to read traditional texts and particularly helped them to understand the meanings of the stories. Medwell found that children who used the electronic versions of the books learned more than those who only used print versions, but that the most learning was achieved by children who read the print versions with their teachers and then used the electronic versions by themselves. This suggests that, although electronic books can help children to progress in reading, they complement rather than replace the role of the skilled teacher of reading.

Reading to learn with the computer

In many ways, information text was made for computerised presentation. Most readers do not read information books in the linear way they approach fiction text and use an approach centred on the contents or index page, from which links are made to other pages. Having such text on a computer simply makes this approach more efficient. Rather than having to physically turn the pages of a book, the reader can just click on a link to move to the relevant information.

One of the unfortunate by-products of this is that the already significant tendency of children to copy from information books is likely to be worsened by the use of electronic information text. After all, selecting, copying and pasting material from a CD-ROM or the internet, or just printing out sheaves of pages from relevant websites is a lot easier than having physically to write out material from a book. There are a number of tried and tested strategies for helping children avoid straight copying when they use information books and many of these are fully described in Chapter 9. These strategies work just as well with computer-based materials.

REFLECTIVE TASK

Look back at the relevant parts of Chapter 9 and think how you might adapt some of the strategies described there to help children to read and use computer-based information text more effectively.

The thinking that pupils are encouraged to do **before** they begin to use information sources is crucial in avoiding such copying. Ask children to think about what they already know about a topic before they develop some questions to which they would like to find answers. This then lessens the possibility of their approaching information sources looking to record everything they find. You might use a strategy such as a KWFL grid for this (see Figure 9.9) to record the process of their information research.

Also, when children are reading information text, you need to make sure they read actively. One strategy to help achieve this is to get them to mark text that they think is significant. In printed text, this can involve the use of highlighter pens and there is usually an equivalent to this for screen-based text. In Microsoft Word, this involves clicking the Text Highlight button, selecting a highlight colour and then using the mouse to select appropriate text. More than one colour can be used in the same document, thus allowing information relevant to a number of questions to be picked out.

Another active reading strategy is for children to restructure the information they have read into one of a variety of other forms. They might go to information sources armed with a word-processed grid, which they keep open in a window on the screen while they browse information sources in another window. The grid both guides them in their information search and helps them structure the information they find for subsequent reporting. An example of such a grid can be seen in Figure 11.1.

The planets			
Name of planet	**How far from the Sun?**	**How big (diameter)?**	**Could it support life?**

Figure 11.1   A research grid to support internet research

Problem-solving with texts

There is a range of textual problem-solving activities, generically referred to as Directed Activities Relating to Texts (DARTS), all of which have been shown to be useful ways of encouraging children to interact purposefully with printed texts. Activities in this range include cloze, where children work together to suggest possible words to fill deletions in a text, and sequencing, where a group of pupils have to work out a meaningful order for a text that has been cut into sections and mixed up. What these activities have in common is that they involve group discussion of disrupted texts and their main aim is to recreate meaningful text.

An early attempt to adapt activities like this to electronic text was the computer program known as Developing TRAY. This program was written initially for use with secondary students who were struggling with reading. The name derives from the idea of a print gradually coming into focus in a photographer's developing tray. Starting with a screen showing only punctuation and a series of dashes to represent letters, the pupils gradually reconstruct the extract, initially by 'buying' letters then by predicting words or phrases as the text becomes clearer.

RESEARCH SUMMARY RESEARCH SUMMARY **RESEARCH SUMMARY** RESEARCH SUMMARY

A number of research studies, both at secondary (Johnston, 1985) and primary (Haywood and Wray, 1988) levels, have suggested that experience with Developing TRAY involves the use of high-level problem-solving skills, analysis of data, decision making about strategies, the creation and interpretation of meaning and hypothesis forming and testing.

TRAY is now more than 30 years old, which for educational software is old indeed, but the fact that a modernised version is still available is testimony to its abiding usefulness in developing children's reading. It is usually found now as part of text problem-solving suites of programs (often given names such as 'word detectives'), which include computer versions of other DARTs.

A more recent addition to teachers' technological armouries is the interactive whiteboard (IWB) which has a great deal of possible uses in the teaching of reading. The IWB allows the information appearing on a computer screen to be projected onto a much larger surface where it can be interacted with – text can be added with a pen, moved, annotated or deleted. This means that the interactivity that is characteristic of electronic text can now be carried out as a shared activity with large groups of children. A simple example of this is the sequencing activity briefly mentioned earlier. Normally, this is done with sections of printed text that have physically been cut up and children move the sections around, experimenting with possible orders until they find one they can agree on. Because of the size of the text and the need to handle the sections, it is normal for this activity to involve three or four children at most. With an IWB, however, the sections of text appear in large type on the board and each can be moved around using the board pen. This makes possible whole-class discussion of a text in this way.

Literacy software is available that exploits the potential of the IWB, and supplies teachers with a large range of texts for shared work. The software includes tools such as highlighter pens, instant cloze text makers and a range of word and phonic banks.

Writing electronically

For a number of reasons, writing was one of the first aspects to be significantly affected by the development of personal computers and other new technologies. The vast majority of the writing that gets done in the world, at least the commercial world, today is done through the medium of information technology. The sheer prominence of on-screen, as opposed to paper-based writing means that we need to familiarise children with the skills and possibilities of this medium if they are to use it confidently. However, ICT also makes possible a number of beneficial approaches to the **teaching** of writing. Evidence suggests that the use of computers as tools for writing can significantly enhance children's understanding of, and competence in, all forms of writing.

ICT has, therefore, a dual role in teaching and developing writing. On the one hand, it can effectively help children learn how to write in **traditional** forms. On the other, it extends these forms by adding new possibilities for writing.

Using word processors

Even quite young children quickly learn how to use word processing programs, and seem to be able to improve the quality of their writing by doing so. What is it about word processors that leads to this improvement?

To answer this question, we need firstly to look at the ways in which our understanding of the process of writing has changed over the last few years. Perhaps the most significant feature of this change has been the realisation that to expect children to produce well thought-out, interesting writing, correctly spelt and punctuated, grammatical and neatly written, at one sitting, is to expect the impossible. Even experienced adult writers do not work that way, and will confirm that any writing other than the most trivial goes through several drafts before it is considered finished. Many teachers encourage their children to approach writing in this way, that is to write drafts which can then be revised, shared with other readers, discussed and edited before reaching their final versions. The use of the word processor as a writing tool reinforces this drafting process. Writing on a computer screen does not have the permanence of writing on paper. Everything about it becomes provisional and can be altered at the touch of a key.

A significant reason why children may find it difficult to fully accept the idea of writing as provisional when it is done on paper is the fact that, if they wish to change their writing, this will usually involve rewriting it. The sheer physical effort of this will persuade some children to adopt a much more studied, once-and-for-all approach to their writing. With a word processor, however, alterations can be made on the screen and there is no need to rewrite. This facility for immediate error correction allows children to approach writing more experimentally. They soon become prepared to try things out and alter them several times if need be. They also begin to be able to live with uncertainty. If, for example, they are unsure of particular spellings, they can try an approximation and check it later, without breaking the flow of their writing ideas. 'We'll do the spellings afterwards' becomes a familiar strategy.

Another significant feature provided by word processing is the facility to electronically cut and paste text. Sections of text can easily be moved around the piece of writing. This allows writers to re-sequence their writing with little effort and to experiment with different sequences.

REFLECTIVE TASK

Look at the following story, written by two six-year-olds after reading *A Troll at School* by Elizabeth Walker.

Once upon a time a troll lived in a bucket of paint. One day he went to my friends school and he bit my friends hand and she shouted miss brown that is her teacher. Her teacher said go to the head teacher. My friend is called Sarah. The head teacher said sit on the prickly mat. Then it was time to go home and when we went to bed we heard noises going like this bump bump bump bump bump and bump. Guess who it was. You are right it was the troll. He was green and slimy with red eyes.

If you were their teacher, how would you advise the girls to change their story, using cut and paste on the word processor, to improve its quality?

After discussing this with their teacher, and eight key presses on the word processor, this is the story the girls ended up with.

Once upon a time a troll lived in a bucket of paint. He was green and slimy with red eyes. One day he went to my friend Sarah's school and he bit my friends hand and she shouted miss brown that is her teacher. Her teacher said go to the head teacher. The head teacher said sit on the prickly mat. Then it was time to go home and when we went to bed we heard noises going like this bump bump bump bump bump and bump. Guess who it was. You are right it was the troll.

It would, of course, have been possible to achieve this with pencil and paper by using arrows, or with scissors and glue, but neither of these methods compares with the simplicity of the word processor. Again, this facility increases the provisionality of writing. Not only can text be changed at will, it can also be rearranged in any number of ways.

Most word processors also have the facility to search through texts for particular words or markers and then replace them with other words. This can assist children's writing in a variety of ways. Firstly, it allows them to change their minds easily. If, for example, they have written a story about a boy called Pete and suddenly decide they really want it to be about a girl called Mary, these details can be altered throughout the text by a couple of key presses.

Secondly, it provides a way of dealing easily with consistent misspellings. If, for example, a child regularly spells 'occasion' as 'ocassion', or 'should' as 'sholud', they can be asked to check these words after finishing their writing. Having ascertained the correct spelling, they can then use the word processor to alter every occurrence of the misspelling at one go. Most word processors allow the user to decide whether each individual occurrence should be altered. This can be useful if there are words the child regularly confuses, such as 'there' and 'their' or 'hear' and 'here'. Being asked to consider each one in turn encourages children to become more aware of the contexts in which each one is appropriate.

A further use of the search and replace facility is to eliminate some of the distraction caused when children search for the spellings of words they are unsure of. These can be entered at first using a marker (such as ***). When the first draft is done, the children can then find the correct spellings and use the replace facility to change their markers.

Children's word-processed text can be rearranged in various ways. This makes it possible for their writing to emerge looking very much like that in 'real' books, with consequent benefits for their motivation to write. The aspect of this which is usually discovered first is justification.

The effects of this can be seen in the following example of the writing of a six-year-old. Her story first looked like this:

> once there was a dragon called Ace he was a friendly dragon and Ace met a boy called John and the dragon said will you have a fight with me because if you do and you win I will take you for a ride yes said John I will have a fight against you John won the fight and the dragon took John for a ride to the moon they came back with straw so they did not hurt themselves.

This was then corrected, justified and the line spacing altered to produce this:

> Once there was a dragon called Ace. He was a friendly dragon. Ace met a boy called John and the dragon said, will you have a fight with me? Because if you do and you win I will take you for a ride. Yes, said John. I will have a fight against you. John won the fight and the dragon took John for a ride to the moon. They came back with straw so they did not hurt themselves.

The child was delighted with the look of this and commented that it was just like in her reading book.

This ability to rearrange text can be taken further by altering the format of the text. If the writing had been done for a class newspaper, it could be formatted with narrower columns, or it could be changed to one of a variety of type styles or fonts. So, the above story might be produced as:

> Once there was a dragon called Ace. He was a friendly dragon. Ace met a boy called John and the dragon said, will you have a fight with me? Because if you do and you win I will take you for a ride. Yes, said John. I will have a fight against you. John won the fight and the dragon took John for a ride to the moon. They came back with straw so they did not hurt themselves.

Such features can enhance children's writing a great deal, and all have the effect of making children enjoy writing more. You do have to guard against font overkill, though. Imagine reading the following:

> Once there was a dragon called Ace. He was a friendly dragon. **Ace met a boy called John and the dragon said, will you have a fight with me?** **Because if you do and you win I will take you for a ride.** Yes, said John. I will have a fight against you. John won the fight and the dragon took John for a ride to the moon. They came back with straw so they did not hurt themselves.

Then imagine this with every letter or word a different colour! Children love to get carried away in this fashion!

Word processors can also be used as teaching devices in the context of children's writing, with consequent improvements in quality. An example of this can be seen in the following piece written jointly by two seven-year-olds. After hunting for minibeasts in the school field, the two boys wrote:

> today we went out side to look for little creatures and we found an ant and one was red and jamie russ found a big black spider and daniel jones caught it in his pot and we also

caught a centipede and it was red and it went very fast and mrs wilkins caught a earwig and two caterpillars but one caretpillar escaped from the yoggat pot and we found some slugs and they made a slimy trail on the white paper

Their teacher asked them to read the piece to her, and they were all struck by the over-use of the word 'and'. The teacher used the search and replace facility of the word processor to exchange the 'ands' for markers, and asked them to look at the writing again.

today we went out side to look for little creatures *** we found a ant *** one was red *** jamie russ found a big black spider *** daniel jones caught it in his pot *** we also caught a centipede *** it was red *** it went very fast *** mrs wilkins caught a earwig *** two caterpillars but one caretpillar escaped from the yoggat pot *** we found some slugs *** they made a slimy trail on the white paper

This revision produced the following finished article:

Today we went out side to look for little creatures and we found ants. One of them was red. Just then Jamie Russ found a big black spider. Then daniel jones caught it in his pot. We also caught a centipede. The centipede was red like the ant. The centipede went very fast like the ant. Mrs Wilkins caught an earwig and two caterpillars but one escaped from the pot. Then we found some slugs and they made a slimy trail on the white paper.

The improvement in quality is quite clear. This may have happened without the use of the word processor but it is doubtful whether the process would have been so simple, or the children so eager to do it.

Shared writing

A word processor can be used as a medium for shared writing, although, of course, the presentation device used will need to be sufficiently large for the writing on it to be read easily by the whole class. This requires either a very large computer screen, a data projector to project the image onto a large screen or wall, or an IWB.

Here are a few examples of possible shared writing lessons that you might adapt for your own purposes.

1. Word-level work – Year 4
Objective: To spell regular verb endings *-s*, *-ed*, *-ing*.

Set the word processor to display a large font, e.g. 28 point, and type in the following list of words: *care, come, face, file, give, glue, hope, ice, joke, like, live, love, make*. Type *ing* after the first few, using a different font. Explain the rule about dropping the final *e*, and delete the spaces between the word and the suffix. Finally delete the *e* as well, giving a dynamic demonstration of how the joining of stem and suffix and the deletion of the final *e* are part of the same action. Do this with a couple of examples.

give	*ing*	**give***ing*	**give***ing*	**giv***ing*
hope	*ing*	**hope***ing*	**hope***ing*	**hop***ing*

Now let individual children come to the computer to carry out the same action. If you have a talking word processor, you can listen to the sounds of the words and then compare them to some common spelling mistakes such as 'comming' and 'hopping'.

2. Sentence-level work – Year 4

Objective: To identify common adverbs with an *-ly* suffix.

Set the word processor to display a large font, e.g. 28 point, and type in the following list of *-ly* adverbs: *quickly, slowly, swiftly, sluggishly, rapidly, unhurriedly*. Highlight the *ly* and then increase the size (on most word processors this can be done by holding down Ctrl + Shift and > (greater than) and decreasing the size is achieved by holding down Ctrl + Shift and < (less than)).

quickly   *quick*ly *quick*ly *quick*ly

Let some children try this with other words. Such animations are a good way of fixing certain letter strings in children's minds.

3. Sentence-level work – Year 3

Objective: To recognise the function of verbs in sentences, and to use verb tenses in writing.

Use a large font size and write some simple sentences without their verbs, for example:

Alexander all the chocolate bars.

Ask the children what is missing. Where should the missing word go? What possibilities are there for this missing word or phrase? Type one suggestion into the sentence, using a bold font. Use copy and paste to reproduce the same sentence five or so times. In each sentence, use a different verb or a variation on the same verb.

*Alexander **ate** all the chocolate bars.*

*Alexander **grabbed** all the chocolate bars.*

*Alexander **hated** all the chocolate bars.*

*Alexander **will eat** all the chocolate bars.*

*Alexander **eats** all the chocolate bars.*

*Alexander **has eaten** all the chocolate bars.*

Discuss all the different meanings that this creates. Children should now be in a position to write their own versions of this changing sentence.

As an extension to this activity, you could try adding adverbs. Does a different position affect the meaning of the sentence?

*Alexander **quickly** ate all the chocolate bars.*

***Quickly,** Alexander ate all the chocolate bars.*

*Alexander ate all the chocolate bars **quickly**.*

4. Sentence-level work – Year 5

Objective: To investigate clauses through understanding how clauses are connected.

Have on the screen/IWB some examples of jumbled sentences, that is sentences in which the main and subordinate clauses do not match.

> *Walking slowly along the road Libby finally forced herself out of bed.*
>
> *When Mum shouted upstairs James suddenly heard the hoot of a car behind him.*

Discuss these sentences and demonstrate how, using 'drag and drop' or 'cut and paste', they can be sorted out.

Try moving the subordinate clause to a different position in the sentence and discuss any changes to the meaning that this causes.

> *Walking slowly along the road James suddenly heard the hoot of a car behind him.*
> *James suddenly heard the hoot of a car behind him, walking slowly along the road.*

Children can then be asked to construct their complex sentences using this pattern, and experiment with different clause positioning.

Group work with word processors

There are many other ways in which on-screen activities can support shared writing at word and sentence levels and even whole-text work. Some of these include asking groups of children to:

- identify different categories of words, e.g. highlighting all nouns pink, all pronouns green, etc.;
- alter existing text using, for example, alternative adjectives, verbs, synonyms, etc. and using different coloured text for any changes;
- use 'cut and paste' to reinstate the correct order of a short story in which the order of the paragraphs has been changed;
- use the 'find and replace' function to replace overused words such as 'said' and 'nice';
- use the 'find' function on its own to search for common spelling patterns, e.g. all words ending in 'ing' or containing 'ea'.

Desktop publishing

The past 30 years have seen the dramatic growth of the use of computer systems for desktop publishing, that is the production of books, journals, newspapers and leaflets by writers themselves, without the intermediate stage of specialist typesetting. The technology to make this possible had a vast impact in the commercial world, especially on those sections of the workforce such as print workers whose skills were thereby made redundant.

Schools were quick to see the potential of desktop publishing as a vehicle for the production of their children's work. Desktop publishing can be seen as providing extra facilities for the output of children's work and has some features that make it particularly useful for realistic writing formats. One of the most important of these is the 'cut and paste' facility. By using this, sections of pages can be electronically lifted from one place and moved or copied to another. This is an extension of the provisionality of writing mentioned earlier. Anything children produce can always be changed in a number of ways, and they quickly grasp the power of this and experiment with format.

Another feature that desktop publishing makes possible is the combining of text and pictures. Users can grab pictures from camcorders and digital cameras and import these into the desktop publishing environment. Once under the control of the software, these pictures can be manipulated in various ways: stretched, enlarged, reduced, rotated, reversed, chopped into pieces and overlaid or interspersed with text. This is a facility of immense potential, which enables users to produce pages that are almost indistinguishable from those of commercial products.

One group of Year 5 pupils used their class digital camera to take pictures of some toys. These pictures were then imported into Word to illustrate a story that they had written collaboratively for the Year 2 class in their school. One page from this story is given in Figure 11.2.

The dragon roared as the brave knight charged across the castle drawbridge.

Figure 11.2   Part of a desktop published story

THE BIGGER PICTURE   THE BIGGER PICTURE   **THE BIGGER PICTURE**   THE BIGGER PICTURE

When you are planning to use desktop publishing, remember that it is not just useful for literacy texts but also to publish children's work in other subjects, for example the results of investigations in maths, science and PE, and research projects in geography and history.

Hypertexts

Electronic technology also makes possible a kind of writing that could not be done using traditional print and paper methods. We have all become very familiar, through our use of the internet, with the texts that characterise the world wide web – hypertexts. Traditional texts are usually designed to be read in one way. They are linear, with a well-defined start and a well-defined end. Hypertexts, on the other hand, are designed to be non-sequential. By using links, the reader can navigate to different parts of the text and the sequence in which the text is read is determined by the reader. The reader is put in control of their own reading of the text to a greater extent and passive reading is all but impossible.

This active involvement with a text's shape and meaning blurs the traditional distinction between reader and writer, but it does, in turn, make the job of the reader more complex. Not only does the reader have to make active decisions about how to proceed through a hypertext, but they also have to contend with a range of alternative textual material. Readers may be familiar with pictures and diagrams in traditional texts, but hypertexts, being computer-based, can also include segments of audio, video and other moving graphics, all of which contribute some extra potential meaning to a text.

If the reading of hypertexts poses extra problems for the reader, then the writing of successful hypertexts also poses difficulties for the writer, but involving pupils in creating their own websites, for example, can significantly enhance their abilities to read critically and effectively the new texts they are presented with through ICT.

As a first step to this, many teachers offer pupils the chance to design and write their own web pages. Figure 11.3 shows the page designed by eight-year-old Marisa to display her poem about Winter.

Winter Silhouette

By Marisa

Snowball fights

Neatly pack snowballs

Oh, everybody likes to play in the snow.

Wow! the snow is deep.

Boy the snow is feeing soft.

And

Lovely to

Look at.

Figure 11.3   Marisa's web page

This page was designed in a specialised web page creation program and, in addition to the skills demanded in the writing of traditional text, it required Marisa to:

- scan and save her winter picture;
- embed this picture electronically within her poem;
- locate a snowflake picture on the internet and embed this within the poem;
- select a suitable font for her poem;
- decide on a layout for the poem and implement this within the software package;
- publish her poem to her class website.

These are all complex skills and there are many adults, accomplished in other aspects of writing, who would not have a clue how to start with any of them.

However, that is not all there is to website design which, principally, involves the creation of hypertexts. Like conventional writing, a hypertext requires planning. A collection of pages randomly linked together provides neither pleasure nor enlightenment for the reader. Nor will it allow the writer to transmit all their ideas fully to the reader. In planning a conventional essay, the writer builds a linear trail for the reader: the points should follow each other in a straight and logical line; but a genuine hypertext involves planning spatially and thinking about which pages (or parts of pages) should be linked to each other or to external sources. A useful way of beginning to create this kind of text is to draft out on paper an outline of how the text might develop. You can encourage pupils to do this graphically by drawing their main introductory screen in the middle of a large page, and then sketching out the subsidiary pages and indicating the links by arrows. They can then draw on a separate sheet the design for each page as a storyboard.

Hypertext is a mixed medium. It can involve varying fonts, sizes and colours. It can also use graphic elements such as photographs, clip art, scanned drawings, etc. Even more importantly, the writer needs to think about breaking up the page into blocks of text, each of which relates to other blocks but which could, potentially, stand by itself.

In hypertext, writers compose small units of text and link them together. On the one hand, this eases the stress of writing, allowing the writer to work on discrete units, rather than a single long text. On the other hand, it means that hypertext writers need to pay particular attention to 'arrivals' and 'departures' – the first sentences their readers encounter in arriving at a text block and the last sentences they encounter as they leave. Each text block, of whatever length, needs to be shaped like a mini-essay, with a beginning, a middle and an end.

This is not the place to give a full analysis of the difficulties of writing readable hypertext, but hopefully enough points have been raised to suggest that this medium for writing brings with it its own challenges and problems. Writing is no longer quite the same process, and in that fact lies much of the excitement of the medium.

EMBEDDING ICT EMBEDDING ICT EMBEDDING ICT EMBEDDING ICT EMBEDDING ICT

When you are using ICT with your class, you must always be aware of safety protocols and follow the school's internet safety policy, especially when setting research tasks as an independent task or for homework. This is a key safeguarding issue, so it is worth sending a reminder home to parents to encourage them to supervise their children's browsing of sites and to set appropriate parental controls to block unsuitable sites and materials.

Social networking technologies

There are many new varieties of electronic text and forms of communication emerging as technology develops. Blogs, instant messaging, mobile phone texting, wikis, tweets and social networking sites provide ever-expanding types of electronic text and ways of keeping in touch. Their use is only just beginning to be explored in educational contexts and there has been concern about privacy and about who can access information outside the person's chosen contacts. One of the risks is that, without hearing or seeing the other person, you cannot really identify him/her or know if their motivation for making contact is innocent. Social networking can also provide a forum for 'cyberbullying'. This is a term used to describe the use of the internet or mobile phones to harass others. It is very upsetting for victims because there is no escape. Incidents can take place at all times of day or night, and at any location, even within the 'safety' of the home. There is guidance for schools on managing the issue, in the document *Safe to learn: embedding anti-bullying work in schools – Cyber bullying* (published 2007, and available via www.teachernet.gov.uk).

EMBEDDING ICT EMBEDDING ICT EMBEDDING ICT EMBEDDING ICT EMBEDDING ICT

Just as you must protect and safeguard the children in your care, so you must also take care over your own privacy. When 'off duty', you may want to keep in touch with friends using social networking sites. Be careful what information you share on these, including any photographs of your social life. Remember that children and parents may look you up! It is not appropriate to accept them as friends on such sites. It is important to follow all relevant guidelines on communicating with children and their parents/carers, for example on using your own personal mobile phone, including those guidelines issued by your school, the local authority or nationally. The Child Exploitation and Online Protection (CEOP) Centre is a useful resource for guidance on cyberbullying, and the safe use of social networking sites and the internet. It has materials suitable for children of different ages and advice for parents and carers and for professionals working with children and young people. See their website (www.ceop.police.uk) for further details.

A SUMMARY OF **KEY POINTS**

➢ Literacy now includes digital literacy – the reading and writing of electronic texts – as well as the skills of working with paper-based texts.

➢ The reading and writing of electronic texts is not the same as the reading and writing of paper-based texts; this means that we need different teaching approaches to these texts.

➢ Accessing electronic versions of books helps children's reading to progress.

➢ There is a wealth of electronic information texts but children need active reading strategies to use these effectively.

➢ Directed activities relating to texts (DARTs) can help children to interact purposefully with electronic texts.

➢ Writing electronically has benefits for shared and independent writing.

➢ Desktop publishing and hypertexts give valuable opportunities for children to present their work in a range of ways.

M-LEVEL EXTENSION > > M-LEVEL EXTENSION > > M-LEVEL EXTENSION

Teachers have varying views on the validity of using electronic sources such as those referred to above in the classroom. Some believe that it is important to use and value all opportunities for children to read and write electronic texts; others that 'text speak' encourages poor grammar and creates bad habits such as lack of punctuation and use of non-standard spellings. Talk to colleagues about this issue to seek their views, and source research on both sides of the debate. What do you think is the way forward?

Now have a look at the work of Clare Wood and her colleagues at Coventry University (*Wood et al.*, 2013), who suggest from their research that, far from making children's reading and writing worse, the use of text messaging can actually improve it.

FURTHER READING FURTHER READING FURTHER READING FURTHER READING

DfE (2013) *Teachers' Standards*. London: DfE. (https://www.gov.uk/government/uploads/system/uploads/attachment_data/file/208682/Teachers__Standards_2013.pdf)

Medwell, J. (1996) 'Talking books and reading', *Reading*, vol. 30(1), pp. 41–6.

Medwell, J. (1998) 'The talking books project: some further insights into the use of talking books to develop reading', *Reading*, vol. 32(1), pp. 3–9.

Ofcom (Office of Communications) (2006) *Media Literacy Audit: Report on media literacy amongst children*. Available at http://stakeholders.ofcom.org.uk/market-data-research/other/media-literacy/archive/medlitpub/medlitpubrss/children/

Wood, C., Kemp, N. and Plester, B. (2013) *Text Messaging and Literacy: The Evidence*. London: Routledge.

Wray, D. and Medwell, J. (2003) *Easiteach Literacy: Content Pack*. Abingdon: Research Machines.

12
Including all children

TEACHERS' STANDARDS

A teacher must:

1. **Set high expectations which inspire, motivate and challenge pupils**

   - **set goals that stretch and challenge pupils of all backgrounds, abilities and dispositions**

2. **Promote good progress and outcomes by pupils**

   - **be accountable for pupils' attainment, progress and outcomes**

5. **Adapt teaching to respond to the strengths and needs of all pupils**

   - **know when and how to differentiate appropriately, using approaches which enable pupils to be taught effectively**

   - **have a secure understanding of how a range of factors can inhibit pupils' ability to learn, and how best to overcome these**

   - **demonstrate an awareness of the physical, social and intellectual development of children, and know how to adapt teaching to support pupils' education at different stages of development**

   - **have a clear understanding of the needs of all pupils, including those with special educational needs; those of high ability; those with English as an additional language; those with disabilities; and be able to use and evaluate distinctive teaching approaches to engage and support them.**

Introduction

Schools and teachers have a responsibility to provide equality of opportunity for all children – boys and girls, children with additional and special educational needs, children with disabilities, children from different social and cultural backgrounds, children from different ethnic groups (including travellers, refugees and asylum seekers), those from diverse linguistic backgrounds and vulnerable children and groups, including those who are looked-after children (by the local authority, foster carers or by members of their extended family). This includes equality of opportunity in their language and literacy learning (reading, writing, speaking and listening). In this chapter, we consider some of the key points relating to the task of including all children.

PRACTICAL TASK PRACTICAL TASK **PRACTICAL TASK** PRACTICAL TASK **PRACTICAL TASK**

The schools in which you teach should have policies for the inclusion of:

- children with special educational needs (SEN) and/or disabilities (SEND), including the able, gifted and talented;

- children with English as an additional language (EAL);
- looked-after children (LAC).

All schools will have an inclusion leader or SEND co-ordinator and they may have other staff responsible for other aspects of inclusion, for example, home/school support workers. This will not be the only additional staffing. The majority of children with special educational needs receive the teaching they need from classroom teachers in mainstream schools. Teaching or learning support assistants provide support to teachers in the classroom. A proportion of these will provide support for children with special educational needs as well as assisting the class teacher with day-to-day support.

There may be teaching or learning support assistants for particular children and specialist language teachers for children with EAL or for traveller education, as well as adults who can translate community languages.

It is very important that you discuss roles with these staff in schools so that you understand exactly how they work in class and out of formal learning situations. You also need to familiarise yourself with all relevant school policies, including anti-discriminatory policies for gender, culture, religion, sexual orientation, race and so on.

Planning for children with SEN

Some children in any class will be working significantly below the level of their class or group and this presents you with some challenges when designing meaningful literacy tasks for whole classes, groups and individuals. In most cases, the range of achievement will be such that you will use general differentiation techniques in your planning to ensure the literacy tasks meet the needs of your children. The focus in the *Draft SEN Code of Practice* (2014) is on working co-operatively with parents and children to understand and meet their needs. For the majority of children with SEN or disabilities, literacy needs can be met through a combination of well-differentiated teaching and school-based planning for support.

There are a number of ways that you might differentiate literacy learning provision for children in your class, including the wide range of abilities found in most classes and the needs of most children with SEN. These include the following.

- *Presentation* – planning to use a variety of media to present ideas, offering vocabulary or extra diagrams to those who need more support. Writing frames might be a form of presentation to help writers who need extra support, where more confident writers do not require such support.
- *Content* – selecting appropriately so that there is content that suits most children with additional content available to some. This might mean some children completing twelve comprehension questions where others complete ten.
- *Resources* – use resources that support children's needs such as writing frames or word banks for poor spellers. For children with EAL, you might need to ensure that target vocabulary is available in a written form.
- *Grouping* – grouping (or pairing) children of similar ability for targeted support or pairing with a more able child, teaching assistant (TA) or language support teacher.
- *Task* – matching tasks to children's abilities. This can mean different tasks for different children. It is sometimes a good idea to offer different tasks that address the same objectives to different children so that they can achieve success.

- *Support* – offering additional adult or peer assistance, from a TA, language support teacher or more experienced child.
- *Time* – giving more or less time to complete a given task can make the task more suitable to the particular children.

EMBEDDING ICT EMBEDDING ICT **EMBEDDING ICT** EMBEDDING ICT **EMBEDDING ICT**

ICT can be used for all types of differentiation, including providing a range of methods to support the drafting process in writing and how the finished piece of work is published, ways of varying the actual content of the task and producing resources that support children's particular needs. It is also integral in many targeted interventions, in providing motivating programs for practising skills and in diagnostic and formative assessment. For more on assessing English, see Chapter 14.

In literacy teaching, there is a great advantage in choosing to set learning objectives for all children. This allows children with SEND or EAL to work at the same level as the other children (possibly with additional support) so that they can learn from the demonstrations and models in whole-class or group sessions. In discussion activities, shared or guided reading and writing activities, children may learn as much from the performance of other children as they do from direct teaching by the teacher. If children always work in small groups or in one-to-one provision outside the classroom, they will miss many of the speaking, listening, reading and writing activities which are shared as a class. This means they will miss experience not only of those texts but of the models of how teachers and children tackle them. Where children have additional support with language or other special needs, it may be beneficial to include this in class lessons.

However, literacy learning objectives should be right for each child at each stage of their learning and development. If, with appropriate access strategies and support, a child cannot work towards the same learning objective as the rest of the class, you may want to track back to an earlier objective. You may also want to discuss this child's progress with the SENCO, to ensure you are making the most of the options available to you within the school provision.

The first step in the cycle of planning for individual children or groups of children is assessment evidence. This will include not only tests and more formal assessments but also informed observation and formative assessment (assessment for learning), which is based on knowledge of the priorities for these children. This means knowing the current learning targets of each child and balancing them with the class targets. For most of the time, it will be appropriate for children to work on objectives that are similar and related to those for the whole class, with the learning provision differentiated for their needs. However, at other times you will also have to consider whether the children have other priority needs that are central to their learning, for example a need to concentrate on some key skills, which mean they have specific, different, learning objectives from the rest of the class. It may be, for instance, that some children in your Year 1 class have an identified need to learn the key grapheme–phoneme correspondences and that they undertake additional phonics group work led by a teaching assistant. This is such an important priority that it might be undertaken at a time when others in the class are doing a different activity.

In your planning for spoken language and literacy you will need to include oversight and integration of any provision or programmes in school which are available to support the language or literacy skills of children in your class, even where these are planned to work for groups of children across classes. If children who need this extreme form of differentiated provision can be helped to 'catch up' with their peers, and supported to maintain that progress, they will achieve much better than if they are left to struggle.

In a few cases children in your class may have an Education, Health and Care (EHC) plan, which is accompanied by additional provision specific to that child. This may mean additional assistance with some aspects of learning through interventions such as inclusion in support groups, additional intervention such as speech and language therapy or one-to-one support in the classroom. Where a child has an EHC plan, you will work with the school SEN co-ordinator (SENCO) to ensure you meet the child's language and literacy needs and to maintain close contact with parents and with the child themselves, so there is a clear, shared understanding of how you are supporting this child's language and literacy within and outside the classroom.

In many classes you will encounter the 5–10 per cent of children classed as gifted in English. These children will not always be those performing at the highest levels in the class. However, they, like the children who are working well above the overall level of their class or group, will benefit from additional planning that can:

- add breadth (for example, enrichment through a broader range of content, tasks and resources);
- increase depth (for example, extension through complexity);
- accelerate the pace of learning by tracking forward to future objectives within or across key stages.

Your skills for teaching literacy and English to children with SEN and/or disabilities are important. You should review your skills and address any issues you feel unsure about to make sure you can teach all learners.

Key skills include:

- planning and teaching for inclusion and access to the English curriculum. This will mean making any necessary adjustments to give children with SEND the opportunities their peers experience. This might include recording spoken instructions, enlarged and simplified texts, provision of time, additional support and all the differentiation strategies discussed above;
- behaviour management, and an awareness of the emotional and mental health needs of pupils (to build their self-esteem as learners). Behaviour and mental health issues do not mean children are less able to learn English. However, if these issues are not addressed properly, they can throw up barriers to effective learning. The behaviour of your class of children and your relationships with individuals make a real difference to your effectiveness as a literacy teacher.
- assessment for learning (learning skills). This is the basis of your differentiation and focused teaching. If you find yourself concerned with the literacy achievement of individuals, despite careful planning, differentiation and support, you should seek the advice of the SENCO.
- an understanding of when professional advice is needed and where to find it. Know the personnel in your school and understand their roles. There are complex areas of SEN you may not be equipped to recognise and your SENCO will help you to keep the records and access the expertise of professionals who can help you.

Planning for children with EAL

Children learning EAL must be supported to access curriculum content while also developing cognitive and academic language within whole-class, group and independent contexts.

With the exception of children learning EAL who also have learning difficulties, it is critical to maintain a level of cognitive challenge consistent with that of the rest of the class.

RESEARCH SUMMARY   RESEARCH SUMMARY   **RESEARCH SUMMARY**   RESEARCH SUMMARY

The work of Cummins (2000) and that of Collier and Thomas (1998) has been central in developing the theory, principles and practice of language and learning of young bilingual learners. They refer to the work of Vygotsky (socially constructed knowledge), Bruner and Maslow (self-actualisation) to point out that young learners are affected by attitudes towards them, their culture, language, ethnicity and religion in and out of school. It is not only cognitive and academic development that will impact on their language development, but also their cultural and social experiences. Supporting young bilinguals means considering all these aspects of their experience.

Cummins has developed models of the relationship between language development and the cognitive and academic domain. He used the metaphor of an iceberg to illustrate these ideas. At the tip of the iceberg, and easily identified, is the child's 'Basic Interpersonal Communicative Skill' (BICS). Less obvious is the base of the iceberg, the 'Cognitive and Academic Language Proficiency' (CALP). The ability to use this language for academic purposes and cognitive development is the key to realising academic potential.

Children who are or have become conversationally fluent in English (BICS) will continue to require explicit attention to the development of the academic language associated with the subject (CALP) and this includes the language of literacy, which is highly abstract and symbolic. Your literacy planning should identify the language demands of the objectives and associated activities. Making sure that EAL learners know and can use the language demanded by the curriculum content of the unit or lesson then becomes an additional objective.

To identify the language demands of a task, teachers and practitioners must consider the language children will need to understand in order to access an activity. This should take account of the language children require to be able to produce, either orally or written, to demonstrate success in achieving the learning intentions. A simple start is to ensure that you begin each lesson by explaining the key vocabulary being used and offer EAL pupils a visual version of a glossary of terms to put into their books.

The development of language is not the only aspect of EAL provision that supports children's literacy learning in school. The ethos of the school, class and lessons is also central in creating a sense of belonging. Children's ethnic, religious, social and cultural backgrounds should be represented across the curriculum so that the school truly represents the community it serves and welcomes its members. Ideally, children should see staff from their background in school and parents and carers should be welcomed and included in school life. Make sure that you carry out some basic research into the cultural and personal backgrounds of the EAL pupils in your class.

RESEARCH SUMMARY   RESEARCH SUMMARY   **RESEARCH SUMMARY**   RESEARCH SUMMARY

In a very famous study, Jane Elliott (1968) told her class of nine-year-olds that blue-eyed children were better than brown-eyed children in order to teach children how it would feel to suffer discrimination. She created a negative stereotype by characterising the behaviour of the brown-eyed children as 'slow', badly behaved, etc. The achievement of the brown-eyed children was affected immediately and the children themselves said it was because they felt bad about themselves. This is an experiment to remember! (You can watch Elliott's original video on YouTube at http://www.youtube.com/watch?v=D0qKDiq1fNw and see some commentary about it at http://www.youtube.com/watch?v=Hqp6GnYqljQ)

Including children in the school extends to your English teaching. You will need to consider how language is represented in class, what languages are spoken and your choice of texts. Displays and the use of languages in these displays should reflect the cultural and linguistic diversity in school.

Find out the languages spoken by the children in your class so that you can show places in the world where these languages are spoken, include a sentence or two in a display, and just know a few facts about the language.

Consider the texts you choose for your class: to read to them and to use for shared and guided reading and writing.

The range of **fiction** should include:

- stories including British-born characters from various ethnic, cultural and religious backgrounds;
- stories set in children's heritage countries;
- traditional stories from children's cultures;
- dual-language books;
- poetry and drama from a range of cultures;
- biographies of people from diverse backgrounds who have made a great contribution to society;
- stories exploring discrimination, isolation, racism, friendship, change, living in two cultures, etc.

The range of **non-fiction** should include texts which:

- teach about bias, stereotyping, racism, sectarianism and human rights;
- emphasise the achievements and contributions of people from a range of ethnic backgrounds;
- explore global development issues past and present, and social and economic issues of migration and displacement, etc.

These are English teaching issues because you will use these texts for your literacy teaching, for practising literacy skills and also for teaching across the curriculum.

You should also consider your own use of language very carefully to meet the needs of your EAL pupils. Sometimes you may need to moderate your speed of delivery to meet the needs of these pupils. Make sure that you repeat and summarise instructions and requests, but be careful not to vary your language too much when you repeat yourself. This can inadvertently pose a whole new set of comprehension challenges which throw up barriers for the EAL pupils. Wherever possible give practical demonstrations to your pupils, including your pupils with EAL. Supporting your words with actions is a highly effective way of conveying a message to them. It is also useful to use drama and action-based tasks with your class, including your EAL pupils, to give them chances to achieve in ways which do not offer linguistic challenges. Every pupil with EAL is different, has a different language background and learning experience, so there is no 'one size fits all' provision for pupils with EAL. You must show your pupils with EAL that you have high expectations for them, and that you will support them to meet those expectations.

LIVERPOOL JOHN MOORES UNIVERSITY
LEARNING SERVICES

THE BIGGER PICTURE   THE BIGGER PICTURE   **THE BIGGER PICTURE**   THE BIGGER PICTURE

When you are planning for the inclusion of all children, remember that there are sources of advice within your school (class teachers and teaching or learning support assistants who work with the children, and the inclusion leader or special educational needs co-ordinator) and from local authority services (such as those for children with additional and special educational needs, for those with English as an additional language and for traveller and minority ethnic children).

A SUMMARY OF **KEY POINTS**

➤ Schools and teachers are required to provide equality of opportunity for all children.

➤ The learning needs of most children should be met through high quality teaching for the class.

➤ There are a number of ways that you might differentiate literacy learning provision for children through presentation, content, resources, grouping, task, support and time.

➤ Seek SENCO advice in supporting the additional needs of children with EHC plans.

➤ Know, celebrate and include the range of languages spoken by children in your class.

➤ Differentiate to support children with Cognitive and Academic Language Proficiency (CALP) so that children with EAL can achieve their academic potential.

M-LEVEL EXTENSION   > >   M-LEVEL EXTENSION   > >   M-LEVEL EXTENSION

When you encounter a school placement, make a point of finding out how the school and/or teacher handles the issue of the inclusion of children with a variety of distinctive needs and characteristics. Key questions to answer are:

- Is the inclusion merely social (children are taught in the same physical space but in fact they follow a quite different curriculum) or educational (efforts are made to ensure all children are working to the same learning goals)?
- How is differentiation planned and evaluated?
- How does the teacher maintain high expectations for all the children in their care?

FURTHER READING   FURTHER READING   FURTHER READING   FURTHER READING

Conteh, J. (2012) *Teaching Bilingual and EAL Learners in Primary Schools*, London: Learning Matters SAGE.

Cummins, J. (2000) *Language, Power and Pedagogy: Bilingual Children in the Crossfire*. Clevedon: Multilingual Matters.

DCSF (2008) *New Arrivals Excellence Programme CPD Modules.* Nottingham: DCSF. (http://webarchive.nationalarchives.gov.uk/20130903170901/http://media.education.gov.uk/assets/files/pdf/n/new%20arrivals%20excellence%20programme%20continuing%20professional%20development%20modules.pdf)

DfE (2013) *The National Curriculum in England.* London: DfE. (https://www.gov.uk/dfe/nationalcurriculum)

DfE (2013) *The 2014 National Curriculum.* London: DfE. (https://www.gov.uk/government/collections/national-curriculum)

DfE (2013) *Teachers' Standards*. London: DfE. (https://www.gov.uk/government/uploads/system/uploads/attachment_data/file/208682/Teachers__Standards_2013.pdf)

DfE (2014) *Draft SEN Code of Practice: for 0 to 25 years*. London: DfE. (https://www.gov.uk/government/uploads/system/uploads/attachment_data/file/251839/Draft_SEN_Code_of_Practice_-_statutory_guidance.pdf)

Gravelle, M. (ed.) (2010) *Planning for Bilingual Learners: An inclusive curriculum*. Stoke-on-Trent: Trentham Books.

Leung, C., Creese, A. and NALDIC (2010) *English as an Additional Language: A Guide for Teachers working with linguistic minority pupils*. London: Sage.

Pim, C. (2012) *100 Ideas for Supporting Learners with EAL*. London: Continuum.

PNS (2006) *Keys to Learning in Literacy and Mathematics*. London: DfES.

PNS (2006) *Learning and Teaching for Bi-lingual Children in the Primary Years*. London: DfES.

Rose, R. (2009) *Identifying and Teaching Children and Young People with Dyslexia and Literacy Difficulties*. Nottingham: DCSF. (http://webarchive.nationalarchives.gov.uk/20130401151715/https://www.education.gov.uk/publications/eOrderingDownload/00659-2009DOM-EN.pdf)

The following documents were originally produced by the DfE but are now available elsewhere:

- *A Language in Common* (2000): http://www.naldic.org.uk/Resources/NALDIC/Teaching%20and%20Learning/1847210732.pdf
- *Marking Progress* (2005): http://dera.ioe.ac.uk/5743/1/markingprogress.pdf
- *Supporting Children Learning English as an Additional Language* (2007): http://www.foundationyears.org.uk/wp-content/uploads/2011/10/Supporting_Children_English_2nd_Language.pdf
- *English as an Additional Language and SEN* (2009): http://www.naldic.org.uk/Resources/NALDIC/Teaching%20and%20Learning/Documents/eal-sen-trainingfile.pdf

13
Organising and resourcing English at Key Stages 1 and 2

TEACHERS' STANDARDS

A teacher must:

1. Set high expectations which inspire, motivate and challenge pupils

    *   establish a safe and stimulating environment for pupils, rooted in mutual respect

2. Promote good progress and outcomes by pupils

    *   demonstrate knowledge and understanding of how pupils learn and how this impacts on teaching

3. Demonstrate good subject and curriculum knowledge

    *   have a secure knowledge of the relevant subject(s) and curriculum areas, foster and maintain pupils' interest in the subject, and address misunderstandings
    *   demonstrate a critical understanding of developments in the subject and curriculum areas, and promote the value of scholarship
    *   demonstrate an understanding of and take responsibility for promoting high standards of literacy, articulacy and the correct use of standard English, whatever the teacher's specialist subject

4. Plan and teach well structured lessons

    *   impart knowledge and develop understanding through effective use of lesson time

5. Adapt teaching to respond to the strengths and needs of all pupils

    *   know when and how to differentiate appropriately, using approaches which enable pupils to be taught effectively
    *   have a secure understanding of how a range of factors can inhibit pupils' ability to learn, and how best to overcome these
    *   demonstrate an awareness of the physical, social and intellectual development of children, and know how to adapt teaching to support pupils' education at different stages of development

8. Fulfil wider professional responsibilities

    *   make a positive contribution to the wider life and ethos of the school
    *   develop effective professional relationships with colleagues, knowing how and when to draw on advice and specialist support
    *   deploy support staff effectively

Introduction

Organisation for the English curriculum is about making sure that children have the most effective environment for their language and literacy learning, both inside and outside literacy sessions and in the wider context of the teaching of English. This means making key decisions about the way you organise your classroom, and being creative and flexible in your planning, so that you can set up the best possible arrangements for learning. Successful organisation is, however, about more than planning appropriate lessons. It is about sharing your enthusiasm for English by creating a classroom in which speaking, listening, reading and writing are an enriching part of children's everyday school life.

This chapter aims to help you to make decisions about the use of space, time and resources, and offers you ways of thinking about how you can organise groups of children for different aspects of English teaching at Key Stages 1 and 2. You can implement ideas imaginatively in any classroom, whether you teach in an old Victorian building or a modern open-plan unit. The ideas are also applicable to classrooms for all ages of primary children. You can decide how to vary the content of activities so that they are appropriate for your particular class.

The chapter begins by discussing the general organisation of the classroom to support literacy learning, taking account of the available space, the organisation of time, and the use of other adults in the classroom. It then focuses specifically on the organisation and resourcing of the classroom for the teaching and learning of speaking and listening, reading and writing.

Organising the classroom space

Planning an exciting and stimulating school and classroom environment that supports and extends opportunities for English is a challenge. Many of us have seen large unpromising Victorian school buildings, whose walls and classrooms were never designed with displays or group work in mind. With some imagination, these can be transformed into language-rich, colourful and animated environments by teachers and children with energy and vision.

Each school year, teachers have the luxury of starting afresh, transforming their empty classrooms into environments that promote learning and reflect the curriculum back to the children. It is often helpful to create an outline of what you want. Bear in mind that the environment is for children to use and to learn in. They should feel at ease when they are reading, writing, discussing, exploring, touching, listening, asking questions, solving problems and making decisions. Getting children interested in their environment also means helping them to take responsibility for feeding pets, watering plants and tidying displays, so that they develop a pride in and sense of ownership over their classroom. Children can devise a simple rota system showing the monitors for the week and listing the duties involved. Groups of children can work together drawing up instruction sheets that show how often plants should be watered and how much light they need. Displays may need information sheets and labels that could be researched and written by children during literacy group activities.

When you take up your first post you may find it useful to make a plan of your room, initially by marking in those fixtures that are permanent. Using this bare outline, you can experiment, deciding where you want particular areas that are concerned with language and literacy learning. These include an area for shared activities, a library or book corner, a listening area, a writing area and a role-play drama area. Some of these areas may already be designated in your room; you will not be able to move carpets, shelving and pinboards; but there are nevertheless things you can do to organise sensibly, for example:

- put noisy activities away from the library and listening areas;
- cordon off quiet areas with dividers made from moveable bookshelves or trolleys;
- check that the listening area is close to plug sockets and has space for a table and chairs;
- check that your computer area is close to plug sockets and away from messy activities such as sand and water play and art work;
- make sure that all areas can be used as active working spaces as well as for displays by providing appropriate furniture.

Remember that you can change environments that you have developed at the start of the year in response to the needs of the children and the curriculum. You can also exchange resources with other teachers in your age phase. Moveable furniture might at one time provide facilities for group work and at another time be used for individual, group or whole-class activities.

THE BIGGER PICTURE   THE BIGGER PICTURE   THE BIGGER PICTURE   THE BIGGER PICTURE

When you are planning to reorganise your classroom, keep in mind the requirements of health and safety (of both children and adults, including your own!). Take advice from other teachers and senior staff, and the site manager or caretaker. Also, bear in mind the safeguarding agenda, for example don't cover external or corridor windows and glass panels in doors completely with displays or posters. It is considered safer for children to have sightlines available, and it is also in your best interests as it reduces the possibility of any misunderstanding or false allegations. Always adhere to school policies in these areas.

A community space for the class

Many primary classrooms have a carpeted area where children can sit as a group. Identify the community area in your classroom and cordon it off if possible with bookshelves and trolleys. This will mark it out as a visibly important meeting place for the class and a focus of shared activity, including whole-class and plenary work in literacy sessions. Remember that even in the best organised classrooms, chairs and tables have a habit of moving onto the edge of the carpeted area and the community space can get smaller and smaller – so make sure it is always there to be used.

If your room is particularly small, you might not be able to designate part of the area for shared activities, and pupils might have to remain seated at their tables during whole-class shared literacy activities and at other shared times. If this is the case, you will need to ensure that all the children can see the texts you use. Enlarge them on a computer or use your interactive whiteboard.

The role-play/playspace area

How you set this area up will depend on the age and experience of the children. Many Key Stage 1 classrooms have an area set aside for role-play. Printed texts can be put in here too so that children can incorporate them into their play (e.g. magazines, telephone directories, comics, calendars, recipe books – the kinds of print that children are likely to see around them, both in English and in the child's first language if this is not English. (Ask parents to bring in examples of the kinds of print their child sees and uses at home.) Children can use this area for writing, so make notebooks and paper available for messages and shopping lists, and provide calendars to write on and forms that can be completed.

Some of the most successful and lively role-play areas are set up by the children as a result of something they have become involved in – a café, a railway station, a shop, or a scene from a book the class has particularly enjoyed or has studied as a literacy text. Changing the setting gives opportunities for you to introduce new kinds of language and print for children to read and write; for example, in a railway station they can design and make signs, labels, tickets and timetables. The café scenario gives opportunities for reading and generating signs, menus, order forms and recipes. Businesses and supermarkets are often generous in providing schools with forms, advertisements, price lists and so on. If appropriate, you can put computers, typewriters and telephones in this area to encourage different forms of writing and talking. Sometimes, the role-play theme can extend across the whole classroom so that it becomes transformed into a hospital or a supermarket. Children can be instrumental in this transformation, using layout sheets to design each element and taking responsibility for its co-ordination.

It is less likely that such transformations will take place at Key Stage 2, but as part of the literacy activities you can organise older children to write their own play scripts or research areas of interest. These can be linked with visits to museums or heritage centres. Use drama sessions too so that the children can act out their ideas or carry out group role-play.

Puppets

A selection of different puppets, either bought or homemade, will encourage imaginative play and creative language use based on children's own experiences or their own retellings of favourite stories. Key Stage 2 children can use puppets to act out plays you have read during the literacy session and rehearse the scenes during independent group work. Once children are familiar with the format of such texts, encourage them to write their own plays during guided writing, performing them during shared reading or the plenary session of the literacy lesson. You do not need elaborate puppet theatres – children can kneel behind a table with a curtain draped in front if they want to perform their play. Simple puppet sets can be made with stick puppets inside a cardboard box with slits up each side.

Displaying some of the puppets will tempt children to pick them up and use them, and in many classrooms they become a favourite extension activity. Attractive containers clearly labelled with the names of the characters or puppets stored inside, together with copies of favourite books, are also popular. Children do like to create their own characters as well, so provide appropriate materials to enable fresh puppets to be made. You can quickly and easily produce shadow puppets and scenery with the aid of an overhead projector.

Storysacks

These consist of large cloth bags containing a picture-story book with all kinds of support materials – soft toys for the main characters in the book, props to illustrate the theme or the scenery, an appropriate non-fiction book relating to the story (for example, The Three Bears' storysack would contain an information book about bears). The sack will also contain an audio-tape of the story and a language game based on the story. Storysacks can be professionally produced or homemade.

Displays

Two-dimensional displays are often the first things that children notice in the classroom. Walls covered with bright cheerful paintings and posters or advertisements create a warm and inviting atmosphere. Many of these displays are not only a celebration of the children's achievements but also have an important function in the curriculum. Some of the ways in which displays extend English curriculum activities are as follows.

- *The investigative area*. Many schools set aside a particular place, either in a corridor, entrance hall or classroom, for three-dimensional displays. Teachers encourage children to pick up and examine different items, such as shells, a Victorian collection (e.g. shoes, a top hat, old photos, gloves, and a parasol) and things to smell (e.g. spices, a pomander or a lavender bag). Items like this can relate to a class project or to an area of interest being studied by a small group. Teachers often set such displays up themselves, but there is scope for the children to make contributions and even to set up the display themselves. You can help children to plan the layout of such a display in guided literacy activities, with groups deciding what the contents of the display might be, writing the labels and seeking further information through the internet.
- *Wall displays*. These can consist of posters, information sheets, pictures and photographs, all of which can form the focus for shared reading in literacy lessons. Encourage the children to create their own posters or to produce information sheets using reference books, CD-ROMs and the internet.
- *Teacher and pupil displays*. These might be considered the natural follow-on from the formal wall display. What started as a single poster shared by the whole class can be supplemented by writing and information cards. This activity can begin as guided or independent work in the literacy session, and carry over to other curriculum areas through children's drawings, paintings, databases and charts. Activities such as these have a particular value for speaking and listening because you can encourage children to share their work with the class, and to describe and exchange experiences as part of the plenary session of literacy sessions. These displays do not always have to draw on experience from a conventional text. You could put up an art exhibition. Portraits painted by a variety of artists will provide a centre of interest for the class. Invite the children to make their own comparisons, to write exhibition reviews and to take part in a critics' forum.
- *A class noticeboard*. Use this for up-to-date class news and reports, for example the dinner menu, weather forecast, class news, lost and found, for sale and wanted, job applications around the school, a list of volunteers to help with events, children's birthdays and so on.

Organising time

Deciding how much time to allocate to an activity is never easy, even within a carefully structured literacy session, particularly if the class is new, or the activity is one you have not tried before. Here are some general guidelines.

- Give a group enough time to complete a task satisfactorily. Within the literacy session this means making sure that tasks you set up are either ones that allow for fast but accurate work, or are planned as continuous activities throughout the week.

- Tell the children at the beginning of the activity when the session is going to end, so they can plan. Say something like: 'You've got 20 minutes to do this, then we'll look at the ideas your group has come up with. I'll tell you when you've got five minutes left.'
- Plan extension activities for more experienced groups of learners who are working independently. This will enable you to spend more time supporting a particular group of children during guided activities.
- Resist putting pressure on those who work slowly. Some need more time than others to think and discuss ideas. It is equally important to remember this during the plenary session of the literacy session when you will have to be sensitive to those who have had difficulty in completing a task.
- Find out what suits individual learners. Observe children at work and talk to them about their learning needs. Older children will often be able to tell you how they learn best. Finding out about learning needs means that you are able to plan appropriate group activities for your class and use your teacher-intensive time to best advantage.
- Build in time for groups to complete tasks, either during subsequent literacy sessions or in extended reading or writing time outside literacy lessons. Remember the importance of allowing children to complete pieces of work. They become frustrated and demotivated if their work is unaccountably abandoned because they have run out of time to finish it.
- Plan to use yourself most effectively by deciding in advance which child or group you are going to work with, and what activity you will do with them. This is fundamental to planning for literacy but is also important for other English activities.
- Plan carefully for the whole class, so that the children who you are not working with directly can carry on with tasks that do not need so much input from you. Many children find it difficult to work independently, so it is important that you give clear instructions at the start and monitor the class regularly to forestall interruptions.
- Use classroom helpers to work with other children, ensuring that these adults know exactly what they are expected to do and how you want them to do it.
- Help the children to learn to respect the time you have to work with each group. Say something like: 'I'm going to work with the red group until quarter past eleven. Please don't interrupt me unless it's something very important.'

Working with adults in the classroom to support literacy learning

You might be fortunate enough to have adults working alongside you in the classroom, perhaps a teaching assistant, a parent, a support teacher, or even a student from a local secondary school on work experience. Classroom assistants or nursery nurses who are permanent members of staff may work alongside you on a regular basis. Their role in the classroom will have to be considered as part of a whole-school plan so that they are used effectively and given opportunities for their own professional development. Other adults, such as parent helpers or secondary school students, will not be part of the regular school staff, even though they might be familiar with school routine. You will have to consider their experience and needs when you decide how they can support children's learning. You may be required to show this organisation in your lesson plans.

Some areas where adult helpers can support children's literacy learning are:

- helping an independent or guided group during the literacy session;
- telling or reading a story to a small group of children;
- listening to a child reading individually;

- making audio-recordings of stories for children to listen to;
- making books for children to write their own stories in;
- helping to put together homemade storysacks;
- observing a child for assessment purposes;
- helping children who are using ICT;
- sitting with children in the reading area and talking with them about the books they choose to read at school or at home;
- keeping records of books borrowed from the school library for children to read at home.

Uses of ICT to support the teaching of literacy

Few teachers would say they have sufficient ICT equipment in their classrooms. You might find that you have to share your electronic hardware and software with other classes, even though many schools have a separate computer suite for whole-class use. Whatever your situation, you will find you have to organise carefully to ensure that each child has an opportunity to use the computer for different purposes. Keep a register of computer use. Many schools now provide printers alongside the computer and children can use word processing packages to produce their own books, magazines or class newsletters.

It is not always possible to tell from the packages just what a program can do or even what age it is suitable for, so make your own records, including notes about the levels of difficulty offered and whether the program is best used by one, two or more children at a time. Some adventure games are specifically designed to provoke discussion and develop problem-solving skills. The ICT subject leader in your school will be able to give you more advice.

Information and communications technology (ICT) covers not only computers, but also more conventional electronic systems – TV, radio, audio and video recorders, telephones, fax machines and cameras. You can use all these creatively to support and develop literacy. CD-ROMs are still available in most classrooms. Select those with interesting text, sound, animation, artwork, photographs or video that are motivating for children and that invite them to read and write for a range of purposes.

Several well-known publishers produce audio recordings alongside popular books, read by accomplished actors, with music and other sound effects. Build up a collection of these and store them on the shelves alongside your books. They can provide a valuable independent activity for literacy sessions.

In addition to commercially produced recordings, make your own of popular books. Encourage pupils to make their own recordings too using a variety of sound effects, and include these in your classroom library. Your class might also like to make story tapes for younger children in the school and this gives them an opportunity to read aloud expressively for a real purpose and audience.

Many popular stories are also produced on DVD and blu-ray and these can form part of a school, class or personal collection, giving access to texts that are difficult to read independently. Again, having copies of these available means that children can enjoy them over and over again and borrow them to use at home.

EMBEDDING ICT EMBEDDING ICT **EMBEDDING ICT** EMBEDDING ICT **EMBEDDING ICT**

It is important to include all new forms of developing technologies, both in your own teaching and to support your children's learning, so that you do not just rely on those with which you are currently familiar. You need to plan for how you will ensure that you keep up to date with the development of ICT and ensure that you can use as wide a range of new media as possible effectively in your teaching. A great deal of current attention, for example, is being given to the use of mobile technology in the classroom. Ipads and various makes of tablet computers, and mobile smartphones, all have their place, although effective pedagogies for the use of these devices are still being developed.

Environments for fostering speaking and listening

A supportive environment that fosters and develops speaking and listening gives children real purposes for using talk, and allows them the opportunity to investigate, develop and present their ideas. In a supportive setting, children will have a chance to reflect on their own uses of talk and on their role as listeners, and to work collaboratively with other children.

PRACTICAL TASK PRACTICAL TASK **PRACTICAL TASK** PRACTICAL TASK **PRACTICAL TASK**

Display a classroom poster similar to the one set out below to help children to become aware of the purposes of their talk, and to reflect on their own development as speakers and listeners.

> *What kinds of talking and listening am I good at?*
> - *playground talk*
> - *classroom talk*
> - *group talk*
> - *pair talk*
> - *silence*

Sensitive teachers do much more than 'let children talk': your role is to develop a classroom environment that encourages the growth of purposeful talk. In addition, you can support the children by being a good role model yourself. Engage the children in discussions and encourage them to listen and respond. Don't be afraid to intervene sensitively to push ideas in new directions, sometimes using new or technical vocabulary, and introducing different and more complex ideas.

Be a good conversationalist and remember that children are watching and listening as you talk to their parents, to other teachers, the caretaker, the head teacher, the cleaners and to the children themselves. Don't be afraid of being hesitant and tentative yourself when you are dealing with new ideas. This will give you an opportunity to show children that it is perfectly acceptable to use talk to think aloud with. Part of your role is to become a good listener – so listen with care and appreciate what children are trying to express, enlarging on their comments and feeding back ideas to them. This will show the children that you're concerned with their ideas and how they thought them through. The attention you pay to these areas will help them to take their learning seriously and give them a way of sorting out ideas when they are on their own.

Think carefully about the seating arrangements for communal whole-class sessions when you are discussing topics. Sometimes it is appropriate for you to sit on a chair with the children grouped around you on the carpet. At other times you might want to sit on the carpet alongside the children, or you might choose to sit in a circle with them. This is one of the most appropriate arrangements for whole-class discussion, because children can look across at each other, and at you, instead of focusing on the back of another child's head.

As well as whole-class discussions, you will want to organise children into groups for speaking and listening. Small groups that really do work together exemplify co-operation, the sharing of ideas and the justifying of opinions. In order to work like this, you need to involve the group in a joint task, and suggest that they pair off into sub-groups to do independent research. The discussions that take place within these small groups are beneficial because they give a greater number of children the opportunity to offer their opinions than whole-class sessions do. In addition, shy children often make the contributions in small groups that they are unwilling to make in front of the whole class.

Obviously, the composition of these groups varies according to the needs of the task. Research has shown that groups of four generate the most talk. Some suggested groupings for specific purposes are:

- a single-sex group to investigate a relevant issue, e.g. aspects of gender stereotyping;
- a group containing an 'expert' on the topic to be investigated;
- a group where a particular child has a good knowledge of a certain task, like word processing, editing or illustrating, and can share their expertise;
- a group where a shy child is given confidence by other group members.

Some ideas for group talk are listed below.

- *Focused suggestions*. Given a fixed amount of time, children in a large group, or even the whole class, contribute ideas off the top of their heads, related to a particular subject or problem. List all contributions without comment, and then ask the children to use their list to select tasks or topics for further work.
- *Jig-sawing*. Children are organised into 'home groups' of about six to look at a topic – for example, creating a newspaper page. Each child in a home group is allocated one aspect of the newspaper page to investigate or to write, and becomes the 'expert' for that group – for example, an editor, a layout artist, an illustrator, a roving reporter, a cartoonist. The children then go into 'expert' groups from time to time, comprising all those from the home groups who have the same job description. After discussion, the 'experts' then return to their own home groups to discuss with the others what they have found out, and to play their part in putting together the final product before reporting back to the whole class.
- *Twos to fours*. Children work together in pairs, perhaps on a mathematical problem or a science investigation. They then join another pair to explain what they have achieved, and to compare it with the work of the other pair.
- *Rainbowing*. In this organisation, each member of the group is given a number or a colour. When the group has worked together, all children with the same number or colour form new groups to compare and discuss what they have done.
- *Envoying*. If a group needs to check something, or to obtain information, one of the group can be sent as an 'envoy' to the library or to talk to another group and will then report back. Groups can also be invited to

send an envoy to another group to explain what they have done, obtain responses and suggestions, and bring them back.

- *Listening triads*. In groups of three, children take on the roles of talker, questioner or recorder. The talker explains or comments on an issue or activity. The questioner prompts and seeks clarification. The recorder makes notes, and at the end gives a report of the conversation. Next time, the roles are changed.
- *Group observers*. A group member is responsible for observing the ways in which the group works together. Using a simple guide list (which the children can devise) the observer watches and listens as the children work. The group then discusses this information and, as a result, is able to review its work.

You can also use the tape recorder to support speaking and listening. Set up a recorder so that children can listen to stories and poetry they know and like. If you have a headphone set, several children will be able to listen at the same time – a good reason to buy several copies of the same book, so the group can all follow the text together. Make sure there is space for three or four children to sit comfortably and to operate the recorder. A listening centre can contain a selection of audio recordings of fiction, poetry, plays and non-fiction texts – some professionally produced and others recorded by you, other adults or the children themselves. Make these recordings available for children to listen to alongside books during independent time in literacy sessions, and at other times too.

Recording group discussions can provide a valuable activity for independent work in literacy sessions, because children can record their talk and prepare presentations. Recording changes the dynamics of a conversation, because children know that what they say will be given permanence, and can be repeated over and over again. This changes – and frequently enhances – the quality of the talk because they have to think carefully about what they are going to say and how they are going to say it. If children are not used to having their voices recorded they need to experiment to overcome any embarrassment felt at hearing their recorded voices for the first time. Here are some more suggestions for using audio-recording.

- Record children's contributions to discussion and invite them to listen afterwards to what they have said, and perhaps to transcribe part of it. Encourage them to examine their own contributions and to discuss what 'written down' talk looks like, and how it differs from formal written English.
- Organise children to make a recording relating to the main literacy lesson text. These can form part of a reference collection together with books on the same theme.
- Give children an invitation to create and record stories, their own and those already published. Remind them that when they are reading aloud they need to read expressively. Give them an opportunity to practise reading the text with sound effects to a group of children or to the whole class before making the final recording. Stories are often enhanced by the use of sound effects and once children are used to recording, they may want to include sound effects and music. Working in pairs, encourage the children to scan the text they have chosen to discover where sounds would be most effective and to experiment to find the most appropriate ones.
- Ask children to create listening games by recording sounds around the environment and asking others to guess what they are.
- Organise a group to record sound journeys inside and outside the school buildings and to present these to the class.
- Organise children to interview people around the school, such as the caretaker or secretary, other teachers, governors, the head teacher, on particular themes.
- Use one of the group's recordings as your main literacy text. Play it to the class in shared reading or writing time, and use it to generate written language.
- Invite children to create their own radio programmes, based on what they have enjoyed listening to.
- Ask children to devise advertisements to publicise school events using language to persuade and convince.

Creating an environment to support writing

Try to develop an assigned space in the classroom where a group of children can write, either during guided or independent writing sessions or outside the literacy lesson, with everything to hand. Set aside one or two tables alongside a computer and provide different-sized paper, pencils, felt-tip pens, crayons, rulers, envelopes, and perhaps a stapler, scissors, glue and paste. Put an alphabet chart close by and a suitable dictionary and thesaurus. Provide a message board so that children can write letters to each other or put up news items.

Children learn about the different forms of writing by observing the kinds of writing that adults and other children engage in around the school, having other people share this writing with them for different purposes, and by having opportunities to try out this writing for themselves. This means that your writing environment needs to have examples of various kinds of writing (posters, homemade books, letters, book reviews, maps, recipes, scripts, stories, poems, advertisements, and so on). Display these at eye-level for the children to read. Displays of stimulating and exciting writing invite children to write in ways that are significant and hold meaning for them.

With the children's help, draw up lists of the various readers they can write for – you, other teachers in the school, children in their class or in other classes, the caretaker, the headteacher, their parents and relations, the cooks, penfriends, authors of books they have enjoyed, their Member of Parliament, sportsmen and women, and so on. Discussion about readership will help children to become aware of the language they should use when they are writing with a particular reader in mind.

Most children are used to having a choice of writing implements – pencils, biros, felt-tip pens or crayons – but are often given only standard size paper to write on. Provide a range of paper from very small to A3, including lined paper and assorted shapes and colours. The variety may inspire the reluctant writer and capture the imagination of the creative. Young children may improve their manipulative competence by experimenting with fat and thin felt tips and chunky pencils, and different types of writing instruments offer older pupils the chance to develop their calligraphy skills. Fountain pens and bullet-nosed and wedge-shaped felt tips create quite different lines. Display examples of writing styles, including writing patterns and italic script and illuminated manuscripts.

Organising a supportive environment for the teaching and learning of reading

The reading corner

This space has two purposes: it will be both a library and a place where children can go when they want to browse or read; so plan for both. In a small classroom, the community space often doubles as the library and this is another function that needs to be taken into consideration. Provide opportunities for children to visit this area outside shared activity time so that they can browse or sit and read quietly. This kind of activity helps them to develop the reading habit, and is particularly helpful for children who are unable to read at home.

How you furnish this area will depend on materials and space available and on your and the children's ideas of design. Bookshelves are often used as partitions to define the reading corner and to make it private and cosy. Test the shelves for stability – rescuing a child from underneath a bookstand knocked over by some boisterous role-play is not funny. Remember, the emphasis is on cosiness, comfort and safety.

To a large degree, the type of shelving you use will probably have been decided for you but think carefully about how you use it. Plastic covered wire shelving is commonly used but there can be problems if you use it to store large soft-covered books, for these tend to flop over and become permanently curved. Put hard-backed books there instead and use slanted shelves for paperbacks. There are units specifically designed for storing big books, though the inevitable size of these means that you will need to consider where they should be placed.

Many children say that their favourite place to read is in bed, because it is warm, cosy and private, so try to set up similar conditions in your reading corner. A carpet or rug, scatter cushions and beanbags are ideal for children to sit on. Small settees or comfortable chairs are always popular with young readers (parents may donate chairs they no longer need). Decorate the area with plants and posters – ask your local children's bookshop for these – and display posters the children have made themselves to advertise books. You could run a special 'Book of the Month' display linked to a project or particular area of interest in the class and include a section of homemade books published in the classroom by the children themselves.

Organising and displaying books

You will want to have a varied range of reading matter, including literature of different kinds, poetry, non-fiction, and books made by the children themselves. Books used as literacy texts should be on display so that children can borrow or browse through them. Some teachers exchange books with another class each term, so there is always a fresh selection for the children. In addition, you may be able to choose some books to borrow from the Library Service in your area.

How you organise and display books will depend on the space available, the children's reading experiences and interests, and the number and type of books you have. Some teachers ask the children to help categorise and display the books, exploring and developing a system that suits their needs. Displaying books with their front covers visible helps to make the reading corner attractive and inviting at both key stages. This kind of display makes it easier for inexperienced readers to choose books, because they are drawn to the title and the cover illustration. They will instantly be attracted to old favourites, and excited about picking up new and interesting titles. Here are some suggested ways of organising books:

- by author's surname;
- by genre, e.g. humour, adventure, animal stories, poetry, folk tales, historical novels and picture-story books;
- by clearly recognised publishers' sets that children are familiar with;
- by kinds of information, i.e. field guides, reports, auto/biographies, diaries, instructions and recipes;
- by homework sections that link to particular subjects or themes.

Setting up a lending library

Many schools have a main library from where children borrow books to take home. In addition, it is sometimes helpful to set up your own class borrowing system, particularly if you are not able to spend time reading individually with children. A well-organised borrowing system is particularly important for younger children, because they frequently read a book in a single evening. A class library means these children can change their books every day if they wish. It also acts as an informal way of bringing parents into the classroom as they help children to make their choice. Letting them borrow from the class library obviously means that you need a good supply of books, if it is not to be too depleted, and a system that records the borrowers. A ticket inside each book or kept in a file box and simply requiring the child to write their name is usually sufficient. When the book is returned then the child's name can be crossed off. The initial organisation may take some time to develop but with patience the benefits outweigh the disadvantages and parents and children can enjoy stories together.

Book reviews written when children have enjoyed books at home – an ideal homework task – can be kept in the library area. You can demonstrate how to write a review in shared or guided writing time. Remind the children that the purpose of reviews is to inform others and to help them to select books for themselves.

Reading displays

Include in your displays those books you have used as literacy texts as well as books that relate to a current television serial the children are viewing at home or at school. Books by a particular author who has visited the school during book week (see below) are always popular. Texts that follow a topic you are covering are worth displaying too. Invite children to display books that they have read and enjoyed at home, together with a review of the book saying why they enjoyed it.

Organising a book week

Many schools organise 'book weeks' where they invite published writers and poets to meet the children and talk to them about their writing. Although many authors may charge for their visits, others enjoy meeting their readers and may come for a nominal fee. It is worth writing to publishers saying who your children's favourite authors are and which books they particularly enjoyed. Even if they do not sponsor someone to visit your school, they may send free publicity, such as badges, posters and bookmarks. Many schools celebrate World Book Day by adults and children dressing up as their favourite character from a well-known book.

Using environmental or public print to support reading

Your reading resources should ideally include texts other than books – posters, lists and notices, the dinner menu, a weather chart and a rota for watering the plants. These are all a part of class reading, so make use of them and refer to them. Sometimes you might even want to use an important notice as a literacy session text because it contains points you want specifically to discuss.

Children are familiar with a great deal of print they see around them at home and in their community before they even come to school – food labels, TV titles, advertisements, instructions, newspapers, catalogues, calendars, magazines, comics, birthday cards, invitations, letters, bills, tickets, crosswords, coins, bank notes, car number plates and shop names. Such texts are woven into children's everyday lives and can be used successfully to support reading in the classroom. You could, for example:

- take photos of the print that children see around them near school and put these into a book;
- discuss these with the children and write captions together in shared writing time;
- organise children to make their own alphabet books of food wrappers;
- collect different tickets used locally (on trains, buses, at the cinema and so on) and put these into a transparent photograph wallet so that children can read both sides of the tickets and talk about the text together.

Resources for shared and guided reading

In addition to your chosen literacy text, you will need a selection of resources for teaching reading during the literacy session. These will include an easel or frame of some kind to display your big book, a flip chart, a pointer, an overhead projector, sets of magnetic letters (upper and lower case), individual whiteboards and word or letter fans and word wheels for the children to use. Resources for guided or independent reading will include sufficient copies of the text you are studying (or photocopies of the appropriate page/s), pencils/highlighter pens, and ICT equipment, including recording facilities.

Choosing books

Your choice of books, both reading scheme and non-reading scheme, will depend on the objectives you are working to. Read as many books as you can – this is really the only way of knowing them in detail. There are, however, several journals that review children's books, such as *Books for Keeps*, *The School Librarian* and *Signal*.

Here are some general features of different kinds of texts for your classroom. We suggest that you use the general criteria together with the more detailed list for each year group, set out below.

Fiction

Choose books that use language in exciting and challenging ways, with a powerful story to tell, by authors who know how to write well for children. Look for picture books where the text and illustrations come together to make the meaning whole, such as *Rosie's Walk* by Pat Hutchins, and for wordless books where the story is carried entirely through the pictures, such as *The Snowman* by Raymond Briggs. Children love funny books, so include ones with plenty of humour. The comic strip format of books like Raymond Briggs's *Father Christmas* series appeals to the reluctant reader as well as to the enthusiast. Choose books with plenty of repetition for the younger reader, such as *Mr Gumpy's Outing* by John Burningham. Books that are serialised on television are popular, so be aware of them, both on dedicated children's TV and the main channels. Stories can be used to advantage to introduce or enrich project work. Children gain a sense of history through reading a book set in the past or one that crosses time, such as *Tom's Midnight Garden* by Phillippa Pearce, while science fiction offers a glimpse of the future.

Choose books with a variety of print styles and sizes, and look for stories that challenge stereotypes (race, gender and disability) in both text and illustration. Include books of different sizes, some small enough to hold in the hand, (such as the Beatrix Potter series) and others that are large enough to be shared by a small group of children.

Poetry

Choose anthologies and books by individual writers. Poets like Michael Rosen, Kit Wright, John Agard, Gillian Clarke, Jenny Joseph and Charles Causley, all write well for children. Include books of traditional rhymes and poetry from different cultures.

EMBEDDING ICT EMBEDDING ICT EMBEDDING ICT EMBEDDING ICT EMBEDDING ICT

There is a useful website that gives information about poetry that is out of copyright or where living contemporary poets have given permission to have their work performed in videos for the site, including poems by Michael Rosen, Roger McGough, Francesca Beard and Benjamin Zephaniah. Set up by Michael Rosen when he was the Children's Laureate (2007–2009), Perform a Poem is an e-safe site for sharing children's poetry performances. The site, a joint project between Booktrust and the London Grid for Learning (LGfL), is also available to be hosted by other UK grids that are part of the National Education Network. For more information, see the website (http://performapoem.lgfl.org.uk).

Another useful site providing free access to online resources is Project Gutenberg, which has a choice of over 33,000 free ebooks for a variety of platforms, including a 'children's bookshelf' (see www.gutenberg.org).

Non-fiction

The non-fiction books in your school might be housed in a separate library area that serves the whole school. However, younger readers often find it difficult to choose non-fiction from such a huge collection. It might be possible for you to borrow texts from the main library for particular purposes, and you can extend your classroom collection by taking advantage of loans from the public library. The use of digital photography has dramatically raised the standard of environmental science books, for example, but be aware that where a particular detail is drawn to children's attention, a careful illustration is often more appropriate than a general photograph. Extracts from newspapers may also provide additional non-fiction material for literacy sessions and you can add these to your class collection.

Many children watch sophisticated television programmes about various subject areas – natural history is a good example – and they need books that excite them and take their knowledge forward. You might consider that it is better to buy one expensive and beautiful book on birds, written by someone who knows and cares about the subject, than to buy several smaller books which begin by telling the reader, 'This is a bird'! If you work closely with a colleague, you could share the cost of this type of book and build up a collection. Look for books with a contents page, an index and a glossary, and a list of references that tell the reader what to read next for more information.

Instruction books (on kite-making, miniature gardens, cookery, making puppets, simple science experiments, etc.) are popular and help children to read in different ways for a range of purposes. For these to be really effective, children need to be able to borrow them to take home or to find the right material in the classroom to carry out the instructions properly.

Children's own books

Have a collection of books published in the classroom and written by the children themselves. Produce these as professionally as you can and encourage the children to develop their ICT skills by publishing their own texts. They can include a blurb and a section 'About the author'. For example, one child wrote:

> My name is David Smith. I am eight years old and I have been writing stories since I was five. My favourite author is John Burningham and I try to write the kinds of stories he writes.

His blurb read as follows:

> This story is about a little boy who finds a dog on a rubbish tip and takes him home. His mum and dad tell him he can't keep it, but can he persuade them? And what will happen to the dog if he doesn't look after it?

Features of progression in reading texts

This chapter concludes with a suggested set of detailed criteria for fiction, non-fiction, poetry and non-fiction from Reception through to Year 6. It covers progression in each kind of text, taking account of objectives at word, sentence and text levels.

Reception
- Patterned texts with a flowing rhythm and repetition of particular words and/or phrases.
- Use of rhyme in poems and stories to encourage familiarity with spelling patterns and to support prediction.
- Use of regular CVC words to introduce and support understanding of sounds and blends.
- Use of rhythmic language in poems and stories to encourage momentum and increase confidence in reading.
- Use of alliteration to encourage familiarity with initial sounds.
- Stories and poems with familiar themes.
- Simple non-fiction texts to introduce young readers to information presented in different ways (e.g. recipes and instructions).
- Illustrations that help young readers to use picture cues alongside the text to establish meaning.
- Clear layout of text and illustrations which helps children to understand left–right sequencing.
- Alphabet books with lower case letters to help children learn the sounds and names of letters and to introduce them to alphabetical order.

Year 1
- A wider range of stories that reflect young children's experiences and introduce a world of fantasy (e.g. modern picture books, traditional tales, stories from different cultures).
- Books by authors who use interesting and challenging vocabulary and exciting and poetic language that trips off the tongue, is easily recognised and is good to say aloud.
- A widening range of simple non-fiction texts that reflect children's interests (e.g. cooking, school, the garden, people who help us, animals, dinosaurs).

- Texts with good quality illustrations that help young readers to understand the relationship between picture and text, and give them opportunities to discuss the meaning in order to support the development of contextual cues.
- Texts with speech bubbles and thought bubbles as well as conventional narrative text.
- Alphabet books with upper and lower case letters.
- Poetry and stories with patterned rhyme and rhythm.
- Collections of nonsense rhymes with humorous word-play.
- Texts with patterned and predictable language to encourage the use of grammatical (syntactic) cues.
- Simple playscripts that encourage young readers to join in and read aloud together.
- Texts with repeated vocabulary to help young readers to increase their recognition of high frequency words and CVC words.
- Texts with alliteration to help young readers increase phonic awareness of initial letter sounds.

Year 2

- Familiar stories with predictable language to encourage the re-reading of well-known and well-loved books.
- Longer stories using literary language and more complex and sophisticated plots, that allow children to enter the world of their imagination and that encourage discussion, prediction, inference and deduction.
- Stories, poems and plays with patterned and predictable language to increase confidence, fluency and independent reading.
- Stories with an increased use of dialogue to encourage awareness of punctuation and to support reading aloud expressively.
- Picture books with complex pictures for children to look at more closely, where illustrations stimulate the imagination, including good multicultural images.
- Stories and poems containing words with regular phonic patterns to develop knowledge of more complex vowel and consonant blends and digraphs and long vowel sounds.
- Retellings of traditional tales that encourage children to see more than one point of view and encourage them to make links between stories.
- More complex poetry using literary language to introduce children to the use of figurative language.
- Anthologies of poems with an emphasis on rhyme and humour.
- Books of jokes to encourage enjoyment and humour and to introduce children to verbal humour.
- Non-fiction texts written in a variety of styles that increase children's range of experience (e.g. instructions with diagrams, photographs, labels and captions) and with features and devices to help them to learn about how non-fiction is presented (e.g. contents page, index, glossary, headings, bulleted points).
- More sophisticated alphabet books, with upper and lower case letters, possibly with a related theme throughout, to consolidate knowledge of the alphabet and alphabetical order.
- An early dictionary to help young readers learn how to find words and their definitions and to extend their written and spoken vocabulary.

Year 3

- Familiar stories to encourage re-reading of well-known and well-loved books.
- More sophisticated picture-story books that deal with complex ideas and use a range of literary language.
- Contemporary stories that are more subtle and complex, dealing with emotive issues in ways that young readers can handle, and with plots and characters that readers of this age can identify with. Some of these should be longer stories divided into chapters.
- Stories that use the first-person narrative.
- Traditional stories from around the world that use rich literary language and more complex sentence structures.
- Texts that support the development of more complex spelling patterns (e.g. long vowel phonemes) and provide opportunities for young readers to develop their knowledge of grammar (e.g. identifying adjectives).

- Non-fiction texts that extend children's knowledge of the world by offering sophisticated uses of language and more unusual vocabulary, including specialised terminology, and that give readers an opportunity to see how text and illustrations work together to reveal information. These texts should also give children the experience of using different organisational devices, including the use of different fonts.
- A variety of poetry, in anthologies and single-authored collections, offering challenging uses of figurative language, word-play and verbal humour.
- Playscripts to develop children's ability to read aloud with expression and take turns in their reading.
- More complex alphabet books that reinforce the alphabet and alphabetical order and help young readers to extend their vocabulary and their knowledge of grammar (e.g. tenses, punctuation).
- A dictionary that is sufficiently complex to give children an opportunity to learn about organisation (e.g. alphabetical order to first and second places, use of headword and guideword).

Year 4

- Familiar stories to encourage re-reading of well-known and well-loved books.
- More sophisticated picture-story books that deal with complex ideas and use a range of literary language.
- Short novels to give young readers the experience of reading an entire book.
- Traditional stories from around the world that encourage comparisons and introduce discussion of story structure (e.g. comparison between fables and fairy tales) and that give an opportunity to discuss the use of vocabulary drawn from different languages.
- More sophisticated contemporary stories with chapters and chapter titles and features such as first-person narrative.
- Books of jokes and riddles to read and enjoy that help young readers to explore the use and meanings of figurative language in sophisticated word-play.
- Anthologies and collections of single-authored poetry that offer children varied styles (rhyming, non-rhyming, use of figurative language, including metaphor and simile, alliteration and onomatopoeia, a variety of layouts to stress meaning in visual terms, and sophisticated uses of punctuation to enhance meaning).
- Non-fiction texts with sophisticated features (extended narrative, captions, speech bubbles, diagrams, instructions, lists, explanations) and more complex organisational structures (contents, glossary of specialised vocabulary, index, headings, subheadings, numbered instructions).
- A more complex dictionary with many entries (2,000–3,000 words) giving children an opportunity to focus on definitions, word classes and word families to support spelling.

Year 5

- Longer novels, including mysteries and adventures, containing challenging vocabulary and dialogue, more sophisticated plot structures and literary devices to build tension and move the narrative forward (e.g. time shifts, parts of the story told from different viewpoints, first-person narrative and use of the omniscient author).
- Sophisticated picture-story books that reflect the complex relationship between illustration and text and enable children to develop their understanding of visual literacy.
- Traditional stories from a range of cultures using more complex story structure and with rich and varied vocabulary drawn from different languages with their typical structures and use of imagery.
- Poetry using a range of styles, structures and language patterns, with varied rhymes and rhythms, and uses of figurative language.
- A wide variety of non-fiction genres, including biographies, instructional texts and extended accounts that include a range of sophisticated elements (e.g. more complex reports and recounts using specialised vocabulary, text and pictures which help children to make composite meanings, diagrams, maps, charts and labels to support meaning, clearly written advice, instructions, speech bubbles, time lines and lists of primary sources used when compiling the text).
- A good dictionary (5,000–6,000 words) and a thesaurus.

Year 6

- Stories, longer novels and playscripts, based on contemporary, historical, futuristic and fantastic themes, both hard-back and paperback, containing challenging vocabulary and dialogue, sophisticated and complex narrative structures and distinctive literary devices which create suspense and move the narrative forward (e.g. links between the past, present and future, careful organisation of paragraphs and lead sentences to develop characters).
- Traditional tales that extend children's understanding of the literary heritage of other cultures and enable them to understand links between stories.
- Poetry with a variety of forms and styles, structures and patterns of language, that explores complex ideas in a variety of rhymes and rhythms, using humour and figurative language and sophisticated word-play. These styles should include haiku, limericks, couplets, triplets, quatrains, quintets, sestets and octets. Some of these poems should lend themselves to being read aloud using intonation and expression.
- A wide variety of non-fiction genres, including biographies and autobiographies, interviews, diaries, first-hand accounts, extracts from news reports, instructional texts and extended accounts. Some of these should be explanatory and discursive texts that deal with difficult and controversial issues and put forward balanced arguments (e.g. complex reports and recounts using specialised vocabulary, that are supported by a wide-ranging glossary) to encourage children to identify the differences between fact and opinion. These should also reflect widespread use of diagrams, maps, photographs, charts, graphs, footnotes and labels to support meaning, and clearly written advice, instructions, speech bubbles, time lines and a list of primary sources used when compiling the text.
- A dictionary containing at least 10,000 words with definitions, notes on word origins and pronunciation.
- An etymological dictionary to explore word origins and derivations.
- A thesaurus.

A SUMMARY OF **KEY POINTS**

- ➢ **You need to make key decisions about the way in which you organise your classroom.**
- ➢ **The organisation of available space should make provision for a community area for the class, a role-play area, and the use of puppets and storysacks.**
- ➢ **You need to think about the various uses for displays and plan these accordingly.**
- ➢ **You should also consider how to use time effectively in literacy sessions, especially with regard to group activities.**
- ➢ **The work of other adults in the classroom needs to be planned carefully in order to ensure that they support children's learning effectively.**
- ➢ **There are many ways in which ICT can support the teaching of literacy and children's learning in Key Stages 1 and 2.**
- ➢ **You need to develop environments that foster children's speaking and listening skills, promote writing and support the teaching and learning of reading.**
- ➢ **Resources for shared and guided reading need to show progression in all text types.**

M-LEVEL EXTENSION > > M-LEVEL EXTENSION > > M-LEVEL EXTENSION

- Use the points made in this chapter to help you reflect on the effectiveness of the classrooms in which you have worked as environments for English teaching. Think particularly about the following things:
- How was the classroom organised and how did this organisation support or hinder the teaching of English?

- What displays were mounted in the classroom and did these reflect children's literacy work or stimulate further work in English?
- How were other adults used in the classroom to support the teaching of speaking and listening, reading and writing?
- Was ICT firmly embedded in the teaching and learning of literacy and English?

FURTHER READING FURTHER READING FURTHER READING FURTHER READING

DfE (2013) *Teachers' Standards*. London: DfE. (https://www.gov.uk/government/uploads/system/uploads/attachment_data/file/208682/Teachers__Standards_2013.pdf)

Evans, J. (ed.) (2000) *The Writing Classroom*. London: David Fulton.

Goodwin, P. (ed.) (1999) *The Literate Classroom*. London: David Fulton.

Phinn, G. (2000) *Young Readers and their Books*. London: David Fulton.

Books for Keeps online (www.booksforkeeps.co.uk)

The School Librarian journal (www.sla.org.uk)

Signal – the journal of the International Reading Association special interest group network on adolescent literature (available at www.kennesaw.edu/english/education/signal)

14
Assessing English

TEACHERS' STANDARDS

A teacher must:

1. **Set high expectations which inspire, motivate and challenge pupils**

    *   set goals that stretch and challenge pupils of all backgrounds, abilities and dispositions

2. **Promote good progress and outcomes by pupils**

    *   be accountable for pupils' attainment, progress and outcomes
    *   plan teaching to build on pupils' capabilities and prior knowledge
    *   guide pupils to reflect on the progress they have made and their emerging needs
    *   encourage pupils to take a responsible and conscientious attitude to their own work and study.

3. **Demonstrate good subject and curriculum knowledge**

    *   demonstrate an understanding of and take responsibility for promoting high standards of literacy, articulacy and the correct use of standard English, whatever the teacher's specialist subject

5. **Adapt teaching to respond to the strengths and needs of all pupils**

    *   know when and how to differentiate appropriately, using approaches which enable pupils to be taught effectively

6. **Make accurate and productive use of assessment**

    *   know and understand how to assess the relevant subject and curriculum areas, including statutory assessment requirements
    *   make use of formative and summative assessment to secure pupils' progress
    *   use relevant data to monitor progress, set targets, and plan subsequent lessons
    *   give pupils regular feedback, both orally and through accurate marking, and encourage pupils to respond to the feedback.

Introduction

Planning and assessment are the key to effective English teaching. As a teacher, you need to know what a child understands, can do and knows. You can then plan for progression. However, assessment of English is complicated because it serves many purposes and takes many forms. This chapter will consider the purposes for assessing English and then look at three main areas of assessment:

- how the teacher can assess and record English throughout the academic year;
- the statutory assessment requirements you may be involved in for children at the end of the Foundation Stage and Key Stages 1 and 2;
- the reporting of assessment to teachers and parents.

The purposes of assessment

There are several reasons why assessments are made of children's reading, writing, and speaking and listening. We shall briefly describe six of these, as follows:

1. to measure progress;
2. to diagnose difficulties;
3. to help match tasks, materials and methods to particular needs;
4. to evaluate teaching approaches;
5. to compare children;
6. to maintain and improve standards.

Measuring progress

Assessment measures progress. This is important to individual children and their parents, to their teachers and to the school as a whole. The main focus of **formative** teacher assessment is to measure and monitor progress against the learning objectives for English. As a result of this, teachers will regularly pinpoint class targets and individual targets for children. Schools administer a **summative**, or 'snapshot', assessment of their children at the end of each year using teacher assessment and any statutory tests and tasks. They then report these assessment results to parents and record the results in such a way that indicates whether children have made progress over a longer period.

Diagnosing difficulties

A further use of assessment is to identify particular difficulties that individual children may have with English. This can be done at several levels and there is a statutory procedure for diagnosing the difficulties faced by children with special educational needs. Some children who have English as an additional language (EAL) may simply need focused support to learn more English. As a teacher, you will need to be able to mark diagnostically and use processes such as miscue analysis.

Matching tasks, materials and methods to children

As a result of recognising children's progress or diagnosing children's problems, judgements may also be made of the kinds of differentiation, materials and teaching methods that would best fit individual children's needs. Teaching can therefore be tailored to these needs. In this way, assessment feeds into planning.

Evaluating teaching approaches

One of the products of assessments of progress might be an evaluation of the teaching methods and materials experienced by the children. Assessments of children's progress are not the only source of this evaluation. Teachers will also evaluate materials and approaches on the grounds of their complexity, ease of operation and intelligibility. The extent of children's learning is, however, an important and necessary criterion for judging the success of teaching approaches. Evaluation of methods and materials will also take place on a local and national level. For instance, a local authority (LA) might look at the statutory assessment results of its schools to evaluate the impact of interactive whiteboards in school. Nationally, the statutory assessment results are one of the factors against which the success of national strategies have been measured.

Making comparisons between pupils, schools and groups of pupils

Assessments are also used to compare children within the national sample, within LAs or in smaller groups such as school or class populations. These comparisons can be made in order to reveal whether certain groups of children are facing problems. Recently, it was noted that a national comparison of pupils in writing revealed that boys were underperforming. This has led to a national effort to improve boys' writing. Comparisons can also be made within schools and classes, to reveal whether national issues apply in a particular class or school. Such comparisons may be used as a means of allocating resources to particular groups. A school or a local authority may, for example, decide to provide extra teaching equipment or teaching help to a group of children who have been identified as having special needs.

Comparisons between schools on the basis of statutory assessment results are not simple, as school intakes and circumstances differ enormously. School performances are compared with 'benchmarks' of groups of schools judged to be generally similar in circumstances.

Maintaining and improving standards

Rigorous, comparable assessments allow us to know whether English standards have been maintained and improved. This information is important at a national, local authority and whole-school level. The assessments used for this sort of measurement are the results of statutory assessment in English at Key Stages 1 and 2. When compared with data from baseline assessments, a measure of 'value added' – the amount of performance increase between assessments – can be made. In response to this information, the government (or LA or school) sets targets for aspects of attainment that it wishes to improve.

It is apparent from the above description of the purposes of assessment that a range of interested parties have a concern with the English assessments made of children. The five main interested parties are:

- national bodies representing government;
- local authorities, who monitor and support the schools in their area;
- the individual school and its staff;
- individual teachers planning their teaching;
- the children who are actually making progress in English, and their parents.

Assessment serves rather different purposes for each of these groups and a range of forms of assessment are necessary to satisfy all purposes.

Teacher assessment of literacy and oracy

There are three basic sources of data for assessing oracy and literacy:

- what children actually produce – this involves looking at writing, analysing reading aloud behaviour in one-to-one, group or shared reading, and analysing what children say;
- what children actually do – observing writing processes, reading processes and speaking and listening processes;
- what children know – asking children what they know, their opinions and attitudes.

Analysing products

A great deal can be gleaned from analyses of children's language and literacy products. We shall look closely at two aspects of this: firstly at a technique for analysing the product of a child's oral reading, and secondly at the assessment of written products.

RESEARCH SUMMARY   RESEARCH SUMMARY   **RESEARCH SUMMARY**   RESEARCH SUMMARY

American researchers Ken and Yetta Goodman are the theorists responsible for much of the important work related to error analysis (see Goodman *et al.*, 1987, for a full account of miscue analysis). Marie Clay (1979) looked at the reading of younger children and developed a procedure called running record, which is part of the reading recovery programme of early intervention.

According to the theory, reading errors are never simply random. Each error is caused by the interactions between a set of circumstances that include the syntactic, semantic and graphophonic cues used for reading. If a child makes errors, an observer can analyse these errors to see what cues are being used successfully and what cues need more attention. This approach to reading (and spelling) has been very useful and a running record has been part of the statutory assessment at Key Stage 1.

Analysis of reading errors (miscue analysis or running record)

Error analysis is based on the theory that the mistakes a child makes when reading aloud from a text betray a great deal about how that child is tackling the reading task. As an example, the following sentence in a reading book, 'The man got on his horse' was read by a child as, 'The man got on his house'. Because the word 'house' does not make sense in this context, it is fairly safe to assume that making sense was not the chief preoccupation of this child, who seems rather to be attending to the initial letters of the word. Another child read the sentence as, 'The man got on his pony'. This child seems to have been attending more to the meaning, even to the extent of ignoring what the word looked like. These two children seem to have different approaches to the task of reading, which led them to 'miscue' in different ways.

The misreading of one word is not sufficient evidence on which to base a complete assessment. The technique of miscue analysis, therefore, uses a child's oral reading of much longer texts and tries to pinpoint patterns in the kinds of misreading that the child produces. It is usually carried out with the child reading from his/her normal book, and the teacher recording exactly what the child reads onto a copy of the text. There are several suggested coding systems for this recording, although the exigencies of time usually mean that the simplest possible system is most effective (it is also possible to make an audio-recording of the child's reading for later, more detailed, analysis if this is required). The child may then be asked to retell the story just read, so as to provide an indication of comprehension. The miscues the child has made are then analysed by the teacher for patterns, which may indicate particular features of the child's approach to reading. To show how this technique operates, we shall go through an example in more detail.

Two eight-year-old children, Gary and Robert, were asked to read aloud from a text. Their reading errors were recorded using the following system:

//	....	pausing
<u>behind</u>	....	sounding out phonically
~~the~~	....	omission
on		
/	....	addition
make		
~~milk~~	....	substitution
C	....	self-correction

Figure 14.1 shows the record of Gary's reading and Figure 14.2 that of Robert.

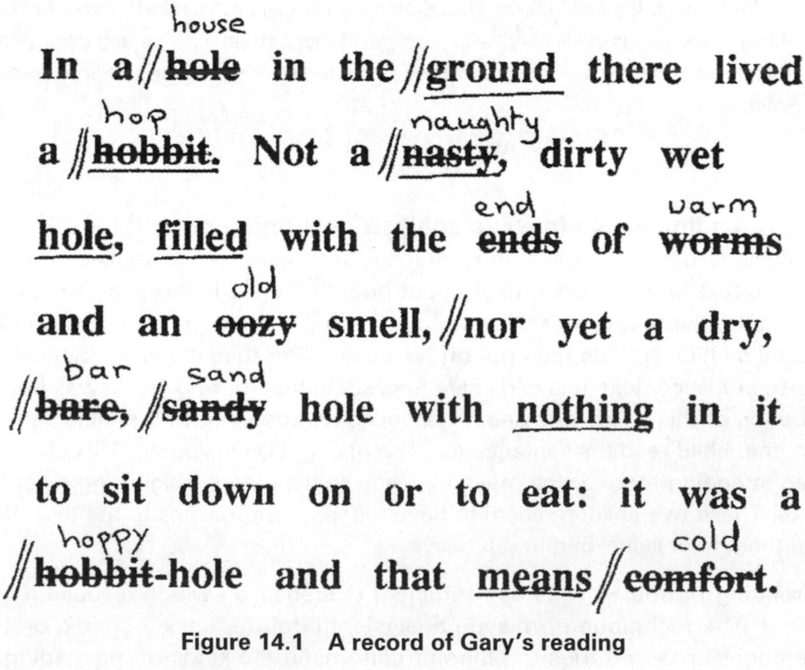

In a // ~~hole~~ in the // <u>ground</u> there lived

a // <u>~~hobbit.~~</u> Not a // <u>~~nasty,~~</u> dirty wet

hole, <u>filled</u> with the ~~ends~~ of ~~worms~~

and an ~~oozy~~ smell, // nor yet a dry,

// <u>~~bare,~~</u> // <u>~~sandy~~</u> hole with <u>nothing</u> in it

to sit down on or to eat: it was a

// <u>~~hobbit~~</u>-hole and that <u>means</u> // ~~comfort.~~

(Gary's handwritten annotations: house / hop / naughty / end / ʋarm / old / bar / sand / hoppy / cold)

Figure 14.1   A record of Gary's reading

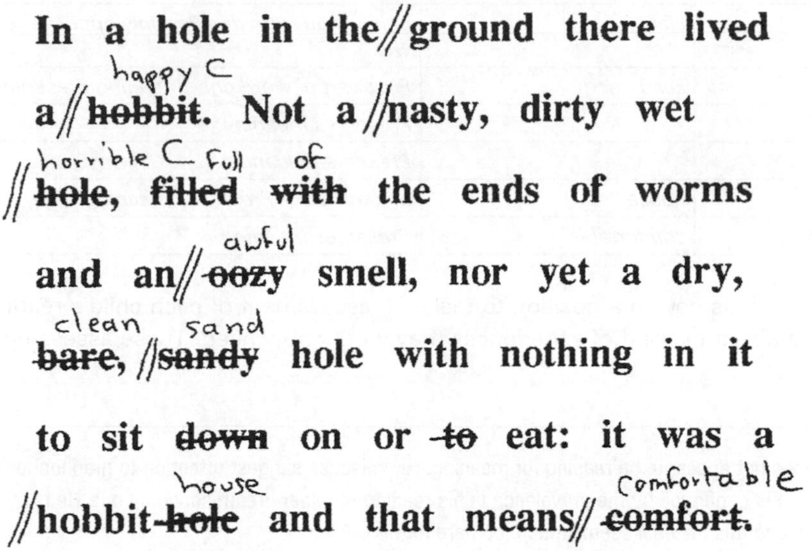
In a hole in the//ground there lived
happy C
a//hobbit. Not a//nasty, dirty wet
horrible C full of
//hole, filled with the ends of worms
awful
and an//oozy smell, nor yet a dry,
clean sand
bare, //sandy hole with nothing in it
to sit down on or to eat: it was a
house comfortable
//hobbit-hole and that means// comfort.

Figure 14.2 A record of Robert's reading

For each child, the teacher completed an analysis form and these are given below.

Gary		
Original word	**What the child read**	**Likely cause of miscue**
hole	*house*	*Guessing from initial sound? Possibly looking forward to 'lived'.*
hobbit	*hop*	*Guessing from initial sound.*
nasty	*naughty*	*Initial sounds.*
ends	*end*	*Only read beginning of word.*
worms	*warm*	*Initial sound.*
oozy	*old*	*Initial sound.*
bare	*bar*	*Initial sounds only.*
sandy	*sand*	*Only read beginning of word.*
hobbit	*hoppy*	*Initial sounds only.*
comfort	*cold*	*Initial sounds only.*

Robert		
Original word	**What the child read**	**Likely cause of miscue**
hobbit	*happy*	*Expecting a further noun. Self-corrected when error realised.*
hole	*horrible*	*Initial sound? Fits tone of sentence. Corrected.*
filled	*full*	*Meaningful response.*
with	*of*	*Responds to meaning of previous miscue.*
oozy	*awful*	*Near synonym.*

bare	clean	Follows on from dry. Possibly opposite of 'dirty wet'.
sandy	sand	First part of word only. Meaning preserved.
down	–	Preserves meaning.
to	–	Preserves meaning.
hole	house	Initial sound? Preserves meaning.
comfort	comfortable	Preserves meaning.

The teacher was now in a position to make an assessment of each child's reading and a statement about the kind of experiences they would now need. These assessments were as follows:

Gary does not appear to be reading for meaning. His miscues suggest attention to graphophonic cues only. This is confirmed by the prevalence in his reading of under-breath sounding out. He is overusing phonics and this material seems much too hard for him.

He needs to be encouraged to read much easier material and to approach it looking for meaning. Simple cloze material may get him to focus more on context cues. We might also use information books more. If he is interested in their subject he might be more inclined to approach them looking for meaning.

Robert clearly realises that reading is chiefly about meaning. His miscues largely suggest a concern for meaning-seeking. At times he is a little cavalier about the actual words on the page, preferring his guess, albeit usually a sensible one, to looking carefully at the words.

His attention to meaning must not be disturbed, but he needs to be encouraged to look more carefully at the words on the page. We could try getting him to read some poetry, especially out loud. Getting the words exactly right is more important in poems.

Hopefully, this example has shown some of the very rich insights into children's reading that the analysis of miscues can provide. A running record is very similar but also records words the child gets right. This makes it more suitable for the younger age range. Following the reading, both running record and miscue analysis should be followed by a discussion about the text, so that the child's comprehension can be estimated and evaluated. This technique, in common with all assessment techniques, is never the sole source of information available to the teacher. Other sources, such as those described below, will be used to confirm, modify or enlarge on the insights gained from miscue analysis. The teacher will build up a battery of assessment techniques, each complementary to the other.

PRACTICAL TASK PRACTICAL TASK **PRACTICAL TASK** PRACTICAL TASK **PRACTICAL TASK**

Looking diagnostically at errors is a very important skill. By doing a miscue analysis, you will change the way you listen to readers. Do a miscue analysis or running record with four or five children using the coding system above.

Select a passage or part of a book. Make sure it is a little difficult for the child. Select a child to read with you and tell them you would like them to read but that you will not help them. The child should do what they normally do if they get to a difficult bit.

- Read the text up to the passage you have selected.
- Ask the child to read your selected passage and mark errors using the code above.
- Read the rest of the story to the child.
- Ask the child to retell the passage and discuss it.
- Analyse the miscues and comprehension as shown in the discussion.

Analysis of written products

Teachers mark and assess a great deal of writing and it cannot all be marked at the same level. When marking any work, the teacher refers to the objectives for that work. If the piece is writing of a particular text type, assessment of writing must begin with a consideration of the aims originally formulated for this piece of work. The product cannot be judged unless these are taken into account. The assessment must also take into consideration the capabilities of the children producing the work. A piece of writing may be good for one child, but well below another's capacity. The assessment should also focus on the intended audience for the writing, and whether it is appropriate for this audience.

Below, you will find guidance for marking and a prompt sheet for use when thoroughly marking a piece of children's writing. This sort of piece might then be put in a portfolio of the child's work to be used for later review of progress or reporting teacher assessment at the end of year. At times, you will want to set particular writing assessment tasks and analyse the results carefully.

Guidance for marking a single piece of writing

1. **Quickly read the writing for a sense of what it is about and an overall impression of how well it responds to the task set.**
2. **Decide which aspects of the analysis are most relevant/useful to you.**
   This varies depending on the age of the child (for example you may not expect Year 2 children to be writing very complex sentences, but you may be interested in their use of adjectives) and the nature of the task (e.g. some descriptions may contain little variation in verbs, but noun groups may be more significant).
3. **Starting with the aspects identified in point 2, read through the writing again. Notice the frequency, variety and appropriateness of the use of the selected aspect.**
   For example, are there many adjectives? Do they vary in terms of specificity/generality, common/uncommon? Do they fit in terms of formality/informality, technical/untechnical?
4. **Make a judgement about the effectiveness of the use of this aspect and tick one of the Yes/No/Partial columns.**
   For example, in an explanation, attempts to join ideas using 'when' or 'after' rather than using 'because' or 'as a result', suggests that the writer has some idea of subordination, but is not confident in using a range of subordinators. This would result in a tick in the 'Partial' column.

5. **Where the analysis has included most aspects on the sheet, look at the patterns of use emerging from columns.**
   For example, there may be evidence of complex sentence construction but only partial grasp of punctuation to mark clauses. There may also be effective appeal to the reader, but little development of content and only partial use of paragraphing.
6. **Look for connections between the different aspects before deciding what to tackle first.**
   In the last example, long rambling sentences and unclear paragraph divisions may work together.
7. **Identify an opportunity in teaching to:**
   - revisit and extend understanding and use of those aspects in the 'Partial' column;
   - focus clearly on any aspects in the 'No' column.

If you are using the sheet for analysing several pieces of writing, look for patterns across the writing as well as within one piece. You can use one sheet to record judgements on several pieces of writing.

Writing analysis sheet

Grammar *Significant features at word and sentence level*	Judgement of effective use		
	Yes	**No**	**Partial**
Sentence structure			
• simple sentences			
• complex sentences			
• variation within sentences			
• co-ordination			
• subordination			
Word choice			
• noun groups			
• verb choice			
• tense			
• adjectives			
• adverbs			
• pronouns			
Punctuation used to demarcate			
• sentences			
• clauses			
• phrases			
• words in lists			
• direct speech			
Organisation and effect *Significant whole text features*			
• appeal to reader			

• development of topic, content, theme			
• openings and closings			
• organisation and length of paragraphs			
• presentation and layout			

Observation

Teachers observe children working all the time. As a result of this observation, they make assessments of children's abilities and attitudes, and plan future work. Yet, when asked about their methods of assessment, they will hardly ever count observation among them. Perhaps because observation is so common an activity and seems so subjective, it is very underrated in terms of the assessment information it can provide. Yet it has a great deal of potential. Its greatest strength lies in the fact that it enables assessments to be made while children are actually engaged in language work, and does not require them to be withdrawn from it into a special assessment situation. It therefore enables direct analysis of the child's process of working, without which assessment must be incomplete.

To use observation deliberately as an assessment technique requires a systematic approach. It also requires some means of recording the information gained rather than relying on memory alone.

A systematic approach will involve first of all knowing exactly what one is going to be looking for. This might mean listing the skills it is hoped to assess, and preparing a checklist of them. An alternative approach is to list the activities the children will be doing, and leaving space for noted observations about their performance.

Observation can be guided by a list of points to look for, suggestions for which are given below. It is important to state that these points are not intended to be simply 'ticked off' as assessments are made. They ideally require a more qualitative response, which can be added to as more information is acquired, and, of course, revised as progress is made. The list of points is divided into three sections, each corresponding to an area of language and literacy. The lists are not intended to be comprehensive, and neither are the points intended to be read as a series of attainment statements. They are intended as points to guide systematic observation.

Reading

Does the child:

- participate in shared and guided reading? How?
- select an appropriate book to read?
- judge when a book is too difficult?
- become absorbed in a book?
- respond to what is read?
- re-read favourite books?
- retell stories previously read?
- use a variety of cues in reading words in shared, guided and individual reading?
- read silently?
- understand the way books and print work?
- have an appropriate language with which to talk about the way they read?

Writing

Does the child:

- turn to writing as an enjoyable activity?
- make independent attempts to write?
- write appropriately for different purposes and audiences?
- participate in revision activities in shared or guided reading?
- revise and redraft writing with or without the help of an adult?
- collaborate with other children in writing activities?
- make attempts to spell and punctuate correctly?
- have good habits of letter-formation, etc.?

Speaking and listening

Does the child:

- participate in large and small group discussion?
- listen to others' points and respond to them?
- articulate ideas in a clear and appropriate manner?
- match their manner of talking to the needs of an audience?

Probing and questioning

To find out what children think and know as they read and write, you may want to have regular, possibly half-termly, conferences with individual children about their reading and writing. You will also ask them directly how they work out words, how they choose words and how they make language decisions in shared and guided reading and writing and in plenary sessions. Three types of probing questions are useful in this.

Looking-back questions

These are of the type, 'Can you tell me how you did that?' They can be useful when looking at children's work alongside them. The children's answers to this question may well reveal a great deal about their perceptions of the processes of language. The following extract from a conversation between a teacher and seven-year-old Clare is an example of this approach. Clare has just written her version of the story of Red Riding Hood in which the heroine is menaced by an alien rather than a wolf.

Teacher:	'Oh, that's an interesting story, Clare! Where did you get the idea from?'
Clare:	'From my book. We don't have wolves here anymore.'
T:	'Yes, that's right. Can you tell me how you started writing your story? What did you do first?'
C:	'Me and Joanne talked about it and … we just wrote it.'
T:	'Did you write it together?'
C:	'Well … at first we wrote the same thing … then Joanne wanted to change hers and I didn't. So we wrote different ones.'
T:	'Did you change your story at all? As you were writing it?'
C:	'I changed some words … Emma told me how to spell them.'
T:	'Oh, Emma helped you too? What did she do?'
C:	'She read the story after I finished it. She told me my spellings.'
T:	'Yes … Now, did you plan to do anything with your story when you finished it? … Who did you want to read it?'
C:	'Put it on the wall?'

As a result of this conversation, the teacher was able to make several observations about this child's approach to and expertise in language processes. Clare had clearly been able to extract information from a book and use it in another context: a fairly advanced skill for a seven-year-old. She had been able to participate in discussion both in planning her writing and in editing it. She was prepared to work on her writing collaboratively although this did not survive the disagreement with her partner. Her approach to the writing process showed some evidence of planning, although this was not extensive. She was unclear about the destination and audience for her writing and saw revision purely in terms of editing spellings.

All these evaluations would require further investigation, but it is clear from this brief extract what a wealth of information the teacher was able to glean simply by asking questions that caused Clare to reflect on what she had done.

Looking-forward questions

An alternative kind of question can be of the type, 'Can you tell me how you will do that?' They ask children to think about their actions before they do them. It is, of course, possible that, because this question makes them think through in advance what they will do, their performance is different from what it would have been without the question. The question may therefore have a teaching role, as well as being a way of seeing whether they know what to do.

Questions such as the following are of this type.

- 'When you go to the library to look for that book, can you tell me what you will do?'
- 'Now, you are going to write your report on sports day for the school newspaper. How will you start?'
- 'This group is going to discuss your puppet play. How are you going to make sure everyone gets a fair chance to say what they think?'

As a result of questions like these, the teacher is able both to make an initial assessment of children's approaches to the process and also to prompt them in a way that may develop their thinking.

Thinking-out-loud questions

These are of the type, 'What are you thinking as you are doing that?' They can help make children's thinking about certain tasks explicit and alert the teacher to faulty approaches. They may include questions such as:

- 'As you make notes from that book, can you tell me why you are choosing those things?'
- 'How did you know that word said "unusual"?'
- 'How can you work out what might come next?'
- 'Now, is your discussion going well? Have you found any problems?'

It is quite likely that, in general, teachers ask too few questions like this. In addition to providing useful information about the way children are thinking, they can have the important effect of heightening children's awareness of the way they are using language. Developing this **metalinguistic awareness** is an important task for the teacher of language and literacy.

Assessing talk

It is important to monitor and assess children's spoken language skills, both formatively and summatively. Approaches might include self-evaluations by children of their own talking, using similar types of question to those detailed above. Children's talking can be recorded for analysis by the teacher; alternatively, the teacher can take notes during discussion sessions, which can be used to inform later assessments, using criteria appropriate to the purpose and focus of the activity. For summative assessment purposes, the National Curriculum level descriptions for speaking and listening can be applied.

Drama in itself can be used as an assessment tool because it often represents the presentation and review of oral (and written) work covered over a period of time. Improvised drama can also be used for assessment purposes, especially if the teacher is observing; when the teacher is in role, brief notes made immediately after the session can be used in conjunction with self-evaluations by the children.

With all assessment activities, it is important that they are integrated as far as possible with other aspects of the work, related to planning, and made transparent to the children themselves so that they are aware of what criteria are being used to assess their speaking and listening. Feeding back assessment findings is also important, so that children can make further progress.

EMBEDDING ICT   EMBEDDING ICT   EMBEDDING ICT   EMBEDDING ICT   EMBEDDING ICT

Increasingly, ICT is used for teachers' record-keeping and to support the assessment process at all stages (including for diagnostic, formative and summative assessments), to handle assessment data (for example to compare and benchmark results, to show 'value-added' and to focus on tracking the progress of vulnerable groups, such as looked-after children) and for creating reports for parents. Make sure that you are aware of the assessment policy and arrangements in your school, including those for data input, as some schools now have a member of the admin team who is responsible for this.

Statutory assessment

Statutory assessment takes place at a number of points in children's development as language users. This chapter describes the requirements of the Early Years Foundation Stage (EYFS) Profile, and at the end of Key Stages 1 and 2. The requirements for Key Stages 1 and 2 were in a transitional period at the time of writing. It is therefore the requirements for 2014 which we will describe.

Baseline assessment and the Early Years Foundation Stage Profile

In September 1998, all maintained primary schools had to implement a scheme of baseline assessment whereby all children aged four or five were assessed within seven weeks of starting school. The assessments included a wide range of observations about children's oracy and literacy abilities and did not ask teachers to 'pass or fail' children, but rather to rate their performance on entering school.

This scheme was replaced by the much more comprehensive Early Years Foundation Stage Profile. The requirements for this are fully described in the Early Years Foundation

Stage Profile handbook (STA, 2013a), which states that the EYFS Profile is designed to summarise and describe children's attainment at the end of the EYFS. It is based on ongoing observation and assessment in the three prime and four specific areas of learning, taking account of the three characteristics of effective learning, as listed below:

The prime areas of learning:

- communication and language;
- physical development;
- personal, social and emotional development.

The specific areas of learning:

- literacy;
- mathematics;
- understanding the world;
- expressive arts and design.

Characteristics of effective learning:

- playing and exploring;
- active learning;
- creating and thinking critically.

A completed EYFS Profile will consist of 20 items of information: the attainment of each child in terms of the 17 Early Learning Goal (ELG) descriptors, plus a short descriptive account of the child in terms of each of the three characteristics of effective learning. These assessments should be based primarily on observations of daily activities and events, but will also take account of a range of perspectives including those of the child, of parents and of other adults who interact with the child. Attainment will be recorded against each of the 17 ELG descriptors in terms of whether a child is meeting the level of development expected at the end of the Reception year (expected), exceeding this level (exceeding), or not yet reaching this level (emerging). This is a much simplified approach compared to previous versions of the EYFS Profile, in line with the recommendations of the Tickell Report (2011).

RESEARCH SUMMARY RESEARCH SUMMARY **RESEARCH SUMMARY** RESEARCH SUMMARY

Marie Clay (1979), in her seminal research into early reading, identified a series of early reading behaviours and used them to develop the 'Concepts of Print Test', arguing that beginning readers need to demonstrate an understanding of particular reading behaviours. You might want to compare the processes she identified with the information required in baseline assessment, and consider how you might build the recording of observations such as these into an early assessment of young children's reading development. Clay's key processes were:

- understanding how to hold a book the correct way up;
- recognising that the words on a page carry the central message;
- knowing how to find the first and last parts of the story in a book;
- understanding that the line of print at the top of the page is to be read first;
- understanding that print is read from left to right;
- knowing that the page number is not part of the story.

Statutory assessment in Key Stage 1

Teacher assessment is the main focus for end of Key Stage 1 assessment and reporting. However, there are some statutory requirements for maintained schools and academies. Schools and teachers are required to administer the Key Stage 1 tasks and tests and the phonics screening check. Full details are given in STA 2013b.

The Key Stage 1 tasks and tests in reading and writing are designed to provide a snapshot of a child's attainment and to help inform the final teacher assessment judgement reported for each child at the end of Key Stage 1. Schools are not required to report these task and test results to their local authority or to another school when a child moves, but the results are made available to parents upon request. The materials to be used for these tasks and tests must be chosen from the 2007 and/or 2009 Key Stage 1 National Curriculum tests and teachers will need to select tasks and tests appropriate to the level at which each child is judged to be working. Copies of these tasks and tests will need to be ordered directly from the Standards and Testing Agency and your school will take responsibility for that.

The phonics screening check is a short assessment designed to confirm whether individual children have learnt phonic decoding to the desired standard. Its aim is to help schools to identify any children who need extra help to improve their reading skills.

The check consists of a list of 40 phonically decodable words and non-words which the child reads one-to-one with a teacher. A short video to support the administration of this check can be found at: http://www.youtube.com/watch?v=IPJ_ZEBh1Bk. It is administered during the summer term with Year 1 children, and, although results are not published, schools must tell parents their children's results and report the data anonymously to the DfE. If Year 1 children are deemed to have 'failed' the check (i.e. failed to read the designated number of words correctly), they are required to retake the check in Year 2.

RESEARCH SUMMARY RESEARCH SUMMARY **RESEARCH SUMMARY** RESEARCH SUMMARY

The phonics screening check has, unsurprisingly, proved to be a controversial addition to the required testing approaches for six-year-olds. The official evaluation of the pilot version of the check (Coldwell *et al.*, 2011) did raise a number of issues in terms of schools' and teachers' responses to the check. It was found, for example, that:

- Three quarters of teachers surveyed felt that the check accurately assessed phonic decoding ability overall for their pupils.
- However, only 62 per cent of teachers felt it usefully identified the decoding abilities of weaker readers.
- The majority (60 per cent) of teachers surveyed felt that the non-words caused confusion for at least some pupils, with an additional 12 per cent feeling that they caused confusion for most pupils.
- Less than half of teachers (43 per cent) indicated that the check had helped them to identify pupils with phonic decoding issues that they were not previously aware of.

Statutory assessment in Key Stage 2

There are two National Curriculum tests for English at the end of Key Stage 2, which are aimed at providing a snapshot of a child's attainment at the end of the Key Stage. Further information about these tests is available on the DfE's website at http://www.education.gov.uk/schools/teachingandlearning/assessment/keystage2/b00208296/ks2-2014. Details about the administration of the tests is given in STA 2013c.

The levels 3–5 tests include:

1. A test of reading in English. The English reading booklet will contain three or four texts, gradually increasing in level of difficulty. Children will have a total of one hour to read the texts and complete approximately 35 to 40 questions about them. The questions will range from:

   - shorter, closed response items (such as multiple choice and matching questions);
   - shorter, open response items;
   - longer, open response items that require children to explain and comment on the texts in order to demonstrate a full understanding.

Questions will be worth 1, 2 or 3 marks.

2. A test of the use of English spelling, punctuation and grammar (SPAG), This test has two components, worth a total of 70 marks:

   - a booklet of short-answer questions;
   - a spelling task.

Paper 1, will contain between 40 and 50 questions assessing grammar, punctuation and vocabulary. Each question is worth one or two marks with a total for the paper of 50 marks. The questions include:

- selected response items (such as multiple choice questions); or
- short, open response items, in which children may have to write a word, a few words or a sentence.

Paper 2, the spelling task, consists of 20 sentences, which will be read aloud by the test administrator. Each sentence has a word missing which the child must complete. The task will be worth a total of 20 marks.

Teacher assessment

Teacher assessment is an essential part of the National Curriculum assessment and reporting arrangements. At Key Stage 2, teachers assign levels for aspects of English and undertake in-service training to check that they are levelling at the same standards. At both Key Stages, speaking and listening is only assessed through teacher assessment. At Key Stage 2, results from teacher assessment are reported alongside the test results. Both have equal status and provide complementary information about children's attainment. The tests provide a standard 'snapshot' of attainment at the end of the Key Stage, while teacher assessment, carried out as part of teaching and learning in the classroom, covers the full range and scope of the programmes of study, and takes account of evidence of achievement in a range of contexts, including that gained through discussion and observation. For children working at levels 1 and 2 in Key Stage 2, teacher assessment provides the sole means of statutory assessment (with the exception of the phonics screening check).

The level descriptions in the National Curriculum are the basis for judging children's levels of attainment at the end of the Key Stage. Level descriptions indicate the type and range of performance that children working at a particular level should characteristically demonstrate. Teachers should use their knowledge of a child's work to judge which level description best fits that child's performance across a range of contexts. The aim is for a rounded judgement that:

- is based on knowledge of how the child performs over time across a range of contexts;
- takes into account strengths and weaknesses of the child's performance;
- is checked against adjacent level descriptions to ensure that the level awarded is the closest match to the child's performance in each attainment target.

Schools are required to keep records on every child, including information on academic achievements, other skills and abilities and progress made in school. They must update these records at least once a year.

Reporting to parents

Headteachers are responsible for ensuring that they send a written report to parents on their child's achievements at least once during the school year. According to current legislation, the following information must be included in the annual report of every child:

- brief particulars of achievements in all subjects and activities forming part of the school curriculum;
- comments on general progress;
- arrangements for discussing the report with the child's teacher;
- child's attendance record;
- the results of any National Curriculum tests taken during that year.

Where information, such as the results of National Curriculum assessments, is not available before the end of the summer term, headteachers must ensure that it is sent to parents as soon as practicable and, in any case, no later than 30 September.

Writing reports to parents

Parents are almost universally interested in their children's school performance and yet do not always feel they have detailed information. This means that reports are very important. Reports should be written for parents in a clear and straightforward way. Most parents want to know:

- how their child is performing in relation to their potential and past achievements, to the rest of the class and to national standards;
- their child's strengths and any particular achievements;
- areas for development and improvement;
- how they can help;
- whether their child is happy, settled and behaving well.

Reports should be personal to the child and there is evidence that some parents dislike statement banks or computer-generated reports when this makes them impersonal. The best computer-generated programs avoid this by offering a wide range of comments. If you do not use a computer-generated comment bank, you should use attainment targets to support your choice of vocabulary. The report should be well written and legible, with correct grammar, punctuation and spelling, but avoiding educational jargon. Comments should be as succinct as possible and use precise and appropriate wording.

A useful school report should concentrate on what the child has or has not learned, rather than what has been taught (many schools will already have informed their parents at the beginning of each term of what will be taught during that term). A report should indicate what standards the child has achieved and whether any comparison is being made with their progress in other subjects, with previous performance, with other children in the class or against national standards. If a system of grading is used, either for attainment or effort, parents need a key or notes which will help them to understand the system, how different aspects, for example effort and attainment, relate to each other and, in the case of attainment, how it relates to national standards.

Reports can be an important way of helping children make progress and become aware of new targets. Children can be motivated by highlighting their strengths and recognising and valuing achievements in different areas of school life, but areas for development should be clearly identified and suggestions made about how these can be improved. It is important not to obscure low achievement or underachievement by the use of faint praise or by avoiding any mention of the problem. Reports should give an accurate picture of current attainment. They can then be used to involve the child in setting clear, achievable and time-related targets for their learning. Even the most able and conscientious child can be given suggestions about how to make further progress.

Parent meetings

Schools will often have termly parents' meetings and for some this will be the only opportunity to discuss their child with the teacher. Remember that some parents will feel daunted by meeting teachers and you will need to put them at their ease. The meeting should provide an opportunity for them to ask questions and learn about their child's performance and attitude. Parents want teachers to be honest about their child's performance; most would rather have the full picture, even if this is uncomfortable.

During meetings with parents, teachers should have available their records of the child's work or scheme of work. These can be used to illustrate standards of work and other points made in discussions. Many parents appreciate specific advice about how to help their child improve, even where their child is already doing well.

Many schools maintain contact about children's progress in English through home-school books or homework books. These can include targets for children and advice for parents about how to help. The parents' meeting is a good time to remind parents about these forms of communications or to discuss misunderstandings.

PRACTICAL TASK PRACTICAL TASK **PRACTICAL TASK** PRACTICAL TASK **PRACTICAL TASK**

As part of your course, you should make sure you write some English reports and discuss them with your school mentor. We suggest you write at least three:

- a report for a child who is struggling with reading or writing;
- a report for a very articulate child;
- a report for a child who you judge as 'average' for the class.

Remember to include all aspects of English performance, with an emphasis on achievements and targets.

PRACTICAL TASK   PRACTICAL TASK   PRACTICAL TASK   PRACTICAL TASK   **PRACTICAL TASK**

Below is an example of an end-of-year report for one Year 2 girl. You might want to read this as if you were the parent of this girl and comment on the level and preciseness of the information it offers.

Tarsem Kaur Daphu

English

Tarsem reads many types of books independently but shows a strong preference for fiction texts. She can give reasons why she likes her favourite authors and why she enjoys them. Tarsem knows how to find answers to questions using information books but sometimes finds the task onerous. In her writing, she chooses words and expressions carefully to create interesting, effective stories. She is less enthusiastic about report writing but is able to select salient points and structure reports well. In general, her spelling is sound, although she is not always accurate when she attempts irregular and unfamiliar words. Tarsem's contributions to class discussions show that she listens carefully. She takes a positive but understated part in group discussion and she is good at helping quieter children take part in joint activities. She is working above national expectations for her age.

THE BIGGER PICTURE   THE BIGGER PICTURE   THE BIGGER PICTURE   THE BIGGER PICTURE

You should get plenty of experience during school placements of making informal assessments of children's progress in aspects of English. It would be hard to teach them appropriately if you did not do this! Try to get experience of the administration of statutory assessments of English. We strongly recommend that you try at least to observe this process, preferably during a summer term assessment period. This might mean making special arrangements with your school and class teacher, but your school-based mentor will understand the need for such arrangements and will usually be sympathetic to your needs in this area. Also ask if you can sit in on any moderation sessions, and to observe a range of types of assessment, including those for children with special educational needs.

A SUMMARY OF **KEY POINTS**

➢ **Planning and assessment are the key to effective English teaching.**

➢ **There are a number of purposes for assessment so it is unlikely that one simple approach will meet them all.**

➢ **There are three basic approaches to assessment: analysing products, observing processes and questioning.**

➢ **Miscue analysis or running records can be very effective ways of assessing children's reading performance.**

➢ **You need to be fully aware of the statutory aspects of assessment and reporting to parents.**

M-LEVEL EXTENSION > > M-LEVEL EXTENSION > > M-LEVEL EXTENSION

Choose a sample of children from your class or the year group that you are working with and ask if you can have permission to look at the assessment records kept for each child over time, which may include seeking parental permission in some cases. Note the types of assessment that have been undertaken on each child. Is there any difference between the range of assessments carried out on children of different abilities, or on particular groups such as able, gifted and talented children, those with additional and special educational needs, children learning English as an additional language or looked-after children? Reflect on the different ways in which assessment is being used to monitor and promote children's learning.

FURTHER READING   FURTHER READING   FURTHER READING   FURTHER READING

Bew, P. (2011) *Independent Review of Key Stage 2 Testing, Assessment and Accountability: Final Report*. London: DfE.

Clay, M. (1979) *The Early Detection of Reading Difficulties*. London: Heinemann.

Coldwell, M., Shipton, L., Stevens, A., Stiell, B., Willis, B. and Wolstenholme, C. (2011) *Process Evaluation of the Year 1 Phonics Screening Check Pilot*. London: DfE. (https://www.gov.uk/government/uploads/system/uploads/attachment_data/file/182621/DFE-RR159.pdf)

DfE (2013) *Teachers' Standards*. London: DfE. (https://www.gov.uk/government/uploads/system/uploads/attachment_data/file/208682/Teachers__Standards_2013.pdf)

Standards and Testing Agency (2013a) *Early Years Foundation Stage Profile Handbook*. London: STA. (https://www.gov.uk/government/uploads/system/uploads/attachment_data/file/249995/Early_years_foundation_stage_profile_handbook_2014.pdf)

Standards and Testing Agency (2013b) *Assessment and Reporting Arrangements: Key Stage 1*. London: STA. (https://www.gov.uk/government/uploads/system/uploads/attachment_data/file/285246/2014_KS1_accessandreportingarrangementsARA_web.pdf)

Standards and Testing Agency (2013c) *Assessment and Reporting Arrangements: Key Stage 2*. London: STA. (https://www.gov.uk/government/uploads/system/uploads/attachment_data/file/278150/2014_KS2_assessmentandreportingarrangementsARA_DIGITAL_HO.pdf)

Tickell, C. (2011) *The Early Years: Foundations for Life, Health and Learning. An Independent Report on the Early Years Foundation Stage to Her Majesty's Government*. London: DfE. (https://www.gov.uk/government/uploads/system/uploads/attachment_data/file/180919/DFE-00177-2011.pdf)

Glossary

alliteration A phrase in which adjacent or fairly closely connected words begin with the same phoneme.

analogy The perception of similarity between two things; relating something known to something new; in spelling, using known spellings to spell unknown words: *night-knight-right-sight-light-fright*; in reading, using knowledge of words to attempt previously unseen words.

analytical methods Approaches to teaching reading in which texts or sections of texts are introduced first, followed by an analysis of their constituent parts such as letters, phonemes and words.

audience The people addressed by a text. The term refers to listeners, readers of books, film/TV audiences and users of information technology.

big book An enlarged text book suitable for use with a group of children during shared reading.

blends The process of combining phonemes into larger elements such as clusters, syllables and words. Also refers to a combination of two or more phonemes, particularly at the beginning and end of words, e.g. *st*, *str*, *nt*, *pl*, *nd*.

composition The process of developing ideas during writing.

comprehension Understanding of a phenomenon. It is usually qualified, e.g. reading comprehension, listening comprehension.

demonstrations These occur when teachers show children how to perform tasks such as reading or writing.

dialect A regional dialect refers to the features of grammar and vocabulary that convey information about a person's geographical origin.

digraph A written representation of a sound using two letters. Consonant digraphs represent consonant sounds (/ch/ in cheese). Vowel digraphs represent vowel sounds but may use letters we usually call consonants (/ae/ in pain, station, say). Sometimes, the two letters making up the digraph are separated (/a/and /e/in late) and this is known as a split digraph. When one sound is represented by three letters (/tch/ in match), this is known as a trigraph.

editing Modifying written work, either own or another's, in preparation for publication. This process takes place after *drafting* (composition) and *revising* (major restructuring) and before *proofreading* (a final check for typographical, spelling errors, etc.). It involves checking of facts, minor improvements to style at sentence level, and checking for accuracy and agreement.

extended writing A piece of writing for which a longer period of time is required than that available within a literacy lesson format.

formative assessment Assessment of pupils' ongoing work.

genre A collection of linguistic practices and narrative conventions that govern the way particular texts are written for particular purposes.

graphic cues Cues used to recognise words in reading which derive from letter shapes and patterns.

graphophonic cues A combination of reading cues using letter shapes and sound–symbol correspondences.

guided reading A classroom activity in which pupils are taught in groups according to reading ability. The teacher works with each group on a text carefully selected to offer an appropriate level of challenge to the group.

guided writing A classroom activity in which pupils are grouped by writing ability. The teacher works with each group on a task carefully selected to offer an appropriate level of challenge to the group.

hot seating A drama activity in which a child is asked to play a particular role and answer questions in that role.

literacy A communication skill. The term *literacy* is most often applied to written communication but it can also be applied to other forms, as in *media literacy, computer literacy, digital literacy*.

metalanguage The language we use when talking about language itself. It includes words like *sentence, noun, paragraph, preposition*.

metalinguistic awareness An awareness of how language works. This is an umbrella term which includes such forms of awareness as phonological awareness, syntactic awareness, etc.

miscue A misreading of a word or group of words. It is possible, using miscue analysis, to determine some of the reasons behind this misreading, which often rest in the reader's use of the cueing systems of reading.

mnemonics A device to aid memory, for instance to learn particular spelling patterns or spellings: *I Go Home Tonight; There is a rat in separate*.

morpheme The smallest indivisible unit of language that has meaning, e.g. cat.

onset The consonant(s) preceding the nucleus of a syllable: s-un. Some syllables have no onset: eel.

oracy The skill of using speaking and listening to communicate. It parallels literacy.

phoneme The smallest contrastive unit of sound in a word.

phonemic segmentation The ability to split words into their constituent phonemes.

phonic cues Clues used to recognise words in reading that derive from knowledge of sound–symbol correspondences.

phonics A method of teaching children to read by teaching them to recognise and use sound–symbol correspondences.

phonological awareness Awareness of units of sound in speech.

prefixes A prefix is a morpheme that can be added to the beginning of a word to change its meaning, for example: inedible, disappear, supermarket.

reading comprehension Understanding of a read text.

register The term used by linguists to indicate the different ways in which people speak to different audiences for different purposes.

revision Making structural changes to a piece of writing one is composing. It should be distinguished from *editing*.

rime The part of a syllable containing the syllable nucleus (usually a vowel) and final consonants, if any – b-*in*.

semantic cues Clues used to recognise words in reading which derive from knowledge of the meaning of the text.

sentence level A level of knowledge about the way text works, which includes knowledge of grammar and punctuation.

sentence-level work Teaching activities focused on sentence-level knowledge.

shared reading In shared reading, the teacher, as an expert reader, models the reading process by reading the text to the learners. The text chosen may be at a level that would be too difficult for the readers to read independently. The teacher demonstrates the use of cues and strategies such as use of letter sounds, re-reading, etc.

shared writing A classroom process where the teacher models the writing process for children: free from the physical difficulties of writing, children can observe, and subsequently be involved in, planning, composition, redrafting, editing and publishing through the medium of the teacher.

Standard English Standard English is the variety of English used in public communication, particularly in writing. It is the form taught in schools and used by educated speakers. It is not limited to a particular region and can be spoken with any accent.

suffixes A suffix is a morpheme that is added to the end of a word to either change the tense or grammatical status of a word, e.g. from present to past (work*ed*) or from singular to plural (accident*s*), or to change the word class, e.g. from verb to noun (work*er*) or from noun to adjective (accident*al*).

summative assessment Assessment of children's work that occurs at the end of a fixed period, e.g. a year, or a unit of work.

syntactic cues Clues used to recognise words in reading which derive from knowledge of sentence grammar.

synthesising methods Approaches to teaching reading in which letters, phonemes and words are introduced first and then used to construct sentences or longer texts.

text level A level of knowledge about the way in which text works, including knowledge of text structure and convention.

text-level work Teaching activities focused on text-level knowledge.

transcription The process of transferring ideas to paper or screen in writing. It is distinguished from composition, which is the process of developing the ideas.

word level A level of knowledge about the way text works that includes knowledge of word construction.

word-level work Teaching activities focused on word-level knowledge.

writing frames Structured prompts to support writing. A writing frame often takes the form of opening phrases of paragraphs and may include suggested vocabulary. It often provides a template for a particular text type.

Adams, M. (1990) *Beginning to Read: Thinking and Learning about Print*. Cambridge, MA: MIT Press.

Ahlberg, A. and Ahlberg, J. (1978) *Each Peach Pear Plum*. Hardmondsworth: Puffin/Kestrel.

Ahlberg, A. and Ahlberg, J. (1980) *Mrs Wobble the Waitress*. Harmondsworth: Puffin/Kestrel.

Ahlberg, A. and Ahlberg, J. (1986) *The Jolly Postman*. London: Heinemann.

August, D. and Shanahan, T. (eds) (2006) *Developing literacy in second-language learners: Report of the National Literacy Panel on Language-Minority Children and Youth*. Mahwah, NJ: Lawrence Erlbaum.

Barrs, M. and Thomas, A. (eds) (1996) *The Reading Book*. London: Centre for Language in Primary Education.

Bissex, G.L. (1980) *Gnys at Wrk: A child learns to write*. Cambridge, MA: Harvard University Press.

Blume, J. (1980) *Superfudge*. New York: Dutton Children's Books.

Briggs, R. (1973) *Father Christmas*. London: Hamish Hamilton.

Briggs, R. (1978) *The Snowman*. London: Hamish Hamilton.

Bryant, P. and Bradley, L. (1985) *Children's Reading Problems*. Oxford: Blackwell.

Burningham, J. (1970) *Mr Gumpy's Outing*. London: Jonathan Cape/Random House.

Canadian Council on Learning (2010) *More Than Just Funny Books: Comics and prose literacy for boys*. Available at: http://www.ccl-cca.ca/CCL/Reports/LessonsInLearning/LinL20100721Comics.html

Cambourne, B. (1988) *The Whole Story*. Leamington Spa: Scholastic.

Carle, E. (1969) *The Very Hungry Caterpillar*. London: Hamish Hamilton.

Carle, E. (1977) *The Bad-Tempered Ladybird*. Melbourne: Puffin.

Chambers, A. (1993) *Tell Me: Children, Reading and Talk*. Stroud: Thimble Press.

Clay, M. (1979) *The Early Detection of Reading Difficulties*. London: Heinemann.

Clipson-Boyles, S. (1998) *Drama in Primary English Teaching*. London: David Fulton.

Coldwell, M., Shipton, L., Stevens, A., Stiell, B., Willis, B. and Wolstenholme, C. (2011) *Process Evaluation of the Year 1 Phonics Screening Check Pilot*. London: DfE. (https://www.gov.uk/government/uploads/system/uploads/attachment_data/file/182621/DFE-RR159.pdf)

Collier, V. and Thomas, W. (1998) *Language Minority Student Achievement and Program Effectiveness: Research Summary of Ongoing Study*. Fairfax, VA: George Mason University.

Crystal, D. (1987) *The Cambridge Encyclopaedia of Language*. Cambridge: Cambridge University Press.

Crystal, D. (1995) *The Cambridge Encyclopaedia of the English Language* (2nd edn). Cambridge: Cambridge University Press.

Cummins, J. (2000) *Language, Power and Pedagogy: Bilingual children in the crossfire*. Clevedon, UK: Multilingual Matters.

Department for Education and Science (DES) (1978) *Primary Education in England*. London: HMSO.

Department for Education and Science (DES) (1991) *Education Observed: The implementation of the curricular requirements of the ERA in 1989–90*. London: HMSO.

Department for Education (DfE) (2012) *Statutory Framework for the Early Years Foundation Stage*. Runcorn: DfE. (https://www.education.gov.uk/publications/standard/AllPublications/Page1/DFE-00023-2012)

Department for Education (DfE) (2013a) *The National Curriculum in England*. London: DfE. (https://www.gov.uk/dfe/nationalcurriculum)

Department for Education (DfE) (2013b) *Teachers' Standards*. London: DfE. (https://www.gov.uk/government/uploads/system/uploads/attachment_data/file/208682/Teachers__Standards_2013.pdf)

Department for Education (DfE) (2014) *Draft SEN Code of Practice: for 0 to 25 years*. London: DfE. (https://www.gov.uk/government/uploads/system/uploads/attachment_data/file/251839/Draft_SEN_Code_of_Practice_-_statutory_guidance.pdf)

Department for Education and Skills (DfES) (2007) *Letters and Sounds: Principles and Practice of High Quality Phonics*. London: DfES.

Dodd, L. (1983) *Hairy Maclary*. Wellington NZ: Mallinson Rendel.

Gentry, R. (1982) 'An analysis of developmental spelling in GNYS AT WRK', *The Reading Teacher*, vol. 36(2), pp. 192–200.

Goodman, Y., Watson, D. and Burke, C. (1987) *Reading Miscue Inventory*. New York: Richard Owen.

Goswami, U. and Bryant, P. (1990) *Phonological Skills and Learning to Read*. London: Lawrence Erlbaum.

Grainger, T. (1997) *Traditional Storytelling in the Primary Classroom.* Leamington Spa: Scholastic.

Graves, D. (1983) *Writing: Teachers and Children at Work*. Portsmouth, NH: Heinemann.

Halliday, M.A.K. (1978) *Language as Social Semiotic: The social interpretation of language and meaning*. London: Edward Arnold.

Halliday, M.A.K. (1985) *An Introduction to Functional Grammar*. London: Edward Arnold.

Harste, J.C., Woodward, V.A. and Burke, C.L. (1984) *Language Stories and Literacy Lessons*. Portsmouth, NH: Heinemann.

Hattie, J. (2012) *Visible Learning for Teachers*. London: Routledge.

Hayes, S (1992) *This is the Bear and the Scary Night*. Boston: Joy Street Books.

Haywood, S. and Wray, D. (1988) 'Using TRAY, a text reconstruction program, with top infants', *Educational Review*, vol. 40(1), pp. 29–30.

Heathcote, D. and Bolton, G. (1995) *Drama for Learning: Dorothy Heathcote's 'Mantle of the Expert' Approach to Education*. Portsmouth NH: Heinemann.

Hutchins, P. (1968) *Rosie's Walk*. London: The Bodley Head.

Johnston, R. and Watson, J. (2005) 'The effects of synthetic phonics teaching on reading and spelling attainment: a seven-year longitudinal study'. Available at: http://www.scotland.gov.uk/Resource/Doc/36496/0023582.pdf

Johnston, V. (1985) 'Introducing the Microcomputer into English: An evaluation of TRAY as a program using problem-solving as a strategy for developing reading skills', *British Journal of Educational Technology*, vol. 16(3), pp. 208–18.

Ketch, A. (1991) 'The Delicious Alphabet', *English in Education*, vol. 25(1), pp. 1–4.

King-Smith, D. (1987) *The Hodegeheg*. London: Hamish Hamilton.

Ko, J. and Sammons, P. (2013) *Effective Teaching: A Review of Research and Evidence*. Reading: Centre for British Teachers. (http://cdn.cfbt.com/~/media/cfbtcorporate/files/research/2013/r-effective-teaching-2013.pdf)

Lee, L. (1959) *Cider with Rosie*. London: The Hogarth Press.

Lewis, M. and Wray, D. (1994) *Developing Children's Non-fiction Writing*. Leamington Spa: Scholastic.

Lewis, M. and Wray, D. (1997) *Writing Frames*. Reading: University of Reading, Reading and Language Information Centre.

Lipson, M.Y. and Wixon, K.K. (2002) *Assessment and Instruction of Reading and Writing Difficulty: An interactive approach* (3rd edn). Needham Heights, MA: Allyn and Bacon.

Littlefair, A. (1991) *Reading All Types of Writing*. Buckingham: Open University Press.

Lunzer, E. and Gardner, K. (1979) *The Effective Use of Reading*. London: Heinemann.

Martin, J. (1989) *Factual Writing.* Oxford: Oxford University Press.

Matterson, E. (1969) *This Little Puffin*. London: Puffin.

Mayne, W. (1992) *Low Tide*. London: Jonathan Cape/Random House.

Medwell, J. (1996) 'Talking books and reading', *Reading*, vol. 30(1), pp. 41–6.

Medwell, J. (1998) 'The talking books project: some further insights into the use of talking books to develop reading', *Reading*, vol. 32(1), pp. 3–9.

Medwell, J., Strand, S. and Wray, D. (2007) 'The role of handwriting in composing for Y2 children', *Journal of Reading, Writing and Literacy*, vol. 2(1), pp. 18–36.

Medwell, J., Strand, S. and Wray, D. (2009) 'The links between handwriting and composing for Y6 children', *Cambridge Journal of Education*, vol. 39(3), pp. 329–44.

Medwell, J. and Wray, D. (2007) 'Handwriting: what we know and need to know', *Literacy*, vol. 41(1), pp. 10–15.

Medwell, J. and Wray, D. (2014) 'Handwriting automaticity: the search for performance thresholds', *Language and Education*, vol. 28(1), pp. 34–51. (http://www.tandfonline.com/doi/abs/10.1080/09500782.2013.763819)

Meek, M. (1982) *Learning to Read*. London: Bodley Head.

Minns, H. (1990) *Read it to me now! Learning at home and at school*. London: Virago.

Morpurgo, M. (1995) *The Wreck of the Zanzibar*. London: Egmont Books.

Nutbrown, C. (2012) *Foundations for Quality: The Independent Review of Early Education and Childcare Qualifications. Final Report*. Runcorn: DfE. (https://www.gov.uk/government/uploads/system/uploads/attachment_data/file/175463/Nutbrown-Review.pdf)

Pearce, P. (1958) *Tom's Midnight Garden*. Oxford: Oxford University Press.

Peters, M. (1985) *Spelling – Caught or Taught*. Abingdon: Routledge.

Purcell-Gates, V. (1997) *Other People's Words: Cycle of Low Literacy*. Cambridge, MA: Harvard University Press.

Qualifications and Curriculum Authority (QCA) (1999) *Early Learning Goals.* London: QCA

Rose, J. (2006) *Independent Review of the Teaching of Early Reading: Final Report*. London: DfES.

Rosen, M. and Oxenbury, H. (1989) *We're Going on a Bear Hunt*. London: Walker Books.

Rosen, M. and Steele, S. (1990) *Inky Pinky Ponky*. London: Picture Lions.

Sassoon, R. (1990) *Handwriting: The Way to Teach It*. Cheltenham: Stanley Thornes.

Seuss, Dr. (1957) *The Cat in the Hat*. New York: Dr Seuss Enterprises.

Seuss, Dr. (1960) *Green Eggs and Ham*. New York: Dr Seuss Enterprises.

Siraj-Blatchford, I., Sylva, K., Muttock, S., Gilden, R. and Bell, D. (2002). *Researching Effective Pedagogy in the Early Years (REPEY) DfES Research Report 365*. Norwich: HMSO. (http://dera.ioe.ac.uk/4650/1/RR356.pdf)

Stahl, K.A. and McKenna, M.C. (2006) *Reading Research at Work: Foundations of Effective Practice*. London: Guilford.

Standards and Testing Agency (STA) (2013a) *Early Years Foundation Stage Profile Handbook*. London: STA. (https://www.gov.uk/government/uploads/system/uploads/attachment_data/file/249995/Early_years_foundation_stage_profile_handbook_2014.pdf)

Standards and Testing Agency (STA) (2013b) *Assessment and Reporting Arrangements: Key Stage 1*. London: STA. (https://www.gov.uk/government/uploads/system/uploads/attachment_data/file/285246/2014_KS1_accessandreportingarrangementsARA_web.pdf)

Standards and Testing Agency (STA) (2013c) *Assessment and Reporting Arrangements: Key Stage 2*. London: STA. (https://www.gov.uk/government/uploads/system/uploads/attachment_data/file/278150/2014_KS2_assessmentandreportingarrangementsARA_DIGITAL_HO.pdf)

Stanovich, K.E. (1984) 'The interactive-compensatory model of reading: a confluence of developmental, experimental and educational psychology', *Remedial and Special Education*, vol. 5(3), pp. 11–19.

Stanovich, K.E. (1993) *The Development of Rationality and Critical Thinking*. Detroit, MI: Wayne State University Press.

Stuart, M. (2005) 'Phonemic analysis and reading development: some current issues', *Journal of Research in Reading*, vol. 28, pp. 39–49.

Stuart, M. (2006) 'Learning to read: developing processes for recognizing, understanding and pronouncing written words', *London Review of Education*, 4(1): 19–29.

Tickell, C. (2011) *The Early Years: Foundations for Life, Health and Learning. An Independent Report on the Early Years Foundation Stage to Her Majesty's Government*. London: DfE.

Wegerif, R., Littleton, K., Dawes, L., Mercer, N. and Rowe, D. (2004) 'Widening access to educational opportunities through teaching children how to reason together', *International Journal of Research and Method in Education*, vol. 27(2), pp. 143–56.

Wells, G. (1987) *The Meaning Makers: Children Learning Language and Using Language to Learn*. London: Hodder and Stoughton.

Wolf, M., Crosson, A. and Resnick, L. (2004) 'Classroom talk for rigorous reading comprehension instruction', *Reading Psychology*, vol. 26(1), pp. 27–53.

Wood, C., Kemp, N. and Plester, B. (2013) *Text Messaging and Literacy: The Evidence*. London: Routledge.

Wray, D. (1981) *Extending Reading Skills*. Lancaster: University of Lancaster.

Wray, D. (1985) *Teaching Information Skills through Project Work*. London: Hodder and Stoughton.

Wray, D. (1993) 'What do children think about writing?', *Educational Review*, vol. 45(1), pp. 67–77.

Wray, D. (2002) *Practical Ways to Teach Writing*. Reading: National Centre for Language and Literacy.

Wray, D. and Lewis, M. (1992) 'Primary children's use of information books', *Reading*, vol. 26(3), pp. 19–24.

Wray, D. and Lewis, M. (1997) *Extending Literacy*. Abingdon: Routledge.

Wray, D. and Lewis, M. (1998) *Writing across the Curriculum*. Reading: University of Reading, Reading and Language Information Centre.

Wray, D. and Medwell, J. (2002) *Teaching Literacy Effectively*. Abingdon: RoutledgeFalmer.

Locators shown in *italics* refer to figures.